DATE DUE

THE DEVELOPMENT OF ARTISTICALLY GIFTED CHILDREN
Selected Case Studies

THE DEVELOPMENT OF ARTISTICALLY GIFTED CHILDREN
Selected Case Studies

Edited by
Claire Golomb
University of Massachusetts at Boston

with a Foreword by Rudolf Arnheim, Harvard University

LEA LAWRENCE ERLBAUM ASSOCIATES, PUBLISHERS
1995 Hillsdale, New Jersey Hove, UK

Lawrence Erlbaum Associates, Inc., Publishers
365 Broadway
Hillsdale, New Jersey 07642

Cover illustration by Joel Rivers

Library of Congress Cataloging-in-Publication Data

The development of artistically gifted children : selected case
studies / edited by Claire Golomb.
     p. cm.
  Includes bibliographical references and index.
  ISBN 0-8058-1524-4 (cloth : acid-free paper)
  1. Drawing ability in children. 2. Drawing ability in
children—Longitudinal studies. 3. Creative ability in
children. 4. Creative ability in children—Longitudinal
studies. 5. Children as artists. I. Golomb, Claire.
  BF723.D7D45 1995
    155.45'5--dc20   94-38746
                                                    CIP

Books published by Lawrence Erlbaum Associates are printed
on acid-free paper, and their bindings are chosen for strength
and durability.

Printed in the United States of America
10 9 8 7 6 5 4 3 2 1

Contents

Foreword

Rudolf Arnheim
Harvard University

To be gifted means to have been given something. But given by whom or by what? It is good that this question is put forward so clearly right at the beginning of this book. It seems to me equally appropriate, however, that the bulk of the contributors do not concentrate on worrying about this problem. It is known by now what conditions are favorable to the development of artistic ability; but it seems to be equally evident that most of the great achievers reached the glories of their work without the help of those favorable circumstances and in fact by overcoming forbidding obstacles. We do not know what brought about the miracle of a Raphael or Picasso in settings that otherwise might have generated mediocrity; and perhaps we never will know.

It is natural for researchers to dig toward the roots of the phenomena they study, and there is a temptation to believe that what they know is all that is needed to know. But it is equally fitting to pause in awe and wonder in the face of happenings that are also creations of nature but beyond our present grasp. I suggest that the psychologists and art educators who present their findings in this book are happily concerned with the best of both worlds, the feasible and the admirable. For although it is wonderful to explore the deeds of the rare geniuses, it is equally rewarding and exhilarating to become acquainted with the ways other human beings strive to observe and to know what they see, their ways of making their feelings and aspirations reverberate in the shapes and stories they invent, and their sense of order and harmony in all these inventions.

All children are gifted with these human distinctions, but there are good reasons for singling out the best among them for description and analysis. Not only that it is encouraging and enjoyable to be in the company of excellence, but also because researchers do well to be satisfied with nothing less than the finest specimens to document their findings. Those specimens are the purest cases, and they display the essential features with striking clarity.

I am not sure how useful it is to draw a line somewhere on the scale between the less gifted and the most gifted individuals and to try and figure out at what level of the scale we better assume the presence of some of that special blessing that makes for the geniuses. Nor should we hamper our vision by trying to determine who is an artist and who is not. Probably the category of artists is best reserved for persons who practice art as their occupation. But when we speak of "art," we need to realize that art is not a category. It is a quality of mind shared by all those who search to cope with their world by exploring and interpreting what they see and by creating form that tells and sings.

The group of leading specialists brought together for this valuable collection of case studies is united in a vision that rises beyond the narrow distinction between the exceptional and the ordinary. The authors envisage the wonderful range of human creativity reaching from the infant to the mature artist and epitomized in the gifted youngsters we meet under their guidance.

Introduction

Claire Golomb

University of Massachusetts at Boston

The idea for a book of case studies of children gifted in the visual arts was born at a symposium on "The Development of Gifted Child Artists" that I organized for the annual convention of the American Psychological Association in 1990. At this symposium we noted the paucity of publications in this field and the need for a concerted effort to fill this gap in our knowlege.

It is perhaps surprising that so little is known about the development of children who show an early promise in their approach to the arts. By contrast to the general study of children's drawings, which by now is a well-established field of developmental psychology, with many publications appearing since the 1970s, the study of children talented in the visual arts and their developmental trajectory has not received the attention it deserves. Unlike the study of precociously gifted children in mathematics, chess, and music, few longitudinally based case studies of children gifted in the visual arts have appeared. There are multiple reasons for this omission, some of which are related to the nature of the domain of art and its symbol system that is less formally organized. As the history of art with its diversity of styles demonstrates, its course does not show an easily discernible "progression," and there are no universally accepted end goals or methods of instruction.

We know from studies of prodigies that talents or potentialities for achievement in artistic or scientific domains most commonly require the sustained support of parents, teachers, and social institutions. This support reflects the interests and values (social, aesthetic, economical, moral) of the larger culture. Artists are not "born," they do not step into the world fully formed, and fostering their talent requires an act of discernment and selection that channels their special aptitude in a direction valued and also rewarded by the culture. The fact that we seem to know so little about prodigies in the visual arts is, perhaps, a reflection of the uncertain status of the artist in our society.

Of course, many fine accounts of the lives of famous artists have appeared, beginning with Vasari's *Artists of the Renaissance*. However, few studies can trace the artistic development of its subject from the early years on; even when samples of childhood works have been preserved, they rarely comprise a sufficiently large body of work that lends itself to a developmental analysis.

Let me pose some of the questions that concern the psychologist interested in the arts and its development. Of course, a first question concerns the "markers" that might identify giftedness in childhood, and their relationship to the child's developmental level. Next, we need to inquire whether the development of talented children follows, in broad outlines, the same general course that characterizes ordinary children, whether the talented skip stages, reverse them, or altogether fall outside common developmental patterns. If one adopts a stage conception of development, does it entail a specific style of representation (realism) as the end goal toward which all children, especially, the gifted are inclined? Above and beyond the issue of "stages" in artistic development, which of our current theories can best account for the general as well as individual characteristics of the art of gifted children?

The motivation to draw and paint is at the core of gifted children's involvement with their art, thus we need to understand how such an interest first develops, and how it becomes a near compulsion to master the medium. To what extent is this desire and determination a function of an intrinsically motivated and fairly autonomously unfolding process, where the child essentially guides his or her own progression, and how much is it the product of early training and guidance provided by adults? The issue of motivation also has some bearing on the question of continuity in style and content over time, and the nature of change and of discontinuities.

This collection of six case studies provides a longitudinal acount of the development of children who can be variously described as *gifted* in the visual arts. We use this term in a very broad sense that includes those who as young adults choose art as their major vocation, as well as children who show an early fascination with drawing, attested by their large output, intense interest and, at times, unusual facility in rendering objects naturalistically. The longitudinal accounts highlight significant individual differences in the personality and style of the young artists reviewed here, and also cast into sharp relief the different perspectives the authors bring to their narratives. The developmental profiles focus on a diversity of motivating factors that propel their subjects to explore their chosen artistic medium and acquire the techniques that enable them to give form to their particular view of the world.

Each one of the authors brings a set of assumptions, explicitly stated or merely implied, to the narrative presentation of the artist. They attempt to define the symptoms or signs of giftedness in the young, raise the issue of continuity versus discontinuity and change in the artist's style and interests, and probe the motivation that underlies the child's artistic pursuit. Beyond factors that seem to inhere in the child, authors address the impact of environmental forces, including the family, schooling, and diverse social, cultural, and economic factors.

The first chapter, "The Changing Concept of Artistic Giftedness," by Diana Korzenik, provides an historical framework and a thoughtful discussion of terms and constructs that figure prominently in the chapters devoted to the case material. The reader is alerted to the conceptual complexity and ambiguity of the terms *giftedness, art, child artist,* and their shifting meaning within the historical context. She calls the reader's attention to the aesthetic preferences and "tastes" that underlie the construction of so-called general theories of graphic development, with authors often unaware that what they consider as markers of developmental shifts are also culture-bound conceptions. Students of child art do not construct their narrative of development as neutral observers who give equal weight to all manifestations. Their accounts are based on a selective reading of the material at hand, and so are the interpretations that reflect the author's concept of art and of the nature of children. Korzenik dates the concept of the "child as artist" to Jean Jacques Rousseau who engendered a new emerging aesthetic of primitivism and fostered a cult of childhood. She claims that "Gifted child artists must be considered in relation to the history of the writing about art, the teaching of art, and of the aesthetics that have shaped these discussions." In her view, conceptions of art and of giftedness coincide with the prevailing attitudes of a particular period; they are terms of praise for what critics and educators value in the art of their own time. Korzenik demonstrates how cultural change in taste, for example, from abstract expressionism to pop art, had its counterpart in the analysis of child art, and with it came a shift from appreciating preschoolers' so-called "abstractions" to valuing the comics produced by the middle- to late-childhood years that rely on graphic conventions.

Chapter 2, "Lautrec—Gifted Child Artist and Artistic Monument," by David Pariser, traces the development of a famous 19th-century artist. This material is of special interest because the gifted child, whose childhood work is quite extensive, grew up to become a great artist, one of the founders of the modernist tradition. The available data, which extend from his childhood to his mature adult works, permit an assessment of the full range of the artist's career.

Within the framework provided by Csikszentmihalyi's model of creativity, Pariser singles out three major determining factors in his analysis of Lautrec's development as an artist. He identifies the young Lautrec's innate graphic gifts, the technical knowledge embodied in the domain he needed to master, and the changing nature of the art world of his time.

On the basis of his reading of Lautrec's childhood work, Pariser argues that his early development follows the same ordered sequence of stages that characterizes the drawings of all children, and that like all talented children, he was hungry for technical knowledge, which he acquired in part by copying extensively from diverse sources. Copying was one of the ways in which he could perfect his graphic skills. Pariser sees a degree of continuity between the child's copying and Lautrec's later habit of "recycling" images from his established repertoire. He also sees a clear link between the vitality of the early lines and the mastery of his later drawings, both of which carry his highly individual signature. Pariser demonstrates significant continuities in Lautrec's collaborative illustrative work, in the treatment of subject matter, and in his experimentation with form and effect.

As one of the defining attributes of childhood giftedness, Pariser draws on Arnheim's distinction between the ability to attend to formal properties of an image and its effect. According to Pariser, "we can see the work of a gifted child whose primary interest is in the relationship between the formal properties of the image and the expressive effect that such properties engender." This special ability, which emerges fairly early in his work, is one of the continuities that mark this artist's career. "What Lautrec the child taught himself about the relationship between form and effect stood him in good stead when he became Lautrec the artist." Beyond an emphasis on internal forces that propelled Lautrec toward an artistic career, Pariser points out that it took more than graphic skills to move into a central place in the history of art, and he analyzes the special circumstances of family, wealth, physical appearance, Bruant, and the changing tastes in the art world that made this possible.

Chapter 3, "Varda: The Development of a Young Artist," by Claire Golomb and Malka Haas, provides a developmental account of a young artist, a sculptor, whose earliest works date from the age of 2. Given the rich collection of drawings from the early preschool years on, the authors focus on the principles that might explain the course Varda's development takes and the kind of transformations that characterize the different phases in the evolution of this gifted child into an adult artist. The conceptual framework that guides their inquiry is largely based on Arnheim's theory of representation, and Varda's childhood drawings document in broad outlines the interpretive power of his law of differentiation and the graphic logic that underlies her art. But beyond the insight derived from psychological laws and principles, the authors portray the artistic development of a gifted child who created her own pictorial language, recognizable in style and content over many years. The authors note that until the late adolescent years, when Varda enters art school, her development is largely self-directed, albeit within a generally supportive family environment.

Despite the highly original productions of young Varda, and the aesthetic appeal of her early work, Golomb and Haas assert that Varda does not skip stages in her graphic development. Her talent matures at its own rate, and its aesthetic appeal lies in an imaginative use of forms, colors, and composition that is congruent with her level of visual thinking, and not in the use of advanced three-dimensional techniques. "Seen over time, there is a continuous enrichment, a restructuring and reintegration of earlier developed forms, themes, and compositional strategies that enhance the expressive power of her work and its aesthetic appeal."

In chapter 4, "Germinal Motifs in the Work of a Gifted Child Artist," Constance Milbrath reports on the development of Joel, a highly gifted youngster for whom drawing was an all-consuming mental and physical activity, at the center of his emotional, intellectual, and social concerns. The author brings to her analysis a theoretical perspective that embraces Piaget's stage-based conception of cognitive development as proceeding from preoperational to concrete operational thought, and culminating in the achievement of formal operations, or more simply put, from a reliance on figural thought to thought based on formal properties and relations.

This theory provides a framework for studying the development of reasoning and productive thinking in general, and as it might apply to graphic representation.

Milbrath's approach to artistic representation is enriched by insights gained from her longstanding study of children gifted in the visual arts, and her intimate knowledge of skills that are domain specific. She examines Joel's artistic development by focusing on two central themes, animals and cartoon characters, and the styles of representation that he evolves over time. Although responsive to instruction when, infreqently, it is offered, Joel is largely self-taught, seeking out relevant information on his own, and engaging in constant, almost obsessive practice until he achieves the mastery he aims for. Striving for a realistic rendition of animals requires the acquisition of extensive anatomical knowledge of his favorite subject matter, dinosaurs, practicing its representation in different orientations and actions, and experimenting with the devices necessary for its depiction as a solid, three-dimensional object. Milbrath attributes his growing competence to changes in his ability to mentally evoke the object and its rotation, which reflects new cognitive capacities. In time, his interest in these prehistoric animals broadens in his quest to understand their environment and the causes for their extinction. He develops an intense fascination with paleontology and evolutionary history, and the drawings explore this knowledge and document it.

Cartooning is the second theme that is consistently explored from the age of 6 until the present time. It captures the changing interests and concerns of the developing individual until the characters express quite sophisticated sociopolitical ideas of the maturing artist. As with his drawings of animals, Joel's cartoon characters are products of fantasy and realism; they show his fine powers of observation and his desire to capture appearances as veridically as he can in a manner that connects their very being with his inner world.

The record of his drawings represents a coherent development over time, pursued with singular dedication. Despite the obvious changes that can be seen in his more recent paintings, there is also much continuity in style and motivation. In Joel's words: "I have had different styles from time to time ... I would draw things as realistically as I could. ... Now I paint ... very interior psychological paintings that have no figures in them ... just furniture and things. I also do cartoon work. I draw from life. All the styles I have ever had are still with me; it's just a question if they are relevant to something I'm thinking about."

Chapter 5, "It Was an Incredible Experience: The Impact of Educational Opportunities on a Talented Student's Art Development," by Enid Zimmerman provides a chronicle of the artistic development of her son, Eric. She provides a vivid description of parents who are art teachers, and whose philosophy of education stresses the acquisition of skills via extensive copying of a variety of sources. In Eric's home, art making, art exhibits, conversations about art education, and artistic achievements were at the center of family life. It was a close-knit family, and Eric's achievements are described by an "insider," who is a privileged participant in his life and also a professional, an art educator who teaches at an academic institution and is much involved in the education of children gifted in the arts. In this environment, Eric's interest in drawing, and his consuming ambition to excel, were nurtured in more than the usual show of parental pride and approval, and included parental advice and guidance, the availability of training manuals, active technical help, and early access to professional teachers.

Zimmerman's approach to art education and to developmental issues is eclectic and pragmatic, and the instructional goal is to help the aspiring young artist acquire the techniques that, traditionally, define the domain of western fine art. She understands the ambition of the young to master the domain, and the frustrations experienced along the way. In her view, talented and caring teachers have a tremendous impact on the developing child, and early training can yield remarkable achievements, an outcome she values and promotes. Of course, in Eric's case there is a dovetailing of parental desires and aspirations and Eric's burning ambition to become an accomplished artist who searches out instruction and, from approximately age 9 or 10, spends a great deal of time drawing at home or in his art classes. His achievements during his high school years, the prizes and scholarships he won, attest to the effectiveness of the formal schooling, and his own commentary lauds those teachers who knew how to inspire him and provide technical assistance.

This case study, with its emphasis on early training and on the role graphic models drawn from the popular culture play in young Eric's fantasy world, highlights the impact of sociocultural variables on children's drawings, and the emotional satisfaction children derive from creating their own fantasy story lines in cartoon format. In the debate of art educators about the educational value of copying, Eric supports the practice, and claims that it provides a deeper insight into the structure of pictorial space. According to Zimmerman, while copying a Picasso "he began to understand how space unfolds and how Picasso established picture planes from different perspectives, and curved space in a variety of directions ... copying art works provided an important means for understanding pictorial space and for acquiring technical skills." Eric tempers these remarks somewhat with reflections on the impact of formal training on the young. "Concentrating on formal design issues can be ultimately damaging to the young artist and result in art work that is 'dry and purely visual' and not connected to the world of the artist's imagination."

In chapter 6, "Eitan: The Artistic Development of a Child Prodigy," Claire Golomb reports on the development of an unusually gifted child who taught himself the major projective drawing systems by the time he was 4 years old, and used them with an expressive virtuosity of line that is quite arresting. Eitan's development is a study in contrast when compared with Varda (chapter 3) in his singular devotion to capture the appearance of his favorite objects, and to depict them as veridically as he can. His drawings are vibrant, they depict the volume and multiple sides of his vehicles (a favorite topic), and capture the action of helicopters, trucks, cement mixers, and construction scenes. His invention of diverse drawing systems and the manner and order in which he transforms them demonstrates the visual logic at work that underlies the evolution of Eitan's graphic solutions, a development that is best understood within the framework of Arnheim's theory.

Like Varda, and perhaps Joel, Eitan did not receive instruction until he reached high school, and even then avoided extracurricular drawing classes. Eitan was determined to follow his own path, specify what problems he wanted to work on, and then go about discovering the means to accomplish his aims. In this process, he invented some of the solutions adult artists have adopted to represent objects and their relations in a pictorial space that captures the three-dimensional aspects of our perceived world.

Like the other young artists in this collection, drawing was a much favored activity, engaged in daily, a record of changing interests and a means for recording his experience and understanding it more fully. Having mastered to his own satisfaction the representation of his favorite objects, which during adolescence include athletic events focused on the human body in action, the desire and perhaps even need to record his experiences visually diminished, as other activities, at which he is equally talented, competed for his attention. While he does not intend to pursue a fine arts career, his love for graphics points in the direction of architecture or industrial design as career options.

Chapter 7, "Nadia Reconsidered," by Lorna Selfe, provides a longitudinal account of the life course of a spectacularly gifted autistic child whose early drawings challenged established conventions on child art and autism. In this chapter, Selfe revisits Nadia, who is now an adult, and reassesses her earlier views of Nadia's art. Nadia came to her attention when it was discovered that this 6-year-old, severely retarded, autistic child created remarkable drawings in linear perspective, using foreshortening and other advanced devices of realism. She drew her favorite objects, mostly animals, from memory, and although she achieved what Selfe terms *photographic realism*, she also embellished her figures, and introduced changes that created a dynamic and vibrant image. She had total control over her use of lines and "at times the search for the line became very dominant and she would go over and over an area until the production looked as if she had employed shading. With the same impulse to achieve the correct line, Nadia would occasionally pick up an old drawing and correct it."

Nadia was a self-taught artist who "appeared happiest with an unrestricted supply ... usually after a second or, occasionally, third session the drawing was complete to her satisfaction." That realism was not her only motive can be seen in her continuous experimentation, for example, with drawings of heads that become smaller and smaller until her riders are headless!

On the advice of the professionals who had diagnosed her condition, Nadia was enrolled in a special school for autistic children. The school emphasized the acquisition of language and social skills, and Nadia seemed to benefit from the instruction. In terms of her drawing, she began to imitate her peers and her interest in photographic realism diminished. This change in the style of her drawing coincided with two major events in her life: the death of her mother when Nadia was 8, and the acquisition of some communication skills. Although Nadia continued to draw, and drawings made at age 12 are quite skillful, "the animation and excitement of her earlier years was totally absent."

Nadia, now in her 20s, lives in a residential home for adults with severe learning difficulties. Her former interest in drawing has waned into extinction. Selfe observes that "Her drawings now are the canonical representations so notably absent in her early years."

Nadia presents psychologists and artists with a seemingly unresolved puzzle: how to account for genius in a severely retarded person, and how to understand the loss, in her adult life, of what appears to have been a spectacular gift in early childhood. Selfe takes us through her earlier efforts to elucidate and explain Nadia's unique gift. She reviews her attempts to explain Nadia's artistry in terms of a compensation for severe language deficts, an accelerated development of representational ability based on deficits in symbolic and conceptual processes, a pathological process due to her autism. "Photographic realism involves one lone viewer surveying a scene from one fixed spot. Such an image of autism is a poetically compelling one ... for this there need not be an apology." Selfe reaffirms her earlier belief that Nadia's drawings were not evidence for an accelerated progress of normal development, but rather a sign of her pathology. She ponders the effect of the death of Nadia's mother, who had encouraged her drawings and prized them. In the end, Selfe, who has studied Nadia's gifts and her life's course closely, acknowledges that Nadia's case is not adequately captured by a reductive analysis.

In chapter 8, "Elusive Profiles: Tentatively Sketched Giftedness," Ronald MacGregor provides both commentary and reflections on art, artists, art education, and the difficulty of making generalizations of highly idiosyncratic developments. He examines the case studies for what they tell us about truly gifted youngsters and proposes to study their artistic endeavors against, what he terms Geertz' *common-sense floor* of the desire to render the world distinct. On the assumption that the gifted "transcend the state of accepting things as they are," MacGregor contrasts the particular qualities of the gifted against the conception of a common-sense floor. He points toward certain commonalities shared by young gifted persons: a strong voice in defining their own identity, ambition, commitment, a crystallizing experience that leads to clearly seeing the road ahead. MacGregor marvels at the artistic intuition of these young artists who discern their path, and pursue it with or without guidance. He remarks on their attention to detail, the richness of their depiction, the themes, and the growing repertoire of techniques. Out of these common behaviors, "a sense of challenge, an appetite for investigation, an openness to new experience, and the acquisition and development of personal metaphors, gifted and talented children forge their individual identities. Their art provides them with a means to orient themselves in the shifting sands of life as lived and life as told."

MacGregor also acknowledges the limits of efforts to generalize beyond the individual cases when considering Nadia, whose art, in MacGregor's view, resembled the drawings of Feliks Topolski, a Polish artist. "Was it possible to claim that Topolski's work had emotional and structural authority, whereas Nadia's, closely related though it was in appearance, lacked that authority?"

In bringing together this collection of cases, our aim was to sketch the variety of ways in which talented children develop their interest in the visual arts. Case studies provide us with a close view of the genesis of artistic creativity and allow us to trace the manner in which universal graphic forms are transformed into the personal vocabulary of the young artist. Where the material dates from early childhood, we can witness the emergence of visual thinking as the child discovers the properties of the graphic medium and the ways in which it can be used to create order and meaning in his world.

To create, to make images, is a basic human propensity that all children share and that can become an absorbing, almost all-consuming activity. In the child's early years, the drawings are fairly autonomous creations, made without much attention to the graphic models presented in picture books or photographs. With the invention of forms, a process of restructuring sets in that yields new levels of competence, awareness, and inventiveness in the manner in which models, the child's own and those of others, are adapted to suit the individual's needs. Gifted children exemplify this general process by their heightened involvement with drawing, and the persistence, intensity, and originality with which they forge their personal style of representation. In their love of drawing and the intensity with which they pursue their art making, they show an affinity to the motives and urges of the adult artist, a proposition that the case studies examine, exemplify, or challenge.

1

The Changing Concept of Artistic Giftedness

Diana Korzenik
Harvard University

This volume is devoted to *gifted child artists*. Collected here are individual cases of developmental sequences of drawing and painting beginning in the earliest years. Because of our position in time, in one case we actually know the mature art produced by the now reknown artist, Toulouse Lautrec. In his case, adult achievements justify our curiosity about his early production. The other case studies are without the "proof" of century's praise of their adult art careers. The authors of these identify and chart the individual child's "gift" based on a quantity of surviving work of those still young or who are in the midst of developing careers in art or an art-related field. The authors of the case studies, whether they be of artists' juvenalia or those who have chosen to pursue art, demonstrate a consensus that the study of gifted child art belongs within the field of psychology.

In my work, I have combined the psychology of art with research in the field of U.S. social and artistic history. My intention in writing this chapter is to complement the other authors' psychological point of view by alerting readers to an adjustment that happens when gifted child artists are viewed in a historical context. In these pages, I make the case for considering the judgment of any particular child's drawings or paintings in the context of the era in which that judgment was made.

In the mid-1970s, I came to college teaching as a painter and art historian trained in the psychology of art. My students were the "class artists" whose success in high school convinced them to come to an art college. As a new teacher, I instinctively and vigilantly avoided such words as *creativity, talent,* and *giftedness* in referring to their work or to that of even younger people they someday might teach. I felt that those words generated more problems than they solved. Over time I decided that I needed to understand why those words seemed to me so misleading and unreliable. Over the years since I have read widely in U.S. and European art history studying how and when people used these terms.

A professional turning point came for me some years after I started teaching. As a then active member of the new Harvard Project Zero, Nelson Goodman and I went to a seminar to discuss a then new study by Carothers and Gardner (1979). The researchers wanted us to respond to data they had pertaining to when—at what age in children's development—one might claim a child's work became art. I saw a problem. What Carothers and Gardner posed as a question in the domain of psychology, I immediately realized was not really a question answerable by psychology. Whether or not a piece was art needed to be examined historically. Aesthetic judgments happen within a culture at a particular time. At what age in children's development one might claim a child's work became art was a question of how adults of a certain era interpreted childhood. To my mind, whatever the judgment, when children's work became art had to be a function of the time when the particular judgment was made.

Because my first degree was in art history, I already was trained to think historically. I understood that the place, time, and culture of a people determined their concepts, actions, values, and the use of words. At that seminar, in the case of the Carothers and Gardner study and others like it, my recommendation was that one needed to examine what was being taken for granted; namely, how the researchers were using the word *art*. The word *art* was broad. It implied it was a culture-free abstraction, whereas in fact art is always a historical artifact.

In that Project Zero meeting, I shifted the course of my professional work. I decided then that I wanted my contribution to the psychology of art to be the addition, the enrichment of the discussion of children's drawing and painting that comes from a historical perspective. Historical inquiry was to be the method of my future work. I was and still am as interested in children's graphic products as ever, but I keep looking to understand that work in the context of culture. History since then has been my means of investigating questions of artistic development.

This book's prepublication title included the words *child artist*. This term is relatively new and hardly defined. Even if we can agree that *child* refers to a measurable chunk of time in the life cycle, the term *artist* allows no such precision. *Artist* is an evaluative word with no objective measure. As soon as we try to apply these words to real children we can see the problems. The domain of art has not always had room in it for any work of children. In what respect today can we say children are artists? What particular behaviors lead us to say children resemble artists? The title becomes even more ambiguous when we add *gifted* to the pair, child artist. What basis have we for identifying one child as more gifted than another? Is there an objective basis for judgment, or does each critic subject the child's product to some tacit standard that evolves with each era's styles and trends? It seems both honest and productive to begin this examination by facing the fact that for experts, parents, and even children this cluster of words, *gifted child artist*, is problematic.

In this chapter, I intend to show how the definitions of *gifted, child,* and *artist* all depend on what connections, if any, people made between their ideas about children and their ideas about making art. Whomever's judgment we read, we need to keep asking what is the bias of the person to whose judgment we refer and what influenced that judgment? Gifted child artists must be considered in relation to the history of the writing about art, the teaching of art, and of the aesthetics that have shaped these discussions.

To reflect on the enterprise of all the authors whose case studies are in this book, it is first necesary to untangle certain assumptions. I do this in four steps and focus on the following issues: (a) taste as the basis of artistic judgment, (b) the child as artist, (c) the artist as child, and (d) giftedness.

TASTE AS THE BASIS OF ARTISTIC JUDGMENT

Occasionally we find an exhibition of paintings by children hung in an art gallery that at another time would be exhibiting adult art. When we do, it is based on certain assumptions that need to be made explicit. They are that (a) the children's work is worth looking at, (b) a viewer will find interest in the time spent contemplating the work, and (c) the children's work is art. As such, it may be appreciated by adults through the same critical sensibility that they bring to adult art. It is assumed that the works on the walls may be appreciated by viewers who have no training in how young children think and feel and how they use materials.

Do children's works become art because of changes that occur at certain times within the development of the child? Or do children's works become art when adults change, when they are culturally influenced by issues in the society so that they choose to construe the children's actions as art? To some degree, both statements are true, but here I provide evidence to support the latter case.

Most contemporary psychological researchers assume that a child who is making a drawing is making art. The words *child artist* are in the literature and they seem to have stuck. Psychologists seem not to have asked themselves, as artist Paul Klee did, if perhaps this was not the case. This is a necessary step in seeing the problems built into the term *gifted child artist*. If we reflect back over time, even over a century, we find that there are many artists, art educators, researchers, who indeed have considered the question and concluded that children's work was not art.

Because we are considering when children's work is called art, we would do well to remember that calling children's work "art" is an act of adult classification. We would remember Goodman's (1968) admonition that there is no innocent eye. "The eye comes always ancient to its work, obsessed by its own past and by old and new insinuations of the ear, nose, tongue, fingers, heart and brain. Not only how, but what it sees, is regulated by need and prejudice" (p. 7). Thus, we must acknowledge that we look at a child's painting with an eye not only influenced by the array of other flat painted surfaces made by adults and called *art*, but by many other influences that generate controversies and vitality with the society as well.

Adult taste is subject to all sorts of influence. The ancient eye that lived through the recent decades could not escape the challenge to European art that arose largely in this country under the label Abstract Expressionism. The shocking appearance of the then radically new art intrigued viewers. Beginning in the mid-1940s, big broad brush strokes became symbols of freedom. Freedom was more than an aesthetic banner. Freedom was also understood in its political sense. Freedom was to be our nation's contribution to the international post-World War II art market. Paris was out. New York was in. This taste did more than sell paintings in the United States and abroad. It enhanced interest in another form of painting that had been there all the while, that of the preschooler.

In my view, the superficial likeness of Abstract Expressionism and child art tended to attract and then blind viewers, so that to many the adult art and the preschool products became fused as two versions of the same enterprise. Adult viewers experienced a form of narcissism. They projected onto the child what they imagined were the motivations of the abstract expressionist adult artists; both types of artists were seen as making expressions of some sort of uncompromised freedom. This projection prevented viewers from seeing what was unique to the child in the painting process. Similarly, they lost track of what was the work of the artists who made the abstract paintings. The outcome of this fusion was exhibitions of child art featuring big broad paintstrokes.

My own dissertation, finished in 1972, grew out of this particular aesthetic moment. I chose my subject precisely in order to clarify what back then I saw as a confusion between what children were doing and what adults do in graphic production. My study was 5- and 7-year-old children's shift from producing ambiguous to readable drawings. The young children's ambiguous images may have seemed to resemble the abstract expressionists' work, but the readable ones certainly did not. My data convinced me that unlike adult abstract expressionist artists, even at 5 when children were making ambiguous, "abstract" shapes, their intent was referential. When viewers had difficulty discerning children's intentions, even at age 5 the children drew with representational intentions!

In the 1970s and 1980s, I already felt a shift away from the rhetoric that fostered and sold Abstract Expressionism. Instead of freedom, art viewers were becoming rhapsodic about graphic conventions, such as the line drawing from the comics, and production systems employed in the mass distribution of images, such as halftone dots from photographic reproduction. Roy Lichtenstein extracted the functional halftone dots from printer's images and used the halftone illusionism in his larger-than-life size painting and sculpture. James Rosenquist, Barbara Krueger, Alex Katz, Red Grooms, and others derived their themes from advertising and other graphic conventions. Curiously, at this time teachers and researchers who watched the art world shifted their interests from the artifacts of early childhood to those created by older children, 9- through 12-year-old children (Churchill, 1970; Pariser, 1977; B. Wilson, 1974). Adults grew interested in more mature behaviors, how children seek out, learn, and then routinize available graphic conventions. They admired this age at which children become proficient cartoonists.

Although this stage drew interest, universally it was not yet prized. Gardner, who in *Artful Scribbles* (1980) was still enamored with the idea that children painted like Abstract Expressionists, saw in the 9- to 12-year stage the nadir of creativity, the deepest dip in what he labeled the artistic U-Shape curve.

But changes in taste, however slowly, do permeate popular art judgments about what children are making. In only a couple of decades, the work that teachers used to apologize for, that caused parents to mourn for their children's lost artistry, that Gardner placed at the nadir of creativity, came to be exhibited and admired. Art educators began to write books on drawing that encouraged children's exploration of graphic conventions such as Superman and Superwoman—that they and their colleagues only a decade or two earlier would have wholeheartedly discouraged (B. Wilson, 1974; M. Wilson & Wilson, 1982).

In the 1990s, entirely different aesthetic issues are in. Instead of the ambiguous, gestural, hard-to-read private graphic expression of the abstract expressionism of mid-century and its colorful reverberations that infused popular taste into the subsequent decades, instead of the proliferation of graphic conventions of pop art, we now face a highly politicized plurality of styles. Appropriation is in. Some artists juxtapose type and graphics from billboards to startle the viewer with new meanings. Others detach the idea of art from any notion of permanence and durability. They make their art not to last. An important attribute of the artwork is its having no saleable product. The process of engaging complex governmental agencies is central to the work of such artists as Christo. His works are events in time that explicitly avoid a permanent vestige. Only drawings and photographs may survive as records.

The art world itself—the art market and the control of taste—has become the subject of art. Politics has returned to art. Artists are challenging viewers to examine their works specifically in terms of the plagues that are AIDS and cancer, and the inequities inherent in social class, ethnicity, and gender. Adult concerns have beome the content of much new art. Even so, Tim Rollins seized this as opportunity for himself and the art he encouraged young people to make. "The Kids of Survival," his adolescent boy artists group, became equivalent to a pop music group. Kids of Survival became all the rage. Rollins' controversial work with the boys in the inner city thereby joined other contemporary art by being inherently political. To my mind, Kids of Survival represented a latter day version, a recent example of the same confusion that led the writers of past decades to merge young children's art and abstract expressionism. Adults keep tapping and admiring in young people's work whatever they can get them to make that will resemble the current art world's taste.

Adults do literally shape what children draw and paint in the choices of what they did and did not give children in the realm of art materials. From my own New York childhood in the 1940s I know that girls and boys were as fascinated with copying and conventions as they were in the 1980s and are in the 1990s, but back then the use of coloring books or any commercial copying device was strictly taboo.

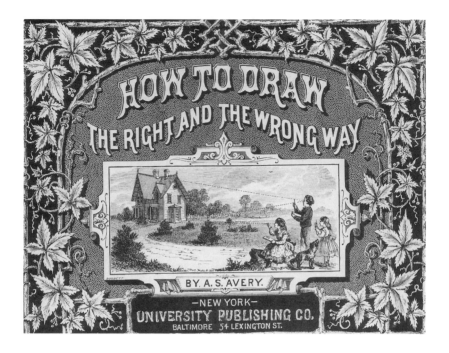

FIG. 1.1. A. S. Avery's "How to Draw, the Right and the Wrong Way," New York University Publishing Co., 1871. Spontaneity had little to do with what Avery prized. Skill was a sure and steady hand. These, put to the task of rendering specific copies, were the mark of the good child artist. The child's ultimate success in drawing was his or her rendering the observed world in correct size relationships. (Korzenik Collection.)

Among parents who were concerned to foster their children's imagination and artistic skills, coloring books were reputed to be destructive. It was said that the use of coloring books contributed to the demise of children's creativity. Like television today, coloring books were blamed for ills from which the young were seen to suffer.

Lowenfeld, a Viennese refugee from Hitler who taught in the United States first at Hampton Institute and then at Pennsylvania State University, provided evidence against using coloring books. In a book he wrote for parents, *Your Child and His Art* (Lowenfeld, 1954), he charged that "because they are so easily obtainable ... (coloring books) ... probably have had a most devastating effect on children and their art" (p. 12). Lowenfeld believed that from coloring books children too easily acquired graphic conventions which spared them having to think for themselves. He believed that if children were shown, for example, simplified formulas for birds in flight, drawn as Vs, they would be likely to imitate these Vs and to name them "birds." Adopting these Vs would substitute for the children's inventing their own forms for representing their experiences of seeing flying creatures. Lowenfeld's pedagogy aimed at getting children to invent forms that expressed what they saw and felt (Lowenfeld, 1952). Some experts concluded that coloring the spaces inside any outlined pictures eroded the children's capacities for imaginative, original thinking. Some went further and distrusted too detailed pictures illustrating the text in school readers. Their ideal was an uncontaminated child, free of adult influence.

Another example is Kellogg (1969), a writer and an early childhood educator at San Franciso's Golden Gate Nursery School who wrote *Analyzing Children's Art*. Active a bit after Lowenfeld, she also worried about the materials adults give to children. She felt that unwittingly we distorted and limited the child's own process. Kellogg distrusted adults who asked children to tell about their pictures. She faulted adults who asked children to title their pictures. But what interests me here is Kellogg's challenging the prevailing use of particular drawing tools. She questioned nursery and preschools providing young children with only fat paintbrushes and thick paint. She felt these promoted only a bold abstract look to the childrens' products. As if to support Golomb's (1974) thesis in *Young Children's Sculpture and Drawing*, Kellogg found that materials determined the forms that children invent to give shape to their ideas. Kellogg believed that giving them wide brushes just prolonged the number of years that young children would keep producing primitive crude-looking paintings. To test her notion, Kellogg began to watch what preschool children drew when she gave them fine-line colored markers. The preschool children's drawings changed and so did the prevailing notions of how children draw. With the fine-line markers the children capitalized on the thinness of the lines to construct tiny, more controlled forms. Small circles and fine stripes replaced the thick round shapes and fat wide lines the children used to make.

Whatever styles shape their adults' aesthetic judgments cannot but so impinge on adults' interpretation of "child art" in general and of "giftedness" in particular. Within each decade, new styles enter and challenge the prevailing tastes. Each decade, adults keep giving or withholding from children certain materials or images that give direction to what the children do.

Meanwhile, very young children are largely impervious to these trends. They keep getting ideas and making their marks. Their work will always be more complex than adults will notice. As the researchers on 16th- and 17th-century painters' early education in *Children of Mercury* (Muller, 1984) suggest, for centuries children's graphic development has resembled today's children's developmental stages. Girls and boys probably have always progressed through certain formal and conceptual uses of drawing, painting, and modeling.

What changes, what is most susceptible to change, is how adults with their never-innocent eyes and intellects, look at, encourage, and interpret what children do. Adult observers choose to see, isolate, and encourage only a small facet of the child's activity they see as art. That is what adults give children permission to make. As children get older and incorporate adults' judgments, whether they be Lowenfeld's or Kellogg's or another's choices, because children exist in a culture with these adults, inevitably they respond to and incorporate the influence of adults' taste.

My research in the history of U.S. art education has convinced me that student exhibitions say from the 1870s, 1930s, and 1960s generated entirely different notions of what young people can draw and paint. Among the innumerable possible forms children may master, products selected for display as children's art always reveal what adults at that time admire. More or less explicitly, adults direct and give children permission to make the forms they make. They tell children what they value. They also guide their efforts by what they pay attention to. Although they may never actually move the pencil in the young person's hand, adults keep reshaping what they take as children's work. What each era selects for its exhibitions of student work never is just an outcome from an uncontaminated hypothetical "pure child." The objects we see hanging in exhibitions always are manifestations of adult taste. The same taste that causes adults to prefer one stage of childhood over another also guides adults' selection of objects to exhibit in young people's art exhibitions. Probably, educators could be more effective if they admitted to their students that much of the knowledge about art that they pass along to them reflects precisely what art they as adults like. Once teachers make this explicit they can be freer to say what it is about a certain style that they personally prefer and why.

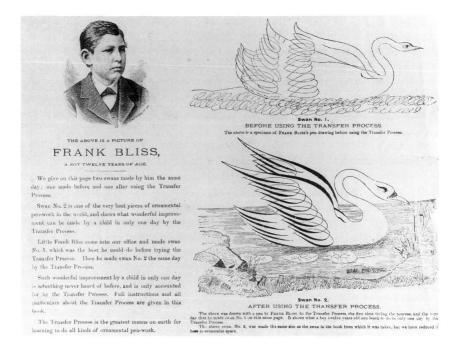

FIG. 1.2. "Real Pen Work—Self Instructor," Pittsfield, Massachusetts, 1881. This 12-year-old, Frank Bliss, learned to picture swans in elaborate pen work in two different systems. His first way was to imitate the marks he saw, the second was a direct transfer process. His cleverness, according to the advocates of this transfer method, was his choice of the "Real Pen Work" transfer process.

To put a frame around this discussion of taste, we need to step back. Not only has children's drawing continually been subject to taste, but so has drawing itself—as a category within art. Over many centuries, the informal sketches that we call *drawings*, have been seen primarily as notes made in the planning stages

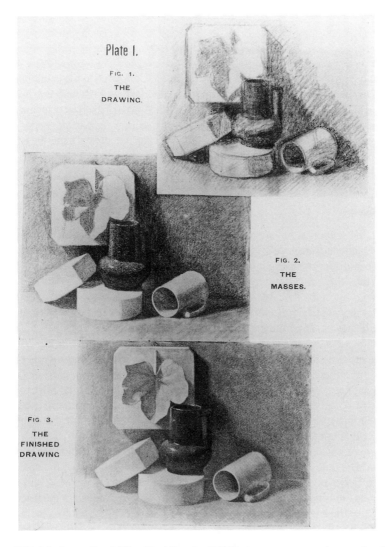

FIG. 1.3. Anson Cross' "Free Hand Drawing," 1897. A century ago, teachers produced and expected their students to produce drawings like these. The skills of a Boston school child astonished viewers. When their drawings came on public exhibition, crowds came to see what children could do. What we might attribute to talent, they knew could be and was taught.

of a work. They were not considered art. In the 18th century, critics and artists launched a debate about whether or not such drawing could be art. Some said thoughts on paper in preparation for art were not art. Only late in that century and early in the next, under the influence of the romantic writers and artists, did those private, preparatory investigations we call *drawings* rise to the level of art. People's then new saving and collecting of drawings is yet another proof that taste keeps shaping what we accept as art.

THE CHILD AS ARTIST

Some changes are swift. Others are of longer duration. Compared to the phenomena just reviewed here, the emergence of the notion of the child as artist has been much slower and more durable. Nevertheless, "the child as artist" itself is a historical phenomenon. All the interpretations of the preceding section on taste, depended on a view that children's work was or could be art. This has not always been the case. The determination that the child could make art—indeed could be an artist—itself was a product of a historical moment.

Rousseau

As I see it, the sequence that launched the notion that the child was an artist began with Jean Jacques Rousseau's writing of *Emile* (1762/1964). That book shaped what two centuries later people still would be seeing and saying about art, about children's drawing, and drawing's role in their psychological and educational development. In *Emile*, Rousseau redefined adult art as bad. Art was one example of his belief that society corrupts, that everything degenerates in the hands of man. He had little good to say for the art of his time.

Nevertheless, Rousseau did write about drawing. In *Emile*, he conjured an imaginary situation in which he and his student, Emile, are drawing together. In Rousseau's judgment, neither draws very well at the start. As a pedagogical device, Rousseau suggested to Emile that the earliest unskilled efforts by both of them should be fitted in grand gold frames, the sort that his contemporaries used to display their most prized works of art. Thereby, Rousseau taught Emile that neither their first efforts nor the artists' paintings that normally would be presented in gold frames were of much worth. Rousseau's rather naughty idea was intended to shock his readers. His gold frame prescription enabled him to ridicule what his society called "art." With one act he could denegrate both beginners at drawing and the adult painters of his time. Rousseau wrote that when either the student or the teacher wishes to disparage the performance of the other, he can condemn it by placing it in a gilt frame. Rousseau's device was a more acidic 18th-century version of 20th-century critics who attacked modernism by saying "Any child could do that!"

Rousseau's ridicule of the art of his time was a necessary component of his articulation of a new aesthetic, an aesthetic of primitivism. Boas (1966), in *The Cult of Childhood,* charted Rousseau's challenge to his time and to those of us who followed. We were to seek the beautiful in the untrained, the naive, the primitive, in whatever was least contaminated by Western European society. Boas sees the United States as having been particularly receptive to this ideology. Perhaps because as a culture we are younger than those of Europe, we have been particularly fertile soil for the "primitivist" arguments. Rousseau's ideas have deeply pervaded our notions about children. Boas argued that we as a nation have idealized childhood and we sought to prolong it as long as possible. He warned readers that "primitivism" or the cult of childhood was but one of many possible ways of thinking about the human being's first years.

Boas sees the key to Rousseau's aesthetic appearing right in his start of *Emile*. He begins with the statement that, "Everything is good as it comes from the hands of the Creator; everything degenerates in the hands of man" (p. 55). Given this premise, children have a priviledged status. They have less experience in and exposure to society. Children are closer to God having lived less time. Rousseau posited that children were purer and better and less contaminated than adults who have lived in human society many more years. It follows that whatever children do spontaneously and uninstructed, should be superior to that which adults do having had a lifetime of guidance and acculturation from others within their society. Aesthetic of primitivism or the cult of childhood is a form of "agism," in which one generation is pitted against another.

Although the child was closer to all that was good, Rousseau did not call the child an *artist*. The term *artist* was just too closely associated with society's many institutions: monarchy, aristocracy, and the church. All these had negative and destructive effects on people. So, although Rousseau valued the child's capacity to draw, the child was not an "artist" nor was the drawing a production of "art."

What Rousseau did value was drawing as a process that engaged children's young avid minds. Even as Rousseau ridiculed the ambitions of artists of his time, and those who collected and displayed their products as ornaments in gold frames, he did value the drawing process. Drawing could be an aid to independent, individual observation, a tool for the study of phenomena that attracted the young person' inquiring eye. Drawing could become a tool in the hands of children for internalizing new knowledge. Rousseau believed that the children who drew would be those who would possess their own active minds, stored full of whatever they observed. Talent had nothing to do with this enterprise. The activity he admired and would have cultivated was that which came naturally to most young people. Their capacities normally permit them to use drawing as one of the many ways human beings have for taking in new experiences. For Rousseau drawing was a valuable means and a prized record of the mind's enjoyment and engagement with nature. So, although Rousseau used *Emile* to show the benefits to the child of engaging in drawing, never would he describe a child as a *child artist.*

Parker

In the late 19th-century United States, Parker (1894), an enthusiast of Rousseauian ideas, refined Rousseau's ideas into his own pedagogy known through his *Talks on Pedagogics*. A Civil War veteran, Parker became reknown as one of the United States' foremost educators. He urged teachers to balance children's learning by continually engaging them in two processes: attention and expression. Attention was the children's process of taking in to their minds experiences of the world. Attention involved seeing, listening, touching, and the use of such mediated processes as reading books and listening to stories. Expression, by contrast, was the children's more active process. It necessitated a transformation of whatever was taken in, by the child's having paid attention. Expression required the children's actually using and transforming the material taken in through the processes of attention.

For Parker, drawing became a perfect example of the process of expression. Children may look at flowers, hear about their structure, learn about their form and their growth. But until they draw the flowers, they have not yet really understood, or digested what they have learned. One needs to draw what one has understood about the flowers. To both Rousseau and Parker, drawing is a tool for "study skills." Since their time, this study skills approach has become a tradition of classroom teaching as is documented in *Art Making and Education* (Korzenik, 1993).

Although Parker and Rousseau shared this appreciation of drawing as a pedagogical tool, Parker departed from Rousseau in enthusiastically calling the child an *artist*. Gone is the disparagement of the artist. To Parker, the child has an inborn artistic nature. As is shown in *Drawn To Art* (Korzenik, 1985), to Parker every child was a born artist. "The child has the art element born into him" (p. 119). To Parker, the child's cognitive processes of attending and expressing are exactly analogous to what artists do. Attention and expression together encompass the art-making process. Although both Rousseau and Parker shared the cult of childhood, one century after Rousseau, Parker encouraged Americans to think of children as artists.

With all their differences, those who followed Rousseau in Europe (Pestalozzi and Froebel) and their advocates here in the United States (Alcott, Peabody, Krusi, Parker, and Dewey) kept refueling the notion that drawing and painting were ways children learned. With permutations, the notion of the *child artist* seems to have held up to our time. Despite severe budgetary constraints, crayons and colored paper remain staples in our late 20th-century elementary schools because of our continuing adherence to the romantic conviction that children are artists. We would do well to keep in mind that this idea is a relatively new one in the broad sweep of history.

THE ARTIST AS CHILD

The durability of the notion of the child as artist is a function of another charged and controversial idea. It is that artists really are grown-up children. Some believe that artists think like children and act like children. To be imaginative is to be childlike. To love to get one's hands into materials is seen as childish. To join together two elements in an unconventional way, is associated with the play of children. Some artists themselves have actively contributed to this notion.

Others object to this characterization. They find this description offensive. To them, this profile of artists maligns people who devoted a lifetime to acquiring their skills and judgments. We need to become sensitive to the implications of both sides of this debate because they impinge on our use of the term *child art*. Psychologists

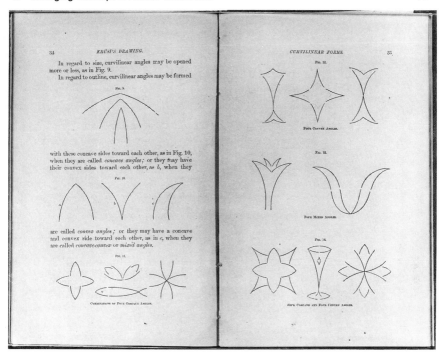

FIG. 1.4. Herman Krusi's system of drawing for Invention, 1874. Originality was prized in this sytem of drawing. Invention involved manipulation of small units of shape, reminiscent of the "Gifts and Occupations" developed by Frederick Froebel for the kindergarten. (Korzenik Collection.)

as well as artists, critics, and art historians who write about artists, need to reflect on the question: "How, if at all, is it productive to think of artists as children?"

In the 20th century, it has became popular to admire artists for having the creativity and spontaneity of children. Artists who aspired to free themselves from the burdens of the past, reveled in the idealization of childhood. Their inventiveness was to be entirely their own, purportedly uninfluenced by any prior ideas. Picasso purportedly prided himself on the idea that it took him his whole lifetime of making art to get back to drawing like a child.

Critics

But in the 19th century, the appeal of that notion was indeed mixed. The particular connotations of the words *artist* and *child* determined the meaning of people's responses. If they believed that by nature children were limited and rigid, and they prized inventiveness and spontaneity in artists, then calling an artist a child would be a condemnation. But, if they thought of children as having boundless ideas, being flexible and playful with those ideas, and these same qualities were admirable in artists, then saying that an artist was pure child could be a compliment. Both views were espoused within the last century.

FIG. 1.5. Child art and Franz Cizek, 1936. During World War II, the Red Cross published Wilhelm Viola's celebration of Franz Cizek's Juvenile Art Class in Vienna. Here, every child was given the opportunity to be "uninfluenced by adults." The marks of the youngest, because they were least influenced, were believed to be the "purest manifestation of artistic creativeness."

Schapiro (1941), in his essay "Courbet and Popular Imagery," described the critics' debate throughout the mid-19th century regarding the charge of "childishness" that initially was brought against Gustave Courbet. He was faulted for being childish because his critics believed he composed his pictures too rigidly. At that time, *childishness* was a term used to refer to a schematic, inflexible treatment of the human figure. Children's work here is characterized as limited and inflexible. The child at this time was associated with the naive artist who was the maker of popular imagery for the proletarian culture. In 1856, Max Buchon altered this trend in criticism. He praised Courbet and introduced the concept of an "instinctive folk creativeness ... an enormous power of intuition" (Schapiro, 1941, p. 172). This folk power or instinctual aesthetic then came to be associated with the work produced by children.

Through reading 19th-century criticism of adult art, we can track changes in the connotions to both the virtues in childhood and those of artistry. We witness the concept of child shifting from a rigid being to one with the power of instinctive creativeness. One critic, Champfleury, argued for the value of the primitive in art and defended naive art and child art at once, "The stammering of children is the same in all countries. ... It offers the charm of innocence, and the charm of the modern *imagiers* comes from the fact that they have remained children. They have escaped the progress of cities" (Schapiro, 1941, p. 178). So, artists came to be admired for remaining as Rousseau envisioned Emile and children raised in this fashion. Artists were people who explored and flourished in nature, away from and impervious to the damage of cities and their culture.

The artist, according to Champfleury, should be like "the stammering child." He, for the writers then were thinking only of men, should retain "the charm of innocence." The model for the artist is the rural child who escaped formal education, whose unformed speech is only "stammering." The artist gains what the rural child preserves. The artist must be left free of the damage of "progress" overwhelming life in the mercantile, industrialized cities. In terms of aesthetics, "to escape progress" becomes a positive value. The artist should be like the country boy who retains his verve, zest, and vitality. The view that boys and artists left to thrive in the country will retain their artistic spirit was nostalgic.

The term *child* came to be a pun. Nostalgia took on double meaning. The child was a human being in his or her immature, early, undamaged, phase of his or her own individual life. As a rural creature the child also stands for the childhood of Western European culture. The country comes to stand for an early time when agriculture prevailed. The country as a place came to stand for a period in time, before that industrial change that drove people together in congested cities and subjected them to the progress associated with them. The child becomes a symbol of a primitive, spared the contamination of the modern world. From the child's pure nature, something better is generated than what cities can yield. In France, these ideas crystallized the hope and expectation for redemption that some art critics, such as Champfleury, expected from artists who were his contemporaries.

The concept of the child was contingent upon the view that the child must survive by being kept independent of adult society. Champfleury wrote: "Send the gamin to an art school and with his greater knowledge of the object, he will have lost the vivacity and the artistic intention he had possessed before" (Schapiro, 1941, p. 179). So the image of the child requires not only a chronological stage of life, but the deliberate prolongation of it. Precisely this is what Boas describe as "the cult of childhood."

By the mid-19th century, the concept of children expressing their own unadulterated ideas, and the artists retaining their powerful artistic intentions became mutually stimulating, but the concept of the child as artist needed one generation before it appeared in the scientific writing, the psychological writing about child art.

Not everyone liked the idea that the child be seen as an artist. Schapiro interpreted the resistance to accepting the idea of the child as artist, by suggesting that certain *consequences* of the idea were found unacceptable. Schapiro seemed to be saying that it is one thing to speak of "the child." It is quite another to talk about "children." He was showing how it was one thing to idealize and to uphold "the child" as an abstraction, as a model of aesthetic values, and is quite another to see children as parents and teachers see them everyday. To illustrate this point, Schapiro cited that although Baudelaire passionately believed that the child was the prototype of the artist, the art of children, the actual images boys and girls make, held no interest for him. Baudelaire perceived children's picturing simply as deficient, clumsy, and imperfect. For Baudelaire, that clumsiness was an advantage because he suspected that the child's lack of skill in rendering his thoughts enabled the child to live that much more than the rest of us, in a world of incomparable intensity of feeling. It is to Baudelaire that we owe the concept of the child as intensely observant and as having a curious sensibility obsessed with the visual world and the shock of sensation. Although the sensibility and emotionality of the child are seen as artistic, the images children actually make are not.

Schapiro's distinction seems to me crucial. Speaking of "the child" as an abstraction is entirely different from the observation of real children in our daily life with them. Viewing the child in the abstract as being sensitive, having intense emotions and a free imagination, in no way necessitates that the graphic work children generate should be viewed as art. The child in Baudelaire's writing was not a "child artist."

Those critics who did prize children did so in two steps. First they admired the child's temperament, sensibility, curiosity. The next step was to admire children's work for qualities of naiveté, primitivism, the work's seeming imperviousness to culture, particularly that culture that grew in cities. Schapiro sees this in *Reflections. Essays on the Beautiful in Art* by Topffer (1848). Topffer, unlike Baudelaire, avoided comparison of children's drawings with adult standards. His enthusiasm for children's drawings was based on his seeing in them their own unique qualities that were a function of children's expressing their own ideas. Topffer's appreciation of children's drawings grew from his position as an antirealist critic. Children's independence from illusionism was exactly what pleased and attracted his eye. Therefore, with Topffer our very modern taste for "graffitti" first emerges, because as Boas in *The Cult of Childhood* reminds us, Topffer's fascination with children's drawings began with his observation of those marks children leave on the walls of buildings and in the margins of their books. Topffer saw in this scribbling a fusion of the immature art of children with that of the uneducated savage. Both sorts of creations, of children and "primitives," to him had an instinctive sense of beauty, which their makers would forfeit if they were schooled.

Artists

Artists themselves had different relationships to this whole debate of whether the child was an artist. Wittkower and Wittkower (1963), in *Born Under Saturn,* showed that through the centuries artists conformed to the cultural climate that prevailed. Ideas about artistic temperament, dress, manners, even lifestyles, were taken on as one might dress to take on a part in a play. For example, by the 17th century, the proto-Bohemian melancholic artist had gone out of fashion. The great 17th-century masters, Bernini, Rembrandt, Rubens, and Velasquez were described in the ways their predecessors never had been. For them there was no room for the impulsive, brooding, or childish emotionality that again would come back into fashion in the 19th century. That melancholic characterization of artists did not reappear until Romanticism conjured it again and artists, like the German painter Caspar David Friedrick, took on the part.

By the 20th century, painters themselves still wrestled with their own reactions to society's stereotypes and expectations of artists. Klee, Kandinsky, and Picasso are three of the many who struggled with their own relationship to childhood and childishness.

Klee is an example of a single individual who struggled with these issues. Within one lifetime, Klee underwent changes in his own interpretation of childhood. In 1912, Klee stated that " the primordial origins of art are to be found at home in the nursery." By 1930, he said: "Don't relate my work to those of children. These are worlds apart" (Werkmeister, 1977, p. 138). What is the significance of Klee's shift in position? In his early years, Klee's interest in the child grew from the essentially obvious connection he saw between each of us and our childhoods. Klee believed what Erikson (1950) reminded us in *Childhood and Society:* A society is a group of people all of whom were children. Klee's early view led him, in the spirit of Freudian psychoanalysis, to reconstruct his childhood experience. Through this period of retrospection, Klee even made an inventory of his childhood artistic products. From these, he selected some for a catalogue of his collected *oeuvres*. In this catalogue, he included 18 childhood drawings made between the ages of 3 and 10. He accompanied the drawings with a unifying verbal commentary, a diary of 36 memories of childhood. In Klee's process of selection significantly he omitted his school art. Whatever he had produced on the basis of the teachers' instruction, by copying, he did not consider these childhood works to be "art." The others he did. What he valued in 1912 that caused him to preserve and celebrate his work was that it was "free from corruption." In this respect, his view carried forward the ideal of Rousseau, Chamfleury, and Topffer. Klee believed that adult works of art were unnatural and corrupting. He believed that because children had not yet absorbed such works, they were free of the attempt to emulate them. Although conservative art critics at this time may have been name calling when they referred to the German Expressionists as children, Klee chose to take the label, to subvert its meaning, and to defend its use. So adults continuously reinterpreted the concept of child artist.

Scientific Studies

The scientific study of children's art was another enterprise that changed the way artists felt about the idea of the child artist/artist as child. It now seems inevitable that psychologists—hearing all this debate about artists and children—would take an interest in the phenomena the critics were drawing attention to (i.e., children's drawings). The scientific study of drawing came from an interest in capturing and comprehending the nature of children. The pychologists' assumption was that products of behavior could be studied as specimens, separable from the society. Drawing was particularly amenable to study because it was a behavior that left a trace, a record that could be analyzed long after its production. So psychologists started to make large drawing collections in order to study children.

Klee's reversal of his position of whether his childhood work should be taken as art, was in part due to the movement of scientific investigation. One phenomenon that contributed to his change was the start of systematic, scientific research concerning the forms of children's drawings. These studies began in Germany early in the 20th century. The assumption behind this enterprise was that children's drawings were products of a natural, physiologically, and psychologically determined activity. Its growth was believed to be independent of any instruction. In German universities, three scientific projects were undertaken. One, in Munich in 1903 was undertaken by Kerschensteiner. Another in Leipzig in 1904 was undertaken by Lampbrecht. A third, in 1905 in Breslau, was conducted by Stern.

Klee is said to have been the first artist to explicitly make the connection between the research of the German psychologists and the work of artists, and he did not like what he saw. The connection he made was one the psychologists would not have liked. Klee found it necessary to discredit their research and to oppose the theory on which he felt it was based. Kerschensteiner's theory of natural development claimed that there was a pattern in children's growth and development through drawing, and that the progression was in the direction of realism. The child supposedly had an inborn disposition to grow into a realistic artist. Like Topffer before him, Klee saw no such inevitable tendency. He prized an art that was independent of the goals of realism. Klee's opposition to Kerschensteiner actually evolved into a two-pronged criticism. First he objected to the pseudoscience of the study, which pretended neutrality while concealing a strong bias in favor of realism. Second, he objected to the objective of Kerschensteiner's research, which he felt was to refine the principles of instruction on which drawing skills were based so that children would learn realistic drawing. Like many of his predecessors, Kerschensteiner believed that spontaneous children's work was defective and imperfect. He asserted that the early drawings that he collected from children in his scientific research had nothing to do with art and were aesthetically limited.

Whether artists were like children came to hang on a debate about whether children were artists. Klee believed that the studies completely missed the fact that the essence and origin of all art could be found in the early work of children, and he charged that Kerchensteiner was still engaged with "indoctrination of discredited ideas" (Werkmeister, 1977, p. 143). Whether the child was an artist then hung on two rivalling views of art. One, represented by Kerschensteiner, saw that children's work was inevitably flawed and needed to be corrected to grow toward realism. The other one saw in children's work the abundance and expressivity of mind on which all art making depends. If one adhered to the former, the conclusion would be that the child could be no artist. If one believed the latter, the answer would be to the affirmative. In the middle of the 20th century, the latter aesthetic won out. Most educators in Europe and the United States agreed with Arnheim (1954) that the seeds of all art may be found in the work of children.

As if this were not enough to polarize German society on issues of art and the child, there were further controversies. The interpretation of the child and art could not but be shaped by the German concern with the ideology of socialization. Children and their natural development had to be forfeited for what the culture valued in the form of the mature stage of adult development. Natural development was opposed to the aesthetic cultural ideal of realism. According to Werkmeister, Kerschensteiner's research thus became a tool for certain ethics, aiming to discredit a trend in the culture that might otherwise have valued not only child art, but free play and values espoused by Schiller and Kant. In the 1920s, this confrontation of ideals compelled Klee to reassess his whole perspective. Once the cultural climate pegged Klee as an antiartist and discredited him as being only a childlike primitive, he was forced to switch. The politics involved here made a revision necessary. Being set up as an antiartist was an unacceptable slander. To correct for this distortion, Klee in his diaries in 1919 modified his own emphasis on his childlike-ness. He stated that it was his "ultimate professional experience" that enabled him to do the economical reduction of form that others saw as childlike. By 1930, in order to free himself of the previous association of his art with that of children, he said, "Don't relate my work to those of children" (Werkmeister, 1977, p. 138).

The artist-as-child theme repeatedly engaged critics and artists in struggles to define the child, to define art, and in the process to establish values within the culture. The examples cited here are evidence of adults' use of children's drawings, not as the data of childhood, but rather as if they were projections from the adults' own minds. We have seen two centuries of adults using children's drawings as symbols in a debate that keeps engaging new generations.

The discussion of *giftedness* cannot be free of the questions about whether children's work should be called *art*. If one follows Kerschensteiner and sees children's work as flawed until it is trained to realism, then only the child-producers of precocious realistic images will be identified as *gifted*. On the other hand, if one follows the spirit of early Klee or Arnheim or the numerous advocates of their view, one would see in early childhood's invention of forms the seeds of art. The child's free and serendipitous combination of shapes might be what would identify the child as *gifted*.

GIFTEDNESS

Allston

When the early 19th-century U.S. painter Washington Allston (1779–1843) had become a celebrated master, a friend presented him with some drawings by a child. The friend solicited his judgment on the child's talent. "Is this the work of a child you would encourage?" he asked the painter. After a look, Allston said, "No." His friend then admitted his question was a trick. The drawings he had shown Allston actually were the mature artist's own childhood drawings (Flagg, 1892).

To me, Allston's being unable to recognize his own work or any elements in the drawings that were suggestive of the distinguished artistic career he already had behind him, raises questions about the validity and the usefulness of the judgment of giftedness.

What is the reliability of a judgment of giftedness? Who should know better than the artist him or herself what a certain drawing contains? Might we suppose an expert other than Allston might have judged these drawings differently? If so, how? According to what criteria?

And what is the usefulness of such a judgment? I believe this Allston anecdote has been told and retold because it presents us with the connundrum of whether knowing and predicting in his childhood Allston's international fame and exquisite achievements would have made any difference in his life?

When Allston was a boy, he loved to imagine and build little structures with mud, twigs, and sticks. When he reflected on these memories he saw himself much like any other child who might have been allowed to play with such items. Allston so enjoyed this memory, he retold it to William Dunlop who wrote about the artist's august life. But what if an adult had seen the little boy playing imaginatively with the sticks and that person said, "This boy is gifted"? What difference would it have made? Without this label, the young Allston already was subjected to high expectations, already had the benefits of his family's priviledged social position. He already was expected to leave home in North Carolina to pursue an excellent boyhood education in Newport, Rhode Island, from which he proceeded to Harvard. He did get to study in London at the Royal Academy. He did travel and paint in Italy, all without the label of *giftedness* based either on his twigs and sticks or his childhood drawings.

Allston's century was one that took an intense interest in art and childhood. As I already showed, that interest was derived from Rousseau's prizing of Emile's awkward dauds more than all the oil paintings framed and hung in art museums. It seems fitting to launch this last section with the anecdote about Allston, our prototypical U.S. romantic painter. His reflections of his own childhood challenges us to evaluate the usefulness of the label of *giftedness* in the life of a priviledged, imaginative, and productive child.

Other Boys

But what of another boy not born into an affluent family? What opportunities might have happened to his imaginative play? In 1800 how might the label of *giftedness* have altered that boy's life? *Giftedness* as a label only makes sense when there are systems, people, and opportunities to which this label gives access. For example, giftedness would have altered that boy's life only if schools and teachers devoted to teaching the gifted existed. The *giftedness* label would have made a difference if funds were available for such boys to travel and study art.

In the United States in 1800, no consistent system of public schooling existed. Education was based on local towns and districts. Free education was available to boys in winter months when farm work was not calling them to the fields. Whoever was available did teach. Whatever that teacher knew was passed along to the nearby young people. Other schooling was even more subject to family economics. If the parents had some money, they might elect to send their son away to a boarding school. A third option was indenture or apprenticeship. Parents might sign an agreement so that a master coach and sign painter might give their son access to years of training. The boy would live in the painter's home. In exchange for adequate food and shelter, the boy owed the man his time. The master might budget that time so that the boy would perform different tasks. The boy might begin by washing the floors and watching the master work. Slowly, after watching his skilled hands and observing his secrets, the master would ask the boy to take on tasks that were components of the production, say of a finished rectangular wooden panel painted with the name of the customer's store.

What would have made this boy, or the many others like him, ever dream of the opportunities that Allston had? Only access to an artist, someone whose life could make these possibilities accessible to the boy. Even so, family finances would constrain the boy's options.

In the 1800s, older boys could not find their way to art schools in America. Because there were no schools to go to, the label of *giftedness* would not have helped our hypothetical student get a professional art education either. The big opportunity that some young American men dreamed of—if they wanted to become painters—was to sail to Europe. Going to Europe offered them the opportunity of seeing and learning from the art in the great European capital cities. To the young men of this era, access to art in musems and churches was equivalent to a formal art education today. But living and working in Paris or Rome was only possible with money. One of the great Hudson River landscape painters, John Kensett, was able to make a prolonged stay in Europe only because he inherited funds at the time of the death of his grandmother. Otherwise he would have headed home and the history of U.S. art would be quite different.

The young person lacking family money, was dependent on the benevolence or self-interest of a patron who might finance a trip. It was benevolence if the patron financed the trip with no strings attached. It was benevolence plus self-interest if the person required that the art made abroad was to become the patron's property. In the 19th century, finding a patron of either sort may have been akin to acquiring the label of *gifted*, but by this point the young person no longer was a child. This patron was predicting and betting on a young person who already had demonstrated mastery within the domain of his projected life work. That is what made the patron decide the young man deserved the expenditure.

Girls

If the child was neither of a wealthy family nor a boy, the problem of access to training was compounded further. In the early 19th century, a girl who drew or played imaginatively with sticks and twigs as so many do would have had fewer options. Her future was more constrained than a boy's, and like her male counterpart, she too was dependent on family finances. If she went to a local school at all it was in the summer. Girls were admitted to their local schools when the boys were away working in the fields. The teachers, who otherwise would have been teaching the boys, devoted themselves to the girls. In the girls' few months of schooling, some learned about drawing but only if the local teacher had that skill or interest. Most learned to sew and stitch.

If the family had resources, a daughter might have been sent away from home even to another state where a school mistress conducted a private seminary. Drawing and painting might have been part of that curriculum, as a tool for studying geography, botany, and literary studies. Sewing, too, as an "ornamental art" was part of her curriculum. The school had to have adept teachers who could teach these

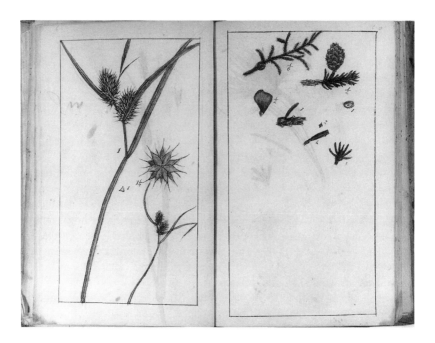

FIG. 1.6. Girl's individual botany sketchbook, painted in water colors. In seminaries in the first half of the 19th century, girls were expected to analyze plants by drawing and painting the plant's forms. Parents paid extra for the expenses incurred in their daughtrs' use of art supplies for botany painting, embroideries, and designing of mythological or historical pictures. (Korzenik Collection.)

skills. Students who were recognized for their artistic skills might have been invited by the seminary head mistress to stay on at the school after graduation to become the drawing teacher for the incoming students. Others went off to open classes either in other schools or in storefront shops. Early in the 19th century, training in ornamental arts yielded prized products. These were the girl's and her parents' proof that the family's money had been well spent on a quality education.

A daughter also had a third option. She too could have had access to indenture or apprenticeship. The agreements generally bound her to household work. At the beginning of the 19th century this involved much of the society's material production. Women were taught to spin and weave, and from the cloth they produced clothing was made. Women also made shoes. The skills the girl might have learned working in another family's home depended on the materials and the skills used by the adults in that household. Many economically viable barterable forms of production involved aesthetic judgment. Indentured young girls were taught these within the other people's households.

For 19th-century young women, too, a ticket to Europe accomplished what we expect the designation of *giftedness* might do for one today. Few women got that, and by the time they did they were old enough to demonstrate significant professional skills. May Alcott Nieriker (1879), Louisa May Alcott's artist sister, was one who did go to Italy and she wrote a book advising her fellow women artists about how to succeed doing this. Those who got to Europe often achieved notoriety for the novelty of their choice. Their celebrity at times obscured the diligence and quality of their work. Like their male counterpart, a young woman's having access to Europe also depended on her having money or someone who deemed the young woman worthy of financial support. American women artists in Italy became curiosities. They used that fact because they also knew that, like their male counterparts, their being in Italy would enhance not only their skills but their fame and reputation once they came home. Being in Europe almost made them be seen as "talented."

By the last quarter of the 19th century, art had become big business in the United States. The Centennial Exhibition at Philadelphia's Fairmount Park was proof of it. There were several galleries and many artists competed there for the limited space. By this time the country could rely on local common schools for mass education. Although some families still did send their children to private academies and seminaries, a system of public schooling had become a significant force in the distribution of educational opportunity. Art education was one of those opportunities.

By 1876, because of its aspirations for international prestige and international trade, the federal government actively encouraged U.S. young people to become artists. Artistic encouragement spread like wildfire. Significantly, nowhere was there designation of classes for the gifted. Everyone was encouraged. Under the title *Art and Industry* (1885), the U.S. Senate published a multiyear national survey that assessed and boasted our offerings in art. Isaac Edwards Clarke gathered and edited data state by state, town by town. *Art and Industry* is a stunning, leather-bound, four-volume, detailed account of the varieties of places anywhere across the country that a late 19th-century young person could go to study art. Art had to be available to everyone because the nation saw art as profitable work for every level of U.S. society. Clarke covered the training of fine artists as the training of a vast class of art laborers. He and most of his contemporaries agreed that artistic skills would enhance the value of every object made or product manufactured in this country.

Today, we rightly are awed to see the average 1880s adolescent students' work. The general level of skill of the ordinary young people seems extraordinary. Students were taught to draw and they learned to draw. Drawing was like writing. Drawing was a complex skill you could learn in school and use to advantage for the rest of the years of your life. No one said, "I cannot learn to draw" any more than they would have said, "I cannot learn to write." They simply did learn. The most popular textbook, Chapman's (1847) *The American Drawing Book*, declared on its first page, "Anyone who can learn to write can learn to draw."

Since the late 19th century, the culture has shifted its priorities. In the 1990s, we are strangers to the fact that drawing is a learnable skill. We seem to have forgotten that the human organism can and has mastered drawing and painting and applied it to a wide variety of needs, from mapping a territory and locating the different

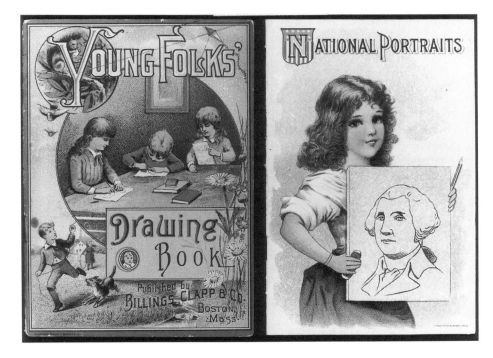

FIG. 1.7. Advertisers' tiny drawing and tracing booklets. Parents wanted their children to draw. Skills in tracing and copying were encouraged. To parents at the turn of the century, the drawing child was a good, productive person. "Young Folks Drawing Book" and "National Portraits" were among a multitude of freebies that corporations gave as premiums to entice parents to buy the products. (Korzenik Collection.)

sorts of trees in planting an orchard, to instructing a carpenter on how to shape a turn in a stairway, to capturing a likeness of a person, to describing a botanical structure of a flower, to announcing visually the products sold in a store. For all these purposes, every day Americans have made remarkably beautiful and effective drawings.

Giftedness

Despite these changes in how art-making skills were acquired and to what uses they have been put, the notion of artistic giftedness keeps cropping up. Why? Kris and Kurz (1979), a psychoanalyst and art historian, respectively, in their book *Legend, Myth and Magic in the Image of the Artist* (first published in German as *Die Legende vom Kunstler*, 1934) offered their interpretations of some reasons why. They proposed and persuasively documented the fact that people psychologically seem to want to believe that the artist is a magical figure. The myth of the master having being born an artist is ancient. They claimed that since ancient time, certain characteristics keep being superimposed on the childhoods of artists. In all these

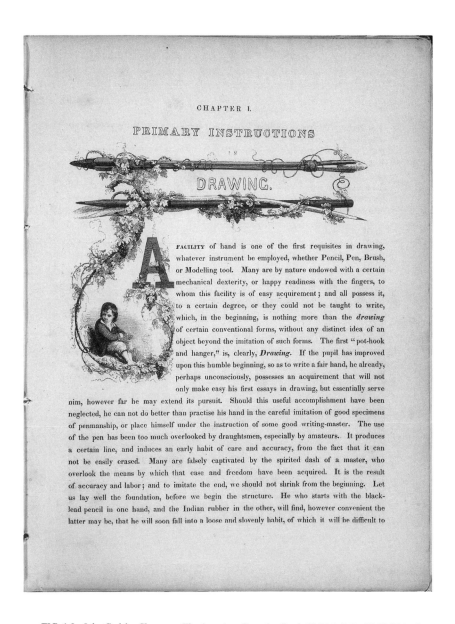

CHAPTER I.

PRIMARY INSTRUCTIONS
IN
DRAWING.

FACILITY of hand is one of the first requisites in drawing, whatever instrument be employed, whether Pencil, Pen, Brush, or Modelling tool. Many are by nature endowed with a certain mechanical dexterity, or happy readiness with the fingers, to whom this facility is of easy acquirement; and all possess it, to a certain degree, or they could not be taught to write, which, in the beginning, is nothing more than the *drawing* of certain conventional forms, without any distinct idea of an object beyond the imitation of such forms. The first "pot-hook and hanger," is, clearly, *Drawing*. If the pupil has improved upon this humble beginning, so as to write a fair hand, he already, perhaps unconsciously, possesses an acquirement that will not only make easy his first essays in drawing, but essentially serve him, however far he may extend its pursuit. Should this useful accomplishment have been neglected, he can not do better than practise his hand in the careful imitation of good specimens of penmanship, or place himself under the instruction of some good writing-master. The use of the pen has been too much overlooked by draughtsmen, especially by amateurs. It produces a certain line, and induces an early habit of care and accuracy, from the fact that it can not be easily erased. Many are falsely captivated by the spirited dash of a master, who overlook the means by which that ease and freedom have been acquired. It is the result of accuracy and labor; and to imitate the end, we should not shrink from the beginning. Let us lay well the foundation, before we begin the structure. He who starts with the black-lead pencil in one hand, and the Indian rubber in the other, will find, however convenient the latter may be, that he will soon fall into a loose and slovenly habit, of which it will be difficult to

FIG. 1.8. John Gadsby Chapman, *The American Drawing Book,* 1847, J. S. Redfield. This, the first page of the chapter on learning to draw, shows the child-as-rustic, for the author stated that because all possess "a facility of hand," drawing should be as natural an act for the child as the curving ivy is natural. (Korzenik Collection.)

stories a discovery myth recurs. The story goes that one day, a great artist is out for his regular stroll and as he walks he happens to see a boy minding his flock of sheep. He (for he is always a man) "discovers" a shepherd boy who is drawing with a stick in the mud. He stops. The boy's drawing is perfect. Accounts vary. Either the boy is drawing a perfect circle or producing a remarkable human likeness. The man is amazed by what he sees. He predicts that this boy will become a great artist someday. The man sees to it that the child has every opportunity for the rest of his life. He sees to it that he has access to the best of an art education so his success in life may be assured.

This myth recurred through the centuries and it crosses cultures. In every edition of Chapman's *The American Drawing Book* since 1847 through 1876, the myth was retold. Even today, the myth is still told. The myth applied to Giotto's life is printed on the back of "Giotto" crayon boxes sold to children in Italy today.

The psychological content of the myth actually transforms two people into magical people. Both the discoverer of the child and the child who is discovered share in being exempt from the constraints of ordinary people's lives. They both participate in a magical process. The attribution of talent or giftedness is the life-transforming act. Once this meeting takes place, and the child's gift is recognized, the boy departs from his ordinary youthful shepherd responsibilities. Now he enters a life of great expectations and unlimited opportunities. Recognition, opportunities, success, and wealth all are his because of that fortuitous moment of discovery

If there is a psychological basis for our wanting there to be "gifted," as Kris and Kurz argued, so also is there an economic one. Like Kris and Kurz, Wittkower and Wittkower's (1963) masterful study *Born Under Saturn* reminds us that the idea of giftedness has been with us since antiquity. In the beginning of the 16th century, when it became particularly common to read about artists being born and not made, these stories had a particular political and economic reason for being. The Wittkowers see the idea of "gift" or "in-born talent" as evolving in the Renaissance in order to solve a problem of status that haunted visual artists. As Arnheim (1969) explained in *Visual Thinking*, whereas poets, musicians, and philosophers were allied with the liberal arts and gained the priviledge associated with their working with their minds and not dirtying their hands, visual artists, whether painters or sculptors, tended to be ranked with other manual artists and trades people.

The Wittkowers showed how in order to gain status and economic advantage, artists needed to detach themselves from the rank of laborers and craftsmen. The idea of *artistic giftedness* became the tool with which artists could differentiate themselves from the other manual workers. If artists were born gifted, the worth of their work should be worth a lot more than labor measured in the number of hours spent working on the job. Instead it was their being a born artist, their inborn gift, that elevated their work above that of others. The gifted, born artist, a sort of cultural prince, never again should have been thought of as someone paid a mere hourly wage! No wonder that for centuries parents have cherished the dream of their children "discovered" for their giftedness. Giftedness had and still has economic consequences!

To my mind, four changes were built into to the transformation of the painter from manual worker to gifted fine artist, and they still seem relevant today. A person classified as gifted is a person subject to greater expectations, she or he is expected to produce superior work. Research studies have show that high expectations often encourage superior work. Such a person is given access to opportunities. If opportunities are scarce, the gifted one gets what little there is. For this person, the gates are open to economic advantage. The gifted one may expect more for his or her work than the prevailing hourly wage. Labor is detached from the notion of the time spent on the task. The price of the work is based on the esteem of the individual's talent. Finally, this person also gains status. The gifted one is elevated to a rank above her or his counterparts. Whether through smaller or greater class distinctions, the gifted one's everyday responsibilities pertain to a priviledged segment of their society.

CONCLUSION

Children probably always have made marks. Depending on the attitudes within the culture, either publicly or secretly children probably always have invented varieties of forms in two and three dimensions. Despite this fact, only when adults took an interest in what children were forming could young people's products rise to the status of art.

But not just any adults' interest alchemically transformed these childhood activities into art. It required the interest of a particular sort of person. Who did notice what children were making? Obviously, the children's caretakers were closest to them. They saw most intimately what children made. Just as they came to know the children's temperaments and pleasures, they noticed the pastimes the children preferred. But caretakers, particularly mothers, no matter how astute they were as observers, usually were not art critics who participated in the art world and the art marketplace where values get established. Only when the critics paid attention to children's drawings did the status of children's works change. Their judgment influenced children's subsequent experiences and opportunities. Only when critics took an interest in artists' biographies and overtly or tacitly interjected the legend of the myth of the born artist, do we find the references to the artist's giftedness. *Giftedness,* like the notion of art itself, keeps propagating the art powerful adults admire. *Giftedness,* like the term *art,* coincides with the attitudes of the time.

Today an obstacle keeps preventing us from seeing ourselves as the creators of our own ever shifting definitions of *giftedness.* We keep using the term *gifted* as if it inhered in the child. In reality, giftedness is an adult concept, like taste, child artist, and artist child. It is a concept shaped by aesthetics current in the mind of the judge. This confusion derives from another mistaken view, that children's mark-making merely facilitates their expressing their inner selves. We see what children make as coming soley from them. Incorrectly, we assume that their enterprises are uncontaminated by adult society. We have acted as if our interests in adult art, our own changes in taste, which are conspicuous in all other arenas of artistic judgment, have had nothing to do with what we value, reward and preserve of children's productions. I hope I have demonstrated that this is patently untrue.

I have written this survey of the ways adult aesthetic preferences impinge and shape our judgments of children to help us be more honest in our interactions with children. As readers proceed to the case studies ahead, notice which characterization of giftedness each author uses.

Is the author referring to children's giftedness in the folk-artlike look of their drawings? Is the author admiring the "stammering" that intrigued Topffer or the primitivism that fascinated Boas as part of that cult of childhood? If so, to what features of the child's art making does the author call our attention? What evidence does the author use?

Is the author referring to functions of the children's minds, their cognitive invention, that comes to be manifest in lines and shapes? Is the author prizing child art in the sense that Parker did? Is the author seeing that it is the child's mind that has the element of the artist born into it, that not the product but the processes of attention and expression makes the child an artist? If so, to what in the drawing process does the author draw our attention?

Is the author referring to the children's capacity to produce images that pertain to the taste of adult art. In that sense, the author would be admiring children's marks in the way that Klee first did, isolating features of his early production that resembled the sort of marks he was then making as an adult. Do authors in this volume isolate particular features of children's work because they remember what is now in vogue, and if so, to what features is our attention being directed?

These three approaches may help readers differentiate the ways adults' ideas of artistic giftedness arise out of our own different concerns and interests. Noticing how each author constructs a concept of giftedness will help us appreciate that no one construct is definitive. As the Wittkowers warned us, "There is a fallacy in seeking a timeless definition of artistic personality" (p. 286). I add the words *artistic gift*.

Like artists, children are enormously varied in what they pay attention to and how they manifest their fascinations in their production of graphic images. Artists, critics, parents and psychologists all have much to gain by studying them in all their grand diversity. The centuries of opinion already demonstrate that. I never want to diminish that fact. What I hope this historical overview has demonstrated is that giftedness as a concept may narrow that wide field. Critics' various designations of giftedness, which subsequently influence parents and teachers, are adult judgments. Giftedness seems to have been their term of praise for qualities in children's production that resemble the art adults see and prize in their own time. Perhaps this is precisely what an education does, drawing children into the aesthetic world of their elders. In that case it may be neither desirable nor possible to suppress this sort of judgment. Regardless of the reader's point of view, it seems to me productive to be on guard to notice when the influence of our own adult aesthetic tastes may be mistakenly defined as what children would do independently of us. This watchfulness may keep us in closer touch with the needs, aims and interests of the children who are the images' producers.

ACKNOWLEDGMENT

Special thanks to Diana Stradzes of the Stanford University Art Museum.

REFERENCES

Arnheim, R. (1954). *Art and visual perception.* Berkeley: University of California Press.

Arnheim, R. (1969). *Visual thinking.* Berkeley: University of California Press.

Boas, G. (1966). *The cult of childhood.* London: The Warburg Institute.

Carothers, J. T., & Gardner, H. (1979). When children's drawings become art: The emergence of aesthetic production and perception. *Developmental Psychology, 15*(5), 570–580.

Champfleury. (1869). *Histoire de L'Imagerie Populaire.* Paris: Michel Levy Freres.

Chapman, J. G. (1847). *American drawing-book.* New York: J.S. Redfield.

Churchill, A. R.(1970). *Art for preadolescents.* New York: McGraw-Hill.

Clarke, I. E. (1885). *Art and industry, education in the industrial and fine arts in the United States, part 1: Drawing in the public schools.* Washington, DC: U.S. Government Printing Office.

Erikson, E. (1950). *Childhood and society.* New York: W.W. Norton.

Flagg, J. (1892). *Life and letters of Washington Allston.* New York: Charles Scribner's.

Gardner, H. (1980). *Artful scribbles.* New York: Basic Books.

Goodman, N. (1968). *Languages of art.* New York and Indianapolis: Bobbs-Merrill.

Golomb, C. (1974). *Young people's sculpture and drawing.* Cambridge, MA: Harvard University Press.

Kellogg, R. (1969). *Analyzing children's art.* Palo Alto, CA: National Press Books.

Korzenik, D. (1985). *Drawn to art: A nineteenth century American dream.* Hanover, NH: University Press of New England.

Korzenik, D. (1993). Education's four competing traditions of art making. In M. Brown & D. Korzenik (Eds.), *Art making and education* (pp. 106–201). Champaign: Univeristy of Illinois Press.

Kris, E., & Kurz, O. (1979). *Legend, myth, and magic in the image of the artist.* New Haven, CT: Yale University Press.

Lowenfeld, V. (1952). *Creative and mental growth.* New York: MacMillan.

Lowenfeld, V. (1954). *Your child and his art.* New York: MacMillan.

Muller, J. (Ed.). (1984). *Children of mercury, the education of artists of the sixteenth and seventeenth centuries.* Providence, RI: Brown University.

Nieriker, M. A. (1879). *Studying art abroad.* Boston: Roberts Brothers.

Parker, F. W. (1894). *Talks on pedagogies: An outline of the theory of concentration.* New York: E. L. Kellogg.

Pariser, D. (1979). Two methods of teaching drawing skills. *Studies in Art Education, 20*(3), 30–42.

Rousseau, J. J. (1964). *Emile.* New York: Barrons Educational Series. (Original work published 1762)

Schapiro, M. (1941). Courbet and popular imagery. *The Journal of The Warburg and Courtault Institutes,1*(3–4), 164–191.

Topffer, R. (1848). *Reflexions et menus-à propos d'un peintre genevois; ou Essai sur le beau dans les arts* (2 vols.). Paris: J. J. Dubochet, Lechevalier et cie.

Werkmeister, I. K. (1977, September). The issue of childhood in the art of Paul Klee. *Arts Magazine.*

Wilson, B. (1974). The superheroes of J.C. Holz. *Art Education, 27*(8), 2–9.

Wilson, M., & Wilson, B. (1982). *Teaching children to draw: A guide for teachers and parents.* Englewood Cliffs, NJ: Prentice-Hall.

Wittkower, R., & Wittkower, M. (1963). *Born under saturn: The character and conduct of artists: A documented history from antiquity to the French Revolution.* New York: W.W. Norton.

2

Lautrec—Gifted Child Artist and Artistic Monument: Connections Between Juvenile and Mature Work

David Pariser
Concordia University, Montreal

Henri de Toulouse-Lautrec is considered—by those who still believe in the notion of personal greatness—a great Western artist. An admirer of Goya and Daumier (Hughes, 1992), he evolved an approach to drawing and printmaking that has had an impact on many subsequent Western practitioners. His distinctive use of line and space is much acclaimed. His prints, paintings, and sketches are still highly valued by museums and collectors and there have been major shows of his work (Bourassa, 1992; Dorment, 1991; Hughes, 1992). Popular attention has not flagged and scholarly and critical interest is strong. Several studies have been published recently on his life and art (Murray, 1991; O'Connor, 1990; Schimmel, 1991). This chapter is a biographical sketch focusing on the connections and continuities between his childhood artistic predilections and those of his adult practice.

Lautrec is of special interest to students of artistically gifted children because a longitudinal sample of his childhood work is available for study and it is evident from the record that he was artistically gifted. Furthermore, Henri, the gifted child, eventually became Henri de Toulouse-Lautrec, the great artist, one of the founders of the modernist tradition.

To initiate this discussion, two contentious notions must be defined: *artistic greatness* and *artistic giftedness*. I address greatness first.

ARTISTIC GREATNESS

It is a tricky task to invoke the term *great* as I do here. The life stories and attributes of Lautrec, Cassatt, Van Gogh, Stein, Gauguin, Picasso, O'Keeffe, and a number of other 19th- and 20th- century artists fuel the romantic vision of the great artist: a marginal person (generally a man), obsessed by demons and devoured by work. In her sociological study of the arts, Zolberg (1990) observed that the romantic conception of the artist as genius was often reinforced by the artist him or herself (Rank, 1989), an image to which Lautrec unwittingly contributed. At the same time, Zolberg warned against the uncritical and stereotypical use of such terms as *alienation, neuroticism,* and *otherness* that, although applying to some artists, are not universal characterizations.

To one critic (Dorment, 1991), Lautrec's way of living and his Montmartre entourage evoke images of a contemporary artist like Warhol who, very consciously, presented himself as an exceptional person. Dorment (1991) pointed out that there are parallels between Warhol's camp followers, marginal crazies and collaborators, all of whom provided the artist with much of his subject matter. In the eyes of censorious critics such as the Hanson and Hanson (1956), it is the notoriously "exceptional" aspect of Lautrec's existence that disqualify him from greatness. They suggest that Lautrec's work has little inherent merit but the sensation associated with his life colors the *oeuvre* and makes it commercially successful.

It is certainly true that the mythic aspects of artists' lives can make it hard to assess their work with any objectivity. To this extent I acknowledge the justness of Zolberg's claim that identifying the modern artist as a genius may be an exercise in applying categories post hoc. Nevertheless, in this chapter, I take it as axiomatic that Lautrec *is* a great artist. By the term *great* I mean an artist who influenced many of his or her successors, who is accepted by knowledgeable viewers as significant, and who still speaks to his or her viewers today (Danto, 1985; Dorment, 1991; Hughes, 1992). I make no claims that Lautrec's contribution will outlast the centuries. My assertion of greatness is tempered by the knowledge that such labels are notoriously fickle—too many great artists have suffered eclipse, rediscovery and oblivion for anyone to make iron-clad pronouncements of immortality.

GIFTEDNESS AND CREATIVITY: A DEFINITION
AND AN APPROACH

Taking Lautrec's present preeminence as axiomatic, in what follows I describe how his visual-artistic endowment, family, social status, historical circumstances, and chance all assisted in his emergence as a creative individual and a great artist. In order to do this I frame the biographical and graphic-development information on his childhood and adolescent work within the psychosocial model for creativity proposed by Csikszentmihalyi (1988).

Csikszentmihalyi suggested a new way of thinking about the emergence of creative individuals—and by extension of giftedness. Generally, the question "Who is creative?" has been framed as though a close study of gifted individuals will yield the secret of their specialness. Instead of asking "*Who* is creative?" Csikszentmihalyi suggested that we ask "*When* is creativity?" In constructing his model, Csikszentmihalyi recognized that notions of artistic preeminence are not only a function of the person's "innate" gifts, strengths, and weaknesses, but also of the social and historical world into which they are born, and the cultural practices and performances that this social world values and supports. Therefore, Csikszentmihalyi invoked a tripartite "systems" model in order to explain the emergence of significantly creative individuals. This three-part model also clarifies the other term that is in need of definition, *giftedness*.

The definition of artistic giftedness that I use draws on all three features of Csikszentmihalyi's model of creativity. That is, an artistically gifted child is one who shows a high degree of drive and technical ability in a socially valued medium or media. The child will likely show an elaborated and refined mastery of the cultural canons of expression, often at an early age, as precocity can be, but is not necessarily, an integral part of the expression of giftedness. Such a child will use his or her skills in the service of a personal project. In the west, such a project is likely to be self-initiated; children will use their artistic skills to explore fantasies, develop imaginary worlds or work through questions of interest (see Clark & Zimmerman, 1992; Golomb, 1992; Wilson & Wilson 1982; Winner & Pariser, 1985). Keeping in mind Csikszentmihalyi's claim that cultures have a differential formative impact on expressions of giftedness (Pariser, 1993), I use the term *gifted* to indicate an individual possessing high levels of skill and drive in an area or domain that is valued by the ambient culture.

One question Csikszentmihalyi posed is: "Why is it that some environments seem so propitious for the emergence of noted artists and scientists?" For example, did 16th century Florence produce more than its share of memorable artists because there was a sudden upsurge in the births of innately artistic individuals? Csikszentmihalyi offered the more parsimonious hypothesis that at all times and in all places the ratio of potentially significant visual artists to nonartists is about the same. Thus, one should entertain the possibility that it was the unusual social conditions in Florence—such as the desire for civic beauty and concurrent recruitment of artists—that helped support the emergence of unusual numbers of artists. Csikszentmihalyi was not suggesting that artists like Michelangelo are simply the chance products of social circumstances. The individual must possess special gifts and capacities, but these capacities alone are not sufficient to ensure that a creative contribution will be made. Creative gifts have to be recognized and valued by the social milieu otherwise individuals possessing such gifts will not flourish.

Two concepts situate Csikszentmihalyi's description of the creative person: In addition to describing the individual, one must describe the domain and the field. *Domain* refers to the intellectual skills and knowledge that the person is mastering (Feldman, 1980). The domain is the structure of knowledge that has to be acquired. Domains can be as diverse as painting, surgery, chess, music, or baseball. The *field* refers to the social world that embodies and adjudicates the special knowledge and skills of the domain. The field is made up of institutions and people who teach, make judgments of quality, certify practitioners and provide support systems for neophytes. Thus, Becker's (1982) art world, comprised of artists, curators, critics, aesthetes, teachers, audiences, galleries, journals, and so forth, constitutes the field for the domain of the artist.

This discussion of Lautrec's artistic development will explore those features of Lautrec's endowment that are clearly "gifts" manifest in childhood and those aspects of his personal history and circumstances that reveal the degree to which his artistic preeminence was a function of chance and social forces.

The first section of the discussion includes a brief biography and an overview of previous research that deals with the juvenilia of significant artists. I consider the primary data: the approximately 2,500 drawings and sketches in various media that come from Lautrec's 6th to his 19th year. This material is analyzed in terms of general graphic-development theories, thematic concerns, and special features such as copying and line quality.

In the second section, I consider the domain of drawing and painting technique as it was structured in late 19th-century France, especially the pedagogy and practice, both academic and informal, which helped to shape Lautrec the artist.

The third section outlines those elements of the art world or field that had an impact on Lautrec's career. I examine some of Lautrec's reasons for entering the world of commercial art much against the wishes of his upper class family.

The fourth section addresses two practices continued from childhood to adulthood: Lautrec's lifelong habit of collaborative illustration that fortuitously threw him together with the popular and influential *chansonnier*, Aristide Bruant; and his longstanding fascination with animals as subject matter. In this closing section, I suggest that in Lautrec's adult work we can find traces of the expression and the touch that he first cultivated as a child. In three cases I trace formal and expressive connections between the marginal doodles and sketches that he drew in late childhood and adolescence and images in a masterpiece. It may be that the copious drawing and sketching that Lautrec practiced in childhood and adolescence was significant for two reasons: His eye and hand became superlatively trained while he began to learn about anatomy and technical matters; and, Lautrec learned how to identify and to control the expressive impact of his drawings. Arnheim (1974) stated that a key understanding for anyone making representations is the distinction between visual effect such as energy, lassitude, happiness, and so on, and the formal means necessary to instantiate such concepts. Arnheim observed that "the difference ... is not primarily between perception and representation, but between perception of effect and perception of form, the latter being needed for representation" (p. 170). I propose that while Lautrec sketched and drew, he was acquiring as much knowledge of form as of effect—and it is the creation of certain effects that link his childhood work with his mature work.

THE INDIVIDUAL: BIOGRAPHICAL SKETCH

Toulouse-Lautrec was born in November 1864 to landed aristocratic parents. His mother was a Tapie-de-Celeyran and his father was the Comte de Toulouse, a well-known eccentric. Henri was the elder of two sons, but the second, Richard, died in infancy. The entire family was interested in the arts as a pastime, and many of Lautrec's uncles drew or sculpted. The quip was that the Lautrecs savoured their wild game thrice: when they hunted it, when they drew it, and when they ate it.

The two bone fractures that Lautrec suffered in 1878 and 1879 were believed to be due to a glandular disorder (*Pycnodysatosis*, according to Dorment, 1991), perhaps a result of the consanguinity of his parents. The disease rendered his bones fragile and affected his physiognomy, making his nose bulbous and his lips protuberant. The only features left untouched were his eyes. By the age of 15, Lautrec had come to terms with the fact that he would never walk properly, never ride well, and never achieve full adult height.

During the course of Lautrec's childhood, his father withdrew more and more from family life, living in a separate chateau. Despite little contact with Henri, there is some indication in the letters of 1886 and 1887 (Schimmel, 1991) that father and son were thinking of sharing a Paris apartment. This plan, although it was not realized, reveals that relations between father and son were not totally severed. It was Lautrec's mother who, throughout his life, provided emotional and financial encouragement for his artistic interests.

In Lautrec's cultivated, upper class family, there was neither the need nor the expectation that he would become a serious artist. As part of the normal course of instruction at his first school, the Lycée Fontanes in Paris, Lautrec received some drawing lessons in the class of Mr. Mantoy. From subsequent events it is clear that Lautrec pursued his love of drawing outside school as well. Between 1879 and 1881 Lautrec and his mother visited various spas and seaside resorts during his convalescence from the second of his two broken legs. During these sojourns, he kept up with his academic studies and found great joy in exercising his talent for graphic observation and satire. He sketched carriages, ships, sailors, soldiers on maneuvers, and the habitués of spas and sanatoria. He put together some of these sketches in a humorous broadsheet called *Les Cahiers de Zig-Zag* (Lautrec, 1931). During the same period (1881), he and a schoolmate from the Lycée Fontanes, Etienne Devismes, collaborated on a story about a horse named Cocotte. The text described the ill-fated relationship between an elderly curate and his horse.

In the spring of 1881, Lautrec began to frequent the studio of a deaf-mute painter with whom he was already quite familiar. René Princeteau (1843–1914) was an artist renowned for his portraits of truly outstanding horses—those that had won big purses or that were of noble lineage. Over the years, Lautrec and Princeteau went to circuses, zoos, and races together. Princeteau urged Lautrec to capture his experiences and impressions in notebooks. From Princeteau, Lautrec picked up the least radical Impressionist techniques and some special approaches to horse painting and sketching. In early 1882, Princeteau advised his pupil to seek the tutelage of a true academic painter.

In March 1882, Lautrec entered the *atelier* of Léon Bonnat (Joseph Florentin, 1833–1922). Here he began to master the skills prerequisite for academic painting. In spite of his posthumous reputation as a free spirit, Lautrec found the regimented demands of the academic approach to painting both challenging and pleasurable.

When Bonnat's *atelier* closed in September 1882, Lautrec moved to the studio of Fernand Cormon (Fernand Piestres, 1854–1924). Here, Henri missed the more demanding style of his previous teacher, noting in a letter to his mother: "My former master's raps put ginger into one—and I didn't spare myself. Here I feel rather relaxed and find it an effort to make a conscientious drawing when something not quite as good would do as well in Cormon's eyes" (Lautrec, cited in Mack, 1938, p. 56).

Murray (1991) pointed out that there is little evidence that in his late teens Lautrec had inclinations that were iconoclastic. In fact, his interests, tastes, and diversions were those of many bourgeois and upper middle-class art students. Thus, there is no reason to believe that Lautrec was restless while he attended the *ateliers*. During this time, Lautrec also became schooled, somewhat more informally, in the bars and bistros of Montmartre—and this of course is the stuff that contributed to the legendary figure of Toulouse-Lautrec. Lautrec's study of the *demi-monde* was by no means an original choice of subject matter. Murray (1991) cited another artist, James McNeil Whistler, as one who encouraged his fellow artists to make sketches in bars and joints. Murray also made the point that it would have been difficult for Lautrec to ignore the pictures of Parisian low life that appeared regularly in the tabloids and journals.

Lautrec began to make a name for himself in part due to his collaboration with Aristide Bruant. Bruant achieved success by insulting his audience and regaling them with ballads about the seamy side of Paris. He bought a nightclub called Le Mirliton, and published a broadsheet by the same name. Some of Lautrec's earliest published illustrations accompanied Bruant's lyrics in this paper. Lautrec's commercial art ventures were not restricted to song illustrations; the posters and lithographs that came later were the fruit of years of commercial work.

Lautrec did not advance very far in the academic art world. He failed to win any important prizes and did not find a place for himself in the *École des beaux-arts*. He became known locally as an eccentric. His talent was employed by local businesses to suggest that a trip up to Montmartre might be a little wicked, but certainly not dangerous (Dorment, 1991; O'Connor, 1991).

During the 1880s Lautrec produced the posters and lithographs that subsequently established him as a master of the genre. In 1891, he made his famous poster for the Moulin Rouge—an image that continues to be the epitome of Montmartre and the Bohemian nightlife of Paris. In 1894, Lautrec confirmed society's jaundiced view of his life and comportment by taking up residence for several months in a bordello. Here he produced a series of lithographic studies of prostitutes (Fig. 2.1). Called Elles, this collection is a remarkable, dispassionate look at a part of the social scene that fascinated many 19th-century literary and artistic figures, among them Flaubert, Zola, and Degas. In Fig. 2.1, we can see a typical scene: The attentive client observes while the prostitute removes her corset.

FIG. 2.1. Henri de Toulouse-Lautrec, French, 1864–1901. "Elles: femme en corset." Color lithograph. 1896. Purchase program for Harvard College. By permission of The Harvard University Art Museums.

In an offhand and typical fashion, Lautrec injected a classical reference and a wry comment by including a picture on the wall of a nymph and a satyr. Later in the same decade the artist went on to paint large canvas studies of the same milieu. Hughes (1992) referred to "the late brothel pictures, which fluctuate with such marvellous ambiguity between desire and repulsion, between the sentimental and the caricatural, while preserving … a strict and aristocratic distance" (p. 55).

In 1899, Lautrec's heavy drinking caught up with him. At his mother's request, he was briefly confined to an asylum to "dry out." In order to prove his return to sobriety and sanity, he made a memorable series of drawings—all from memory—of circus acts and performers. Lautrec's friend and admirer, Joyant, helped him to leave the sanatorium, but the cure was short-lived. In September 1901, Lautrec returned to the castle of Malrome where, with his mother in attendance, he died.

Background: Related Research on Juvenilia

Psychologists (Dennis, 1986; Gardner, 1980; Golomb, 1992; Porath, 1988), art educators (Carroll, 1992; Duncum, 1984; Hurwitz, 1985; Paine, 1987; Pariser, 1991), and art historians (Murray, 1991; Staaller, 1986) all studied the childhood work of noted artists. Because traces of artistic development in the form of sketches and notepads are occasionally left behind as part of the visual record, students making case studies of visual artists are at an advantage over those who wish to study the early work of musicians, actors and dancers—for few traces are left of these early performances.[1] Numerous archival collections of childhood art exist. Early works by Picasso (Staaller, 1986), Lautrec (Paine, 1987; Murray, 1991; Thomson, 1981), three Israeli children (Golomb, 1992), and Wang Yani (Andrews, 1989; Goldsmith & Feldman, 1989; Ho, 1989; Pariser, 1993; Tan, 1993) have been studied.

The results suggest that graphic development evident in even these gifted childhood artists follows a predictable sequence of stages. Some researchers claim to have found a strong correlation between mastery of spatial rendering and performance on cognitive tasks related to spatial reasoning (Case, 1992; Dennis, 1986; Evans, 1977; Lewis & Livson, 1967; Porath, 1988). However, this strong relationship between cognition and representation is questioned by other researchers (Golomb, 1992).

Duncum (1984), too, examined biographical and archival material in his study of 35 well-known 19th- and 20th-century European artists. He looked at how these artists learned various drawing techniques in childhood, identifying such practices as copying, tracing, and drawing from three-dimensional models and two-dimensional images. For his sources, Duncum used collections of juvenilia in *catalogues raisonnés* and in comprehensive reference works. His findings concur with those of the scholars studying the work of Picasso, Lautrec, the young Israeli artists, and Wang Yani. They are further corroborated by the work of Zimmerman (1990) and Robertson (1987), who found no evidence of developmental anomalies in their analyses of the work of artistically gifted children. It appears that there is nothing striking or anomalous about the methods by which these children destined for greatness acquired their early skills. Like other children, they copied, traced, and

---

[1]Wallace (1989) advocated the case study method for looking at the lives of creative people. She lamented the fact that "childhood is that part of life for which the empirical evidence is sparsest" (p .38).

imitated the work of older, more skilled adults. There was, however, accelerated graphic development and significant and consistent productivity.

My own work on the juvenilia of Klee, Lautrec, and Picasso (Pariser, 1991, 1987) relies heavily on their drawings, sketches, and doodles in schoolbooks and sketchbooks. Findings thus far support the idea that Lautrec and Picasso, although technically advanced for their age, were unexceptional in the order in which they acquired certain technical drawing skills such as perspectival rendering. Klee's work is noteworthy for the early emergence of a whimsical tone to which he would return in his mature work.

What we have thus far established is that there are different sources for materials on artistic juvenilia, and that scholars have examined this material from various perspectives. The most noteworthy finding is that graphic development followed the same sequence as that of less-gifted individuals. A second finding is that gifted children use the same array of sources and models as other children. A third finding is that there is no necessary connection between childhood giftedness and eventual artistic greatness—it must be emphasized that both phenomena are socially mediated.

I now describe Lautrec's juvenile material: how it was collected, some of the limitations of the collections, and some observations, both general and specific, about the material.

METHOD OF STUDY: JUVENILE AND ADOLESCENT DRAWINGS—LIMITATIONS OF THE AVAILABLE MATERIAL AND GENERAL TRENDS

This discussion of juvenilia is based on a tabulation of themes and subjects from Lautrec's juvenile period. Aesthetic and historical dispositions can create different cutoff points for the duration of Lautrec's juvenile period. If one embraces a pragmatic criterion for maturity, that is, the mastery of a standard body of artistic knowledge and skill, then one could argue, as I do, that Lautrec's juvenile period ends a little shy of his 20th year. At this time, he was studying in the *atelier* of his last academic master, Cormon. The record suggests that by 1884 he had mastered the basic skills needed for academic drawing, that is, volume, anatomy, and so on. By 1884, he was producing accomplished studies as well as his own more personalized sketches. Space, tone, and articulation were clearly no longer a problem for him.

However, Murray (1991) suggested that one might prolong Lautrec's juvenile period to include the end of his academic training, that is, 1887. In accordance with her social-constructivist view, the judgment of "maturity" is a function of one's critical school and one's aesthetic allegiances. Accordingly, Lautrec's massive painting of 1888, "Le Cirque Fernando" (see Fig. 2.2) would announce Lautrec's mature style. This blend of popular subject matter and "high art" presentation epitomize Lautrec's special contribution to the artistic movements that followed (Visani, 1970).

FIG. 2.2. Henri de Toulouse-Lautrec, French, 1864–1901. "In the Cirque Fernando: The ringmaster." Oil on canvas. 1888. 100 × 161.3 cm. Joseph Winterbotham Collection, 1925.523. Photograph copyright 1993, The Art Institute of Chicago, all rights reserved.

In seeking out juvenilia, the archives and published sources consulted include *L'Amour de l'Art* (1931), Devismes (1953), Dortu (1971), Fermigier (1969), Goldschmidt and Schimmel (1969), Heintzelman (1955), Jedlicka (1943), Lautrec (1938), and Wattenmaker (1976). Of particular interest in the collections at the Lautrec Museum in Albi, France was Lautrec's school exercise book dated 1875–1880. In this book of dictation, translation, and transcription of Latin and Greek authors, Lautrec has doodled and sketched copiously.

The Drawing Collections: Size, Sample, and Dating

As a prelude to the general findings, three concerns with the corpus of drawings must be dealt with: size of the sample, representativeness of the sample, and dating of the materials.

Size of the Sample.   One has to assume that the available drawings are only a fraction of Lautrec's total childhood production. It is not unreasonable to expect that a child who enjoys drawing, if given the opportunity to draw and sketch, will produce roughly 300 to 500 drawings a year—at least up to the age of 9. This estimate is based on a longitudinal collection of drawings made by my own children. Evidence from other sources, such as Szabad-Smyth (1992), indicates that under normal circumstances, children in early and middle childhood can be expected to produce at least 200 graphic works in a year, excluding work done in school. Tan (1993) reported that by the age of 17, Wang Yani had produced some 10,000 paintings, whereas another Chinese painting prodigy, Tan Wen Xi, is reputed to have completed some 37,580 paintings and drawings from age 3 to 16, an output of roughly 3,000 paintings per year. If Lautrec was as productive as some of these children, the 2,544 drawings left as a record of his first 17 years of active artistry may represent only 20% to 50% of his total output.

Selectiveness of the Sample.   It is certain that the sketches and drawings that have survived have passed through many hands. The artist himself, his family, dealers, and good friends probably sorted through the collection, distributing or disposing of works. The existing collection is not a random sample but instead reflects a series of choices and subsequent culling.

Dating.   Paine (1987) is skeptical of the dates attributed by Dortu, one of Lautrec's foremost cataloguers, to some of the drawings. She stated that it is possible that drawings that Dortu and others have identified with Lautrec at age 6 include some made at 4 or even 3 years of age. She commented on the confused sequence and vague dating assigned some of the drawings following the family's move to Paris. Thus, when considering the sample of childhood drawings, it must be noted that it represents only a fraction of Lautrec's total output. Also, as Paine indicated, we cannot be too sure of the exact chronology of some of the drawings. Although little can be done about these concerns, one must keep in mind the possible shortcomings of this sample when considering the observations that follow.

General Findings

Lautrec was inordinately fond of sketching animals, especially horses. He enjoyed spectacles that incorporated people and animals, such as circuses and steeple-chases. Of his childhood drawings, 42% contain animals—with or without people. Drawings exclusively of people—group studies, portraits, academic studies, and anatomical studies—account for another 50%. Landscape and architecture comprise a scant 8% of the drawings; Lautrec's famed prejudice against landscape seems to have been established in childhood. As a mature artist, Lautrec maintained that landscape was "for idiots," at best a foil against which to set off the figure. Caricature and satirical images together make up 16% of the total number of drawings, prefiguring his fascination with caricature in his adult work.

The existing record shows that over time, Lautrec acquired skills in spatial rendering and figure articulation in much the same sequence as other children. For example, in his treatment of animal and human subjects, one sees that, as Henri becomes older, his skill improves. His early attempts, at age 10 (Fig. 2.3) are a little clumsy and unsure. Proportions are off and limbs are sketchily constructed. Ink sketches made years later of the same topic (Fig. 2.4 and 2.5) show a clearer sense of anatomy and more economical use of line—the results of encouragement, time, and practice. The record shows that these skills did not come full-blown from his hand.

Thematic Concerns.   One can divide Lautrec's noncaricatural childhood works into two periods for which roughly the same number of sketches have been preserved: 1,237 from childhood and early adolescence, from 1870 to 1880 (ages 6–16), and 909 from late adolescence, 1880 to 1883 (ages 16–19; see Table 2.1)

If the percentages for the subject matter Categories C through E in the table are combined, an increase can be seen in drawings that have people exclusively as subject matter: a change from 25% in Period 1, to 63% in Period 2. If the category of diverse animal drawings for Periods 1 and 2 are compared, a sharp decline is seen from 42% to 14%. The 3-year period in the early 1880s includes the beginning of his work in the academic *ateliers* of Bonnat and Cormon. Murray (1991)

TABLE 2.1
Lautrec's Noncaricatural Childhood Works

Subject Matter	Period 1 1870–1880 N = 1,237	Period 2 1880–1883 N = 909
Category A: Diverse animals	42%	14%
Category B: People and animals	22%	20%
Category C: People	10%	21%
Category D: Portraits	14%	21%
Category E: Academic studies	1%	21%
Category F: Boats and miscellaneous	11%	3%

FIG. 2.3. Henri de Toulouse-Lautrec, French, 1864–1901. "Horserace." Pencil and water color. 1874. By permission of the Musée Toulouse-Lautrec, Albi.

FIG. 2.4. Henri de Toulouse-Lautrec, French, 1864–1901. Group of horses running (detail). Schoolbook, 1875–1880, p. 86. Pen and ink. By permission of the Musée Toulouse-Lautrec, Albi.

FIG. 2.5. Henri de Toulouse-Lautrec, French, 1864–1901. "Cavalry parade from Devismes' Cocotte. 1881." Pen and ink. By permission of the Houghton Library, Harvard University.

suggested that the shift in subject matter from horses and animal sketches to academic and nonacademic figure studies reflects Lautrec's entry into the world of academic *ateliers.*

Over the two periods (1870–1880, 1880–1883), the total number of caricatures is 413, and the proportion of satirical/caricatural images remained at 17%–18% of the total. Lautrec was a born caricaturist. For example, Fig. 2.6 shows a diminutive elephant flitting across some Greek declensions in his schoolbook. This tiny creature reveals Lautrec's sure grasp of the principles of humorous distortion.

Henri's satirical interest in all aspects of the human comedy is established early, as demonstrated in his letters to his family while he recuperated from his leg fractures (Adhemar & Reff, 1969; Schimmel, 1991). One may compare Lautrec with another 19th-century observer of the social scene—Gustave Flaubert—who also relished the bizarre. It is easy to imagine Lautrec sharing in Flaubert's enthusiasm for the spectacle of the grotesque, celebrating in caricature "the giantesses, the freaks, the dancing bears" (Barnes, 1984, p. 52) found at fairs. Lautrec was at times a spectacle in his own right. He loved wearing masks and, like his father, he enjoyed dressing up, for example, as a choirboy or a Japanese geisha (Bourassa, 1992; O'Connor, 1991).

Paine (1987) mentioned several fantastic juvenile drawings by Lautrec including "some animals attired anthropomorphically in uniform, standing upright" (p. 299). I suspect that these 6-year-old's drawings are based on the work of Grandville

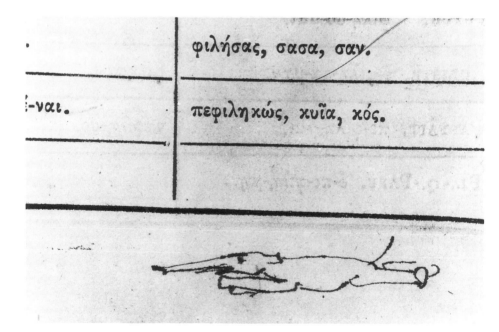

FIG. 2.6. Henri de Toulouse-Lautrec, French, 1864–1901. "Running elephant." Pen and ink. From Chassang, 1875, p. 79. By permission of the Musée Toulouse-Lautrec, Albi.

(Jean Ignace Isidore Gerard, 1803–1847), a popular illustrator who specialized in etchings of people with animal's heads and surreal worlds populated with animated objects. Paine noted "a drawing of a rabbit ensconced in a pot beside a bird, possibly half-human" (p. 300; see Fig. 2.7). This composition (developed in at least two other versions by Lautrec) seems very similar in topic if not handling and style to a Grandville etching called "The Hare and the Wild Duck" (Adhemar, 1975; see Fig. 2.8). At least seven other anthropomorphic drawings exist in the Dortu catalogue (1971, numbers D.8, D.42, D.43, D.102, D.645, D.646, D.510). The existence and provenance of these studies show the young man's interest in Grandville's grotesqueries. Paine viewed these drawings of animal-masked people as an indication of Lautrec's wit.

Henri's steady output of caricatures during his juvenile period (1870–1883) foreshadows his predilection for exaggerated elements in his mature work. There is, for example, one of his many portraits of Yvette Guilbert (Fig. 2.9). Although Guilbert reacted in dismay when she first saw the unflattering likeness, eventually she came to terms with the print and allowed it to be used for advertising purposes. In "Le Cirque Fernando" (1888; see Fig. 2.2), the ringmaster is practically a flat cartoon compared with the modeled realism of the equestrienne and her mount. Henri was as capable of turning his satirical pen on himself as on others. His cartoonlike self-portrait as a parrot (Fig. 2.10) bedecked with a pince-nez and hat is as unflattering to the diminutive artist as his portrait of Yvette Guilbert was to that *chanteuse.*

FIG. 2.7. Henri de Toulouse-Lautrec, French, 1864–1901. "Wild Duck and Rabbit." Charcoal. Lot de croquis 1873–1875. By permission of the Musée Toulouse-Lautrec, Albi.

Fabel 13: Der Hase und die Wildente. 121 × 100
Le lapin et la sarcelle.

FIG. 2.8. Grandville (Jean Ignace Isidore Gerard), 1803–1847. Le lapin et la sarcelle. Etching. 12.1 × 10 cm. From Adhemar, 1975, p. 776. Public domain.

General Graphic Developmental Trends

A close examination of his drawings reveals that Lautrec's graphic development shows no sudden or unexplained leaps in the acquisition of technical skills such as the rendering of depth or anatomy. Thomson (1981) observed that although talented, Lautrec's draughtsmanship did not reach its full potential until at least 1882 (age 18) when he began proper art school training.

Murray (1991) judged Henri's drawings at the ages of 14 and 15 as the promising work of a precocious beginner, although Lautrec was "largely unskilled in drawing and inexperienced in the technique of mixing colors" (p. 9). Despite these temperate appraisals, one feature of Lautrec's graphic development points to the dramatic results of a change of medium. Paine (1987) drew attention to the fact that between the ages of 8 and 10, Lautrec shifted from pencil as the preferred medium to pen and ink for his drawings. According to Schimmel (1991), however, from an early age, most of Lautrec's letters were in ink. It is worth speculating that his exposure

FIG. 2.9. Henri de Toulouse-Lautrec, French, 1864–1901. "Yvette Guilbert." Lithograph. Gift
of Carter H. Harrison, 1931.53. Photograph, copyright 1993, The Art Institute of Chicago, all

FIG. 2.10. Henri de Toulouse-Lautrec, French, 1864–1901. "The Dog and the Parrot" (*Le chien et le perroquet*). Lithograph. 1899. 30.6 × 26.3 cm. Gift of Charles F. Gore, 1927.896. Photograph copyright 1993, The Art Institute of Chicago, all rights reserved.

at an early age to a responsive and fluid medium such as ink may have stimulated his graphic talents. For example, the pencil drawings of horses (see Fig. 2.3) reveal the hesitancy with which the pencil outline is developed. Later drawings in pen and ink (see Fig. 2.5) demonstrate a line quality that is far more fluent and secure. Obviously, some of this difference can be explained by practice and maturity: The two drawings were made at least 4 years apart. His increasing competence can also be attributed to his extensive use of pen and ink, both for drawing and writing.

One may ask if the panache with which Lautrec handled ink might be an example of what Walters and Gardner (1986) identified as a "crystallizing experience." Such an experience is one in which gifted individuals suddenly recognize the skill or medium for which they have a special affinity (e.g., chess players for the chess board or musicians for a particular instrument). Paine (1987) noted that Lautrec's drawings at 14 years old "have greater strength as images, as though Lautrec had become more aware of the sensual qualities of his media, usually pencil or pen" (p. 300). By age 15, "the artistic leap seems gigantic, much influenced by a broadening conception of the nature of art, more intellectual in approach, more uniform in quality and achievement, more confident than ever before" (p. 304).

Paine (1987) observed that at age 16, Lautrec's style, subject matter, and technique began to diversify. Such an observation is consistent with a recent graphic-development theory proposed by Wolf and Perry (1988). They hypothesized that one of the important developmental watersheds for young visual artists is the discovery of the possibility of the multiple versions of the same subject—what Wolf and Perry called multiple *renditions*. Thus, Paine (1987) found evidence for the emergence of technical concerns and technical explorations at a developmentally appropriate time in Lautrec's life. Paine identified three themes that emerge from her perusal of Lautrec's childhood sketches: an enthusiasm for spectacles such as circuses and horse races; an interest in caricature; and a fascination with capturing character. In effect, Paine's observations support the thematic concerns previously mentioned.

Copies. Lautrec, like most young artists and many older ones, copied the work of other artists and "borrowed" images from popular genres. Murray (1991) suggested that in the 1870s, Lautrec's exposure to the work of *animaliers*—artists who depicted animals both domestic and wild—and *les peintres sportifs*—artists who depicted the gentry engaged in sporting pursuits—improved his grasp of equine anatomy and posture. Painters whose works must have been known to, and closely observed by Lautrec include Princeteau (1844–1914), Grandjean (1844–1908), Brown (1829–1890), Du Busson (1859–1933), and Goubie (1842–1899).

Murray demonstrated in her visual analysis that Lautrec borrowed images from two Goubie paintings that hung in his home. One canvas, "Retour d'une chasse aux oiseaux," shows some wealthy gentry entering a coach in a seashore setting, figures and horses from which are echoed in Lautrec's two studies, "Attelage en tandem" and "Monsieur." Even though the painting is still clumsy, the poses and spatial orientation of the horses identify their provenance very clearly. Another Goubie painting, "Vol de la corneille," is the clear inspiration for a Lautrec study after an 18th-century equestrian. The pose and the costuming details are unmistakably the same as the Goubie.

Lautrec also may have been inspired by the illustrations in books known to have been in his household. Citing the memoirs of Mme Attems and Lautrec's own letters from the period, Murray identified two such illustrated books: Dumontiel's *Le jardin d'acclimatation* (1876), about the Paris zoo, illustrated by Victor Gerusez (whose *nom de plume* was Crafty); and a book on sports by A.J. Walsh (whose *nom de plume* was Stonehenge). These two books may have provided the models for a number of animal and sporting images found in his early work, for example, Dortu (1971) catalogue, drawings D.93, D.107, D.125, D.134, D.164, D.173, and D.175.

As Murray made clear, Henri borrowed and studied images from his environment. In this respect, he is no different from most children who are interested in developing their graphic skills. Zimmerman (1990), Gardner (1980), Duncum (1984), Robertson (1987), and Wilson and Wilson (1982) all documented the way in which children appropriate from diverse visual sources. The Wilsons (1977) took the extreme position, based on their interpretation of Gombrich (1967) that all child art owes more to other children's art and to adult art than it does to observation. Although their position has been challenged (Golomb, 1992; Pariser, 1977), there is some basis for acknowledging the importance of borrowed imagery. In studies of juvenile work by Klee and Picasso, I found ample evidence of copying from all manner of sources, both "high" and "low" (Pariser, 1987). For example, in late childhood, Klee made meticulous copies of calendar tear sheets in order to learn about architectural details and costume. Like Lautrec, some of the images that Klee copied were undistinguished, and the impulse that propelled him was a hunger for technical knowledge. This hunger for "how to get things right," noted by Gardner (1980), Burton (1980), and others, is a normal part of the "mastery" phase of graphic development.

Yet even as a mature artist, Henri continued to borrow images from his own stock and reuse them in different compositions. In accord with the procedure advocated by Cormon, Lautrec developed individual sketches and studies from life in the bars and dance halls, and later organized these diverse portraits into compositions in his major canvases in the studio (Murray, 1991). Thus, in childhood the artist was encouraged to recycle other artists' images, whereas in maturity, he also reused his own images.

As an instance of Lautrec's mature "recycling," Murray cited three studies of a seated woman, in profile, wearing a furpiece, with her hair pulled into a topknot. The woman was drawn from life and then incorporated, along with several other figures, into his major painting "Au bal du Moulin de la Galette." This habit of composing larger scenes from individual portraits earned Lautrec some criticism: Lassaigne (1953) saw Lautrec's larger compositions as mere "collections of portraits" (p. 22).

Line Quality.   In addition to Lautrec's penchant for recycling images, a close inspection of his early drawings reveals the quality of his line. In marked contrast to his early teacher, Bonnat, who described Lautrec's drawing as "atrocious," many 20th-century students of Lautrec's work extol his drawing skills. Paine (1987) noted, "it is the confident, barely controlled, yet dynamic quality of line which makes Henri's six-year-old sketches leap to the eye" (p. 299). Polasec (1975) observed that Henri's childhood sketches and cartoons in the copybooks show an ability "to capture a likeness with a few strokes. His 15-year-old drawings reveal an absoluteness of line" (p. 13). These comments suggest that 20th-century viewers find evidence of the early emergence of Lautrec's highly specialized visual intelligence (Gardner, 1985) and an exceptional use of fluid, expressive line.

I have now outlined some of the main properties of Lautrec's juvenile work: the profusion of imagery dealing with horses and other animals, sports and spectacles, along with his predilection for satire and caricature; the early mastery of articulated forms; and a vitality of line. Having looked at these more personal properties of Lautrec's gift, I now return to the two other features of Csikszentmihalyi's (1988) systems' model of creativity, the domain and the field. They refer to the structure of knowledge that Lautrec was expected to master as a neophyte artist and to the social institutions which governed the teaching and evaluation of artistic production.

THE DOMAIN: LAUTREC'S MASTERY OF LATE 19TH-CENTURY FINE ARTS SKILLS

Lautrec was brought up as an amateur artist. He initially absorbed the norms and expectations of the domain of painting and drawing informally, through the paintings and books that were available to him in the chateau, through the artistic pastimes practiced by his relatives, and through the encouragement he received from his family and Princeteau. Copying from "accepted" works and studying from nature were among the prescribed methods of artistic apprenticeship. Princeteau taught Lautrec a very watered down version of Impressionism, a style Henri learned quite quickly. When it became impossible to tell Lautrec's paintings from his own, Princeteau urged Lautrec to start studying in an *atelier* in Paris.

Boime (1986) outlined the routine course of study followed by students in such *ateliers*. Exercises in learning to render faultlessly two-dimensional models were followed by copying engravings of the anatomy. At this point, students were expected to make copies of works of art. Following this apprenticeship in two dimensions, students were given plaster casts to draw and finally, classically posed nudes to study. These studies were referred to as *académies*. After this rigorous training, one at last began painting fully developed compositions in oil on canvas. These paintings were entered in competitions and judged for entry into prestigious *ateliers* such as the *Ecole des beaux-arts de Paris*. Lautrec was quite comfortable with the academic regimen and although he acquitted himself well in life drawing and plaster cast studies, he did not excel. Lautrec never won the prized academic competition for entry into the *Ecole des beaux-arts de Paris*—a vital steppingstone for a truly first-rate "academic" career (Murray, 1991, p. 48). Indeed, as noted previously, his first academic teacher, Bonnat, found Lautrec's drawing ability *lacking*!

It is common knowledge that Lautrec admired some of the Impressionists, notably Manet and Degas. However, his youthful training was at the hands of the *juste milieu* painters such as Bonnat and Cormon, painters who tried to maintain a balance between the wild romanticism of Delacroix and the control of David. While following the accepted path toward academic painting, Lautrec was also developing competence in a parallel domain of endeavor—popular illustration.

Lautrec began to contribute drawings and prints to popular journals in which the criteria for success were rather different from those for academia. One had to be productive, lively, and topical. Lautrec was all of these things. The skill and facility with which Lautrec had captured the gait and movement of horses, riders, animals, and circus acts was now applied to capturing moments of café life. But, initially at least, Lautrec's academic work and his contributions to the popular press were separate, only coming to complement each other in what Murray referred to as his mature work.

It is clear from the modest success that Lautrec achieved among the academic painters that he was judged to have a competent but not extraordinary grasp of the domain of classical painting, a judgment that from our 20th-century perspective is irrelevant. One reason for this incongruence between our own view of Lautrec and that of the "official gatekeepers of the arts" who were his contemporaries is the upheaval in the institutions of the art world at the very time that Lautrec was active in Paris.

THE FIELD: UPHEAVALS IN THE FRENCH ART WORLD AND THE DRIVE FOR RECOGNITION AND SUCCESS

Lautrec was fortunate to have been born into a wealthy family that was prepared to indulge and support his artistic bent. Equally important for his long-term success was Lautrec's good luck in being born into a historical period when the structure of the French art world was undergoing some radical changes. It is to this subject that I now turn.

In his analysis of the Parisian art world of the late 1800s, Huston (1989) maintained that during this period, the criteria for "good art" changed. As the power of the salons and the academy declined, alternative marketing and display venues became ascendant and alternative criteria for critical judgments emerged. Huston claimed that many artists, both within and outside established institutions, had to struggle for a place during this period of transition. The mature Lautrec (and his work, posthumously), however, benefited from this shift in the power base of the artistic establishment. Huston described a critical period in the 19th century when the social criteria for "good art" underwent radical revision: The private patrons lost their dominant role to the state, yet the state was unable to establish its own aesthetic values. During that confusing time, according to Huston, artists whom we respect and admire today, such as Lautrec, were in no way more set upon, or more harshly treated than "mainstream" academic artists. Huston gave as an example the plight of the artist Gérôme, a venerated member of the academy, who was the target of a stinging critical attack. Seeing Lautrec and the "moderns" as the victors in a pitched battle between the avant-garde and the establishment is revisionism guided by hindsight. Huston convincingly argues that at the time, avant-gardistes and academics were equally at risk.

Lautrec was fortunate to have had the financial means to practice his art until the dawn of a period when his unorthodox approach was recognized by institutions that superseded the academy. Persevering in the face of official indifference and rejection (Goldschmidt, 1972), Lautrec cultivated his connections with commercial establishments. Lautrec's first triumphs—his posters (in part inspired by Japanese prints)—took place outside the field of the academic art world. Lautrec owes his posthumous recognition to the fortuitous development of his idiosyncratic style during a period when the French art world had lost its monolithic aspect.

Over and above his "natural" artistic gifts, Lautrec was motivated by personal and social circumstances to seek recognition as an artist. One personal motivation was his dissatisfaction with his physical appearance. The collection of letters compiled by Adhemar and Reff (1969) provides us with Lautrec's critical, if not bitter thoughts on the physical burden he carried. In his letters, he referred to his lack of grace and elegance, to his ugly voice and visage, and he described himself in a letter to his mother as "the abject being who makes for your despair" (p. 9). His self-perceptions were mirrored by mean-minded critics who were quick to use Lautrec's physical deformities as a basis for their aesthetic and moralizing comments. The art critic Edmond de Goncourt described Lautrec as "a ridiculous little man ... whose caricatural deformity is reflected in every one of his drawings" (cited in Adhemar & Reff, 1969, p. 19).

Perhaps to compensate for his dissatisfaction with his physical self, Lautrec actively pursued commercial and critical success. His letters show clearly his hunger for recognition and his acceptance of various commissions. As he was a wealthy man, these business dealings could not have been motivated by financial need. One factor that may have impelled Lautrec to seek commercial ventures was that he did not do well as a "classical artist in training." However, Lautrec's desire for commercial success was not without its complications. He well knew that his patrician family, particularly his father, had great disdain for those artistic "gentlemen" who suffered the indignity of being paid for their work. It may be, then, that Lautrec's dalliance with the commercial art world was motivated by both the positive urge for recognition and the negative desire to affront his family.

Thus, at the personal level, we find several reasons for Lautrec's move in the direction of commercial art work and exhibiting in galleries and public gathering places. Among these are his quest for personal autonomy and self-worth, his ambivalent relations with his family encompassing the desire for distance and differentiation, and an equally strong impulse to gain status in the eyes of his family. Lautrec's involvement with the commercial art world appears quite crucial for his career as it was only within the field of this nonacademic milieu that his work took root and flowered.

To summarize this discussion of domain and field, five factors in Lautrec's personal and social environment contributed to or impelled him along his chosen path. These include his love of drawing and other forms of image-making and a willingness to invest huge amounts of time and energy in this activity; his failure, during his student years in Paris, to achieve significant notice as a promising academic painter; the good fortune to start his career in the Parisian art world at a time when the old closed structures of the academy and salon were losing their power to newer social organizations; his longstanding unhappiness with his physical condition; and his ambivalent attitude toward his family, encompassing the desire for a career as a commercial artist (knowing full well that such a metier would alienate his father) and an equally strong dependency, both emotional and financial, on his family.

In the next section, I address two features of his youthful work that establish important motivational and formal links between his juvenile and mature work. The identification of these features helps describe how childhood giftedness led, in Lautrec's case, to adult achievement. It is important to note that in so doing I am documenting the special conditions and gifts that helped this talented child turn into a noted artist. However, it is likely that descriptions of other gifted child artists who eventually became great artists (e.g., Millais; Warner, 1981) will identify other sorts of gifts and continuities. It is only after researchers have been able to compile a significant number of detailed case descriptions from a wide variety of cultural situations that we can start to think about commonalities among diverse cases. Ultimately, such nomothetic formulations would be very satisfying, but for the present we remain at the level of idiographic studies.

In the case of Lautrec, two important links between childhood efforts and adult work can be documented: an interest in illustration and his treatment of subject matter. From his earliest years, Lautrec was attracted to illustrating text, be it his own words or those of another author. This affinity for illustration remained with him throughout his life and resulted in some fortuitous and important collaborative efforts. In terms of subject matter, we find a persistent attitude toward, and liking for animated and slightly grotesque images. The habits he first acquired in his studies of animals did not leave him when he began to observe the denizens of the Parisian *demi-monde.*

CONTINUITIES

Illustrative Work: Collaboration in Childhood and Adult Work

Throughout his life, Lautrec engaged in illustrative collaboration. As a schoolboy with less than perfect study habits, he left behind a number of richly doodled Latin and Greek textbooks, a dictionary, and several exercise books illustrated between 1873 and 1881. In these books, one finds frequent marginal sketches. In Geoffroy's (1873) *Dictionnaire Elémentaire*, we can observe Lautrec's enjoyment of ink blots. This playful experimentation bespeaks an early fascination with a rudimentary printing process. For example, on the bottom margins of pages 362–363, the young artist blotted a drawing and played with its impression on the other page, creating the profile of a man wearing a cap. On opposite pages of the same dictionary, Henri experiments with sequence and action, notably the acrobats gracing pages 437, 456, 458, and 464. These diminutive figures that balance on the vertical line dividing the columns of print are delightful evidence of Lautrec's early mastery of gesture and movement. In other cases there are clear connections between the content of the text and the image. Lautrec's school exercise book in which he took dictation and prepared for his exams (dated 1875–1880) are filled with sketches of ancient Gauls, chivalric gentlemen, and other figures that complement the material he was transcribing. Some textbooks with narratives also invited illustration. Several tales in his Latin edition of Aesop's fables are accompanied by small pencil sketches (see Fig. 2.11, an illustration of the fable about a greedy but unsophisticated dog).

The impulse to illustrate a narrative—either one's own or someone else's—is often found among visually gifted children. Zimmerman (1990) and Feinburg (1976) cited their own children as examples of inveterate narrative-spinners. Golomb (1992) and Wilson and Wilson (1982) mentioned the frequency and

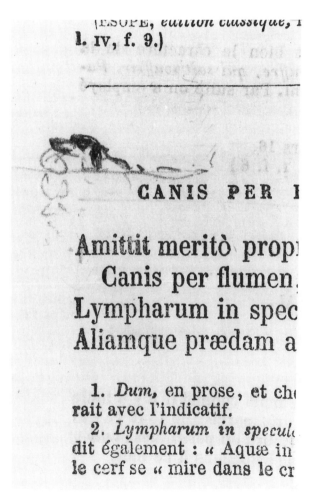

FIG. 2.11. Henri de Toulouse-Lautrec, French, 1864–1901. Dog swimming. Pencil. 18 × 11 cm. From Phedre, 1875. By permission of the Musée Toulouse-Lautrec, Albi.

prevalence of narrative illustrations among visually gifted children. Lautrec's first two illustrated projects—*Les Cahiers de Zig-Zag* and *Submersion* (both 1880) were intended, respectively, as a letter to his cousins and as a diary entry. *Les Cahiers* details—with some satirical force—the train trip and hotel lodgings that Lautrec and his mother endured. Both the pen-and-ink caricatures and the text offer a good taste of Henri's biting and sometimes coarse humor. A letter from the same period attests to Lautrec's knack for caustic observation. In Letter 34 (Adhemar & Reff, 1969), Lautrec described the guests at the spa: "the faces people make while drinking the health-giving 'waters'! … one could fill an album with these expressions" (p. 60). Thus, at this early point in his life, his powers of observation and his delight in the human comedy are well in evidence.

"Cocotte" (Devismes, 1953) was Henri's first fully developed collaborative work. The result of the friendship that grew between Lautrec and another schoolboy, Etienne Devismes, "Cocotte" is a story about an old mare—an ex-cavalry mount—who mortifies her owner, a priest, by joining a cavalry parade with him aboard. The curate is embarrassed and upset and Cocotte's career is terminated. Henri's illustrations are lively, fluid, and show off his ability to capture human and equine character. The 17-year-old artist-illustrator took his task seriously. He evidently pondered the merits of different approaches to a given scene for there exist many preliminary sketches.

In spite of the sentimentality of the tale, Lautrec's sketches are vivid and direct. A pen-and-ink drawing (see Fig. 2.5) shows the moment when Cocotte, carried away by her enthusiasm for her past life, joins the cavalry parade, and Monsieur Le Curé loses his prayer book, hat, and worst of all, his wig—visible at the bottom right of the drawing. Cocotte herself is drawn more sketchily than the other horses. Her gait is agitated and uncontrolled, whereas that of the cavalry horses is measured and orderly. Her eyes roll wildly and the priest grabs for the stability of her neck. The carriages and horses advancing toward the viewer from the right and exiting on the far left of the page are a practiced part of Lautrec's visual vocabulary. One can find numerous contemporaneous examples of the same sorts of equine figures sketched in Lautrec's schoolbook pages (see Fig. 2.4 from his 1875–1880 schoolbook). The foreshortened horses in "Cocotte"—the arched necks of the oncoming carriage horses and the rumps of the animals disappearing into the distance—bear a strong resemblance to horse sketches in his schoolbook.

The "Cocotte" drawings are important for several reasons. They are Lautrec's first collaborative effort—and artistic collaboration is a route that he pursued consistently over the course of his life. They mark the end of the schoolboy period of Henri's life and the beginning of his career as a "serious art student." They are accomplished drawings showing that Lautrec is beginning to orchestrate form and expression.

Later, when Lautrec studied in Cormon's Parisian studio, his master asked him to illustrate two groups of poems by Victor Hugo ("Avertissements et Châtiments" and "La Légende des Siècles," both published in 1884). To Henri's great disappointment, his drawings were rejected by the publisher—an event he mentioned in his letters to his mother. Murray viewed Lautrec's illustrations for the poems

"Chevalier avec Trois Nymphes" and "Chevalier" as examples of Henri's "middle-of-the-road" style—*juste milieu* as it is known. Thus, we have evidence that as late as 1884 (Lautrec's 20th year), some of his work was still conservative. The start of his stylistic break came when he began his collaboration with Aristide Bruant.

It was working with Bruant, according to Murray, that gave Lautrec the impetus to find his mature voice: a blend of close observation, bold design, and biting expression. Bruant, as noted earlier, was the Montmartre entertainer whose performances consisted of bawdy songs and the verbal abuse of his audience. The height of Bruant's career spanned from 1885 to 1895. A middle-class gentleman from the country, he had a knack for rasping out songs about cutthroats, prostitutes, soldiers, and others. He goaded his adoring patrons with a chorus of *"Tous les clients sont des cochons!"* ["All the customers are pigs"](O'Connor, 1991, p. 12). Bruant's favorite haunt was Le Chat Noir, which he eventually bought and renamed Le Mirliton. Bruant's publication, also called *Le Mirliton,* contained some of Lautrec's early illustrations.

According to Murray, these illustrations were an important departure for Lautrec. In order to create them, he familiarized himself with the everyday imagery and themes of the Parisian press, including work by the illustrators of the day, Caran d'Ache, Forain, Heidebrunck, Ibels, Lunel, Rafaelli, Steinlein, and Willette. From these artists and from Bruant, Lautrec acquired a repertoire of "naturalistic" subjects (i.e., low life). This subject matter was especially dear to the popular press because in dwelling upon it, the papers could titillate and edify their clientele. Lautrec's posters advertising the delights of Montmartre drew their inspiration from the same popular press. More than suggestive, his posters were sometimes too close to the bone. Hughes (1992) described the way in which all copies of an advertisement—illustrating a scene from a lurid novel in which a prostitute is kissing a fat banker—were summarily removed by two stockbroker's clerks.

Thanks to such publicity, good citizens flocked to Montmartre to gape at spectacles. Because of his collaboration with Bruant, Lautrec began to assimilate themes from the contemporary press—themes that did not originate with him but that eventually permeated his own work: "his journalistic illustrations of the 1880s were to evolve into the posters and graphic work of the 1890s and eventually 'pop' and 'high' art were to merge in his work" (Murray, 1991, p. 89).

But Bruant's influence may have gone beyond inducing Lautrec to deal with popular topics. Bruant's coarse, harsh, and sketchy songs may have evoked an equally rough and sketchy approach in Lautrec's images (Murray, 1991). Canvas surfaces are rough, materials used on occasion (such as cardboard) are crude and unrefined. Lautrec probably chose to use cheap materials and a crude approach as his way of making a statement: "the use of this cheap coarse proletarian material for formal works must have had democratic connotations. Lautrec probably chose it deliberately" (Murray, 1991, p. 89). Moreover, Lautrec, like other "progressive" painters sometimes used the format of the academic sketch as a finished work despite the fact that in Cormon's *atelier,* he had learned all the steps leading up to a finished painting. His illustrations for Hugo's "Avertissements et Châtiments," for example, were done in accordance with the principles of *l'esquisse peinte,* the painted sketch as taught in the *atelier* (Boime, 1986), yet they are presented as finished works.

Such audacity (which irritated Lautrec's father no end) signaled his early experiments with a "modern" approach to representation, namely a disdain for hiding process and a fascination with rough ignoble materials and techniques—all visible in the final product. These features of Lautrec's modernism, it must be noted, were not unique to his style and had already made themselves felt in France as early as the 1820s (Boime, 1986). However, I claim here that it is due in large part to Lautrec's longstanding taste for narrative illustration and his felicitous partnership with Bruant that his own work began to move in the direction of a "modern" aesthetic. Bruant's subject matter called for the rough visual treatment in which Lautrec delighted.

Lautrec's collaborative ventures did not end with Bruant. For the rest of his life, he continued to illustrate stories and other texts, including humble dinner invitations, episodes from the theater and bestiaries (e.g., Clemenceau, *Au Pied du SinaÇï,* 1897; Renard, *Histoires Naturelles,* 1899). I agree with Murray that it is Lautrec's collaboration with Bruant that initiated his experimentation with significant thematic and formal elements. Thus, Lautrec's continuing interest in illustration provided a format within which he could narrate and document his own experiences. It also gave him the impulse to work with Bruant—a collaboration that was to provide much grist for Lautrec's artistic mill.

Attitude Toward Subject Matter

As noted earlier, of the 2,554 existing drawings and sketches made by Lautrec up to age 19, 42% are of animals or of animals and people. When he entered Bonnat's studio, Lautrec's interest in animal studies began to wane, whereas his interest in figure studies increased. As is seen in Table 2.1, between the ages of 16 and 19 Lautrec made fewer drawings of animals relative to his total output than he had from ages 6 to 16. Yet despite the fact that he was dealing more with people, Lautrec's treatment of his subjects remained the same. The sense of distance that may have obtained between himself and his animal subjects prevailed in the distance he set between himself and his human subjects. In fact, three critics stated explicitly that Lautrec observed people *as though they were animals.* Hughes (1992) said, "he was about as compassionate as a rattlesnake" and that his view of the lower classes was from the vantage point of an aristocratic French male—"he watched them as one might watch fish in an aquarium" (p. 54). In a catalogue accompanying a recent show of Lautrec's work, Matthias Arnold (1985) compared the figure studies by Degas and Lautrec:

> one may say that Degas painted women like horses and horses like women. Something of this odd equation also motivated Lautrec, who spoke affectionately of his prostitute models, "they loll about on sofas like animals." (Thadée Natanson, 1951, cited in Arnold, 1985, pp. 48–49)

In the same vein, Dorment (1991) observed: "sometimes one is reminded of two lionesses, idly pawing each other in play. Like most of Lautrec's brothel scenes, the pictures of lesbians are even more about stifling boredom than they are about sex" (p. 18). The animallike quality of these portraits suggests a psychological link between Lautrec's mature studies and his childhood fascination with animals. The focus has changed, but the distant attitude of the observer remains constant.

Lautrec's attitude toward animals, as loyal but inferior companions, is echoed in his adult experience of Montmartre nightclubs and bordellos in which equally fascinating and equally alien creatures disported themselves. Is it not possible that the attitude that Lautrec cultivated vis-à-vis animals was ultimately transferred to his experience and observation of marginal people? Lautrec enjoyed and copied the animal grotesques of Grandville; these images conflate the animal and human for satirical purposes. This childhood interest also presages an expressive feature of his mature studies.

Several circumstances helped to shift his focus from animals to the nightlife of Montmartre, and the Grandville images may have been one of the steps along the way. Murray identified another transitional subject: the peasants from his own estates of whom Lautrec made several portraits one summer while working in the Paris *ateliers*. Here, we see the first instance in which Lautrec willingly strayed from his standard imagery of animals, spectacles, soldiers, and equestrians. Murray found it significant that Lautrec decided to turn from genteel to rougher and less privileged subjects.

One other factor deserving elaboration when considering Lautrec's noted distant attitude toward his favorite subjects is his class (Hughes, 1992). In addition to the gulf that he felt separated him from able-bodied and well-favored individuals, there was the fact of his noble birth. Although rejecting the outer trappings and the career path of a gentleman, Lautrec's attitudes and values were fundamentally patrician. Murray viewed his *juste-milieu* tastes as one indicator of Lautrec's strong identification with his class. His letters to his family reveal that he was less solicitous of the welfare of his servants than he was of the well-being of his animals. On one occasion, a housemaid was taken ill and Lautrec complained about the nuisance involved in getting her to hospital!

Adhemar and Reff (1969) reported an incident that reveals that Lautrec's sense of himself as a high-born person remained with him to the end. One evening near the end of Lautrec's life, the unhappy man was accompanied by cronies bent on drinking him dry. As the party ended, Lautrec found he had no money to pay for the hotel room and, "unable to come to terms about his bill ... in the ensuing argument declared, 'I am the Comte de Toulouse!'" (p. 22)

Such evidence suggests that no matter how deeply he delved into the hidden worlds of Montmartre, Lautrec thought of himself as a gentleman, with little in common with the ordinary folk he studied. The social gulf between the two spheres was almost as great as that between one species and another. And perhaps it is this combination of a sense of distance and fascination which lends intensity to some of his paintings and drawings. To some degree, this trait is a function of his childhood and adolescent training—as an observer of animals.

Experimentation With Form and Effect

Lautrec's special gift, even as a child, must have been the capacity to note and distinguish between what Arnheim (1974) called the perception of effect of an image and the perception of its form. It is one thing to recognize the emotional impact of an image, and quite another to figure out which elements in the structure of the image give it emotional power. It is this sort of analytic understanding that, Arnheim said, is needed for effective representation.

If one looks at some of Lautrec's sketches in his schoolbooks and textbooks, it appears that in at least three instances the drawings of an inattentive schoolboy foreshadowed some of the powerful renderings that were to come from his mature hand one or two decades later. These sketches suggest that as early as adolescence, Lautrec was beginning to consider the relationship between the formal properties of an image and its effect. On page 86 of his school exercise book, dated 1875–1880 (see Fig. 2.4), one finds the bottom half of the page covered with eight diminutive sketches of horses in rapid motion. The scale of the drawing is tiny: Each horse is no larger than a word on the page. Yet, the vigor and animation with which they are drawn is striking. Lautrec's signature is plainly there. Seven of the horses are foreshortened. Two are without riders. The riderless horse third from the left side of the page is particularly bold, racing toward the left with its neck arched, rear quarters extended. It is studied from a low angle and its anatomy is rendered with economy and assurance. Lautrec used the white space of the page with special skill to model the flanks.

Essentially the same animal appears in the lithograph "The Jockey" (1899; see Fig. 2.12). The horse is displayed, neck arched and rear quarters at eye level, forelegs extended. In the lithograph, the direction of the animal has been reversed, but this can be attributed to the printing process. The 1899 horse was *drawn* facing in the same direction as that in the schoolboy sketch. The basic scaffold for the horse in this lithograph was developed some 20 years earlier. The energy of the sketch and the print are similar as well. As noted earlier, although the record is far from complete, it is certain that Lautrec drew this same animal many times—the effect that he sought is present from its first recorded appearance as a schoolbook sketch.

On page 55 of the same school notebook, there is another horse study (see Fig. 2.13). Here, a heavily muscled rump and arched neck characterize a solid animal. In "Le Cirque Fernando" (1888; see Fig. 2.2), we find the same robust equine anatomy, moving in the same direction, from right to left. The rear quarters are slightly below eye level allowing us to see the broad back on which the equestrienne is sitting. The expression of controlled power epitomized by the heavy rear quarters and compressed neck are already present in the schoolboy sketch. Lautrec added the canted angle of the beast and its cocked hind foot, conveying the idea of motion and controlled force, to his later work.

Another more dramatic instance of Lautrec's childhood experimentation with schema and expression can be found on page 552 of Geoffroy's (1873) *Dictionnaire Elémentaire*. A sketch of a face, drawn below several sketches of ships and a

FIG. 2.12. Henri de Toulouse-Lautrec, French, 1864–1901."The Jockey" (*Le jockey*). Lithograph. 1899. 52 × 36 cm. Gift of the Baldwin M. Baldwin Foundation. By permission of the San Diego Museum of Art.

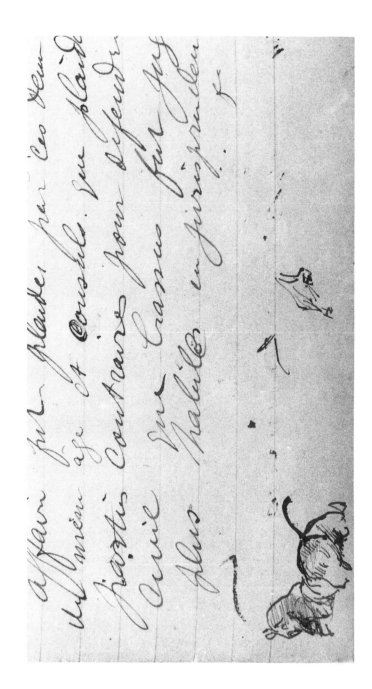

FIG. 2.13. Henri de Toulouse-Lautrec, French, 1864–1901. Sketch of a horse and horse head. School exercise book, 1875–1880, p. 55. By permission of the Musée Toulouse-Lautrec, Albi.

FIG. 2.14. Henri de Toulouse-Lautrec, French, 1864–1901. Sketch of a face (detail) in Geoffroy, 1873, p. 552 (made between ages 11 and 17). Pen and ink on paper. 22 × 15 cm. By permission of the Musée Toulouse-Lautrec, Albi.

coachman, is rendered in a few sure lines (Fig. 2.14, dated about 1878). The closed eyes, wide cheekbones, thin lips, flaring nostrils, high forehead, and strained supercilious expression are striking in their similarity to Lautrec's portrait of Yvette Guilbert, "Linger Longer Lou" (1898; Fig. 2.15). Behind many studies of Yvette Guilbert, we find lurking this same blueprint. Lautrec seems to have formulated the construction of a particular expression that then became part of his stock in trade. This process may be similar to the one that Arnheim (1970) observed in his study of "Guernica." He noted that one of Picasso's earliest sketches for the mural, rudimentary although it may be, contains all of the basic element of the final version. Lautrec's sketchbook experiments, although covering a much longer period of time than Picasso's work for the "Guernica," seem to be another instance of an artist returning to initial images and devices for aesthetic closure.

CONCLUSION

Two youthful predilections provide some of the framework for understanding Lautrec's career as an artist: his penchant for illustration and his lifelong fascination with animals and the grotesque. His habit of illustrating his own narratives or those of others paved the way for his partnership with Bruant. In the same way, Henri's

FIG. 2.15. Henri de Toulouse-Lautrec, French, 1864–1901. Linger, Longer, Lou. Plate VII from The English Set, 1898. Lithograph. 32.2 × 26.4 cm. By permission of The Harvard University Art Museums.

love of animals began as the prosaic interest of a well-to-do child who studied pictures of horses and other animals and images of sporting life. This observant child gradually transferred his acute vision to the human scene. From contemporary artists who worked in a "naturalistic" vein, Lautrec assimilated themes that he recast in a "high art" mold. His mature style emphasized linear qualities in the application of paint, the almost cartoonlike depiction and bold placement of the figures, dense color and empty space, and the use of melodramatic lighting and point of view. Some critics feel that it is the psychological tone of his mature images that makes them memorable. Hughes (1992) described the portrayal of individuals in Lautrec's work as:

> not merely a mask of passion or a symbol of social role. A little bareback rider's squinched up face above the massive churning crupper of a stallion ... the Cyrano nose and signature black gloves of Yvette Guilbert ... these images live on as obdurately as the traits of Dickens' characters. (p. 55)

I maintain that Lautrec's childhood doodles and sketches afforded him the opportunity to hone the expressive skills that critics find so remarkable. I only partly agree with Thomson (1981), who suggested that Lautrec's training in classical drawing was a significant and decisive precursor to his mature work. I would argue that Lautrec's academic training may have helped him in terms of instilling discipline and tenacity. But the technical skills that Henri acquired as he matured and studied with several masters contributed relatively little to the work for which he would be famous. Some of his most important lessons were those he gave himself in his own private childhood studio—in the margins and on the back pages of school texts and exercise books.

In Fig. 2.5, 2.6, 2.13, and 2.14 we can see the work of a gifted child whose primary interest is in the relationship between the formal properties of the image and the expressive effect that such properties engender. "Realism" mastery of perspective, proportions, and "correct composition" were all minor challenges easily overcome, but of no special consequence for his art. What Lautrec the child taught himself about the relationship between form and effect stood him in good stead when he became Lautrec the artist. But it took more than a gift for visual expression, the capacity for phenomenal linear control and the drive for artistic recognition to move Lautrec from the position of an eccentric art student to prominence in the history of art. As we have seen, Lautrec had the good fortune to be supported by a wealthy and loving, if bewildered, family, and to fall into a collaborative endeavor with Bruant who exposed him to the gritty material that was the perfect complement to his preferred way of working. Lautrec was also fortunate to be born into an era when a maverick approach to the visual arts could be recognized and accepted. The academy and its institutions were under siege, and although Lautrec was no radical storming the barricades, he was the posthumous beneficiary of the ensuing battles over artistic doctrine.

ACKNOWLEDGMENTS

Research for this chapter was supported in part by grants from Concordia University and from the Social Sciences and Humanities Research Council of Canada. Thanks to Line Maurel and Wendy Thomas for their excellent assistance. Thanks also to Lon Dubinsky for suggesting references.

REFERENCES

Adhemar, J. (1975). *L'oeuvre graphique de Grandville* [The graphic works of Grandville]. Paris: Arthur Hubschmidt.

Adhemar, J., & Reff (1969). Introduction and notes. In L. Goldschmidt & H. Schimmel (Eds.), *Unpublished correspondence of Henri de Toulouse-Lautrec: 273 letters by and about Lautrec; written to his family and friends in the collection of Herbert Schimmel.* London: Phaidon Press.

Andrews, J. (1989). Wang Yani and contemporary Chinese painting. In W-C. Ho (Ed.), *Yani: the brush of innocence.* New York: Hudson-Hills Press, in association with the Nelson-Atkins Museum of Art, Kansas City, Missouri.

Arnheim, R. (1962). *The genesis of a painting: Picasso's Guernica.* Berkeley: University of California Press.

Arnheim, R. (1974). *Art and visual perception.* Berkeley: University of California Press.

Arnold, M. (1985). Toulouse-Lautrec and the art of his century. In W. Wittrock & R. Castleman (Eds.), *Henri de Toulouse-Lautrec: Images of the 1890's* (pp. 37–77). New York: Museum of Modern Art.

Barnes, J. (1984). *Flaubert's parrot.* New York: McGraw Hill.

Becker, H. (1982). *Art worlds.* Berkeley: University of California Press.

Boime, A. (1986). *The academy and French painting in the 19th century.* New Haven, CT: Yale University Press.

Bourassa, P. (1992). *Toulouse-Lautrec. La collection Baldwin M. Baldwin du San Diego Museum of Art.* Quebec City: Musée du Québec.

Burton, J. (1980). Developing minds series: Representing experience from imagination and observation. *School Arts Magazine, 26–30.*

Carroll, K. (1992). *Beginnings: the work of young Edvard Munch.* Unpublished paper, The Maryland Institute College of Art, Baltimore.

Case, R. (1992). *The mind's new staircase: Exploring the conceptual underpinnings of children's thought and knowledge.* Hillsdale, NJ: Lawrence Erlbaum Associates.

Clark, G., & Zimmerman, E. (1992). *Issues and practice related to identification of gifted and talented students in the visual arts.* Storrs, VT: The National Research Center on the Gifted and Talented.

Csikszentmihalyi, M. (1988). Society, culture and person: A systems view of creativity. In R. Sternberg (Ed.), *The nature of creativity: Contemporary psychological perspectives* (pp. 325–340). New York: Cambridge University Press.

Danto, A. (1985, December). Henri de Toulouse-Lautrec. *The Nation*, 656–660.

Dennis, S. (1986). *The development of children's art: A neo-Piagetian interpretation.* Unpublished doctoral dissertation, Ontario Institute for Studies in Education, Toronto.

Devismes, E. (1953). *Cocotte.* Paris: Editions du Chêne.

Dorment, R. (1991). Lautrec's bitter theatre. *The New York Review of Books, 38*, 15–18.

Dortu, M. (1971). *Toulouse-Lautrec et son oeuvre* [Toulouse-Lautrec and his work] (6 volumes). New York: Collectors' Editions.

Duncum, P. (1984). How 35 children, born between 1724 and 1900, learned to draw. *Studies in Art Education, 26*, 93–102.

Evans, D. (1977). *A Piagetian perspective on artistic development.* Unpublished doctoral dissertation, Ohio State University, Columbus.

Feinburg, S. (1976). Combat in child art. In J. Bruner & K. Sylva (Eds.), *Play: Its role in development and evolution*. New York: Basic Books.

Feldman, D.H. (1980). *Beyond universals in cognitive development*. Norwood, NJ: Ablex.

Fermigier, A. (1969). *Toulouse-Lautrec*. New York: Praeger.

Gardner, H. (1980). *Artful scribbles. The significance of children's drawings*. New York: Basic Books.

Gardner, H. (1985). *Frames of mind: The theory of multiple intelligences*. New York: Basic Books.

Gardner, H. (1990). Multiple intelligences: Implications for art and creativity. In W. Moody (Ed.), *Artistic intelligences: Implication for education* (pp. 11–31). New York: Teacher's College Press.

Geoffroy, J. (1873). *Dictionnaire élémentaire français-latin (nouveau)* [Beginner's French-Latin Dictionary (new)]. Paris: Jules Delalain.

Goldschmidt, L. (Ed.). (1972). *Henri de Toulouse-Lautrec: Letters 1871–1901*. Paris: Gallimard.

Goldschmidt, L., & Schimmel, H. (Eds.). (1969). *Unpublished correspondence of Henri de Toulouse-Lautrec: 273 letters by and about Lautrec; written to his family and friends in the collection of Herbert Schimmel*. London: Phaidon Press.

Goldsmith, L., & Feldman, D. (1989). Wang Yani: Gifts well given. In W-C. Ho (Ed.), *Yani: The brush of innocence*. New York: Hudson-Hills Press, in association with the Nelson-Atkins Museum of Art, Kansas City, MO.

Golomb, C. (1992). *The child's creation of a pictorial world*. Berkeley: University of California Press.

Gombrich, E. (1967). *Art and illusion*. Princeton, NJ: Princeton University Press.

Hanson, L., & Hanson, E. (1956). *The tragic life of Toulouse-Lautrec*. London: Secker & Warburg.

Heintzelman, A. (1955). *Toulouse-Lautrec, one hundred and ten unpublished drawings*. Boston: Boston Art Book Shop.

Ho, W-C. (Ed.). (1989). *Yani: The brush of innocence*. New York: Hudson-Hills Press, in association with the Nelson-Atkins Museum of Art, Kansas City, MO.

Hughes, R. (1992, March 9). Cutting through the myth. *Time*, pp. 54–55.

Hurwitz, A. (1985). The U.S. and the U.S.S.R.. Two attitudes towards the gifted in art. *Gifted Child Quarterly 20*, 458–464.

Huston, L. (1989). *L'évolution des expositions d'art et le pouvoir dans la vie artistique 1864–1914* [The evolution of art exhibitions and power in artistic life 1864–1914]. Unpublished doctoral dissertation, Concordia University, Montreal.

Jedlicka, G. (1943). *Henri de Toulouse-Lautrec*. Zurich: Eugen Rentsch Verlag.

Lassaigne, J. (1953). *Lautrec: Biographical and critical studies* (S. Gilbert, Trans.). Geneva: Skira.

Lautrec, H. (1931). Les Cahiers de Zig-Zag appartenant de Henri de Toulouse-Lautrec. *L'Amour de l'art, 12*, 172-176.

Lautrec, H. (1938). *Submersion. Arts et metiers graphiques*. Paris: Curnonsky.

Lewis, H., & Livson, N. (1967). Correlations of developmental level of spatial representation in children's drawings. *Studies in Art Education, 8*, 46–57.

Mack, G. (1938). *Toulouse-Lautrec*. New York: A.A. Knopf.

Murray, G. (1991). *Toulouse-Lautrec: The formative years, 1878–1891*. New York: Oxford University Press.

O'Connor, P. (1991). *The nightlife of Paris: The art of Toulouse-Lautrec*. New York: Universe Books.

Paine, S. (1987). The childhood and adolescent drawings of Henri de Toulouse-Lautrec (1864–1901). Drawings from 6 to 18 years. *Journal of Art and Design Education, 6*, 297–312.

Pariser, D. (1977). A comment on the Wilsons' iconoclasm: Problems with the making-matching hypothesis. *Art Education, 30*, 24–25.

Pariser, D. (1987). The juvenile drawings of Klee, Toulouse-Lautrec and Picasso. *Visual Arts Research, 13*, 53–67.

Pariser, D. (1991). Normal and unusual aspects of juvenile artistic development in Klee, Toulouse-Lautrec and Picasso: A review of findings and directions for future research. *The Creativity Research Journal, 3*, 51–65.

Pariser, D. (1993). The artistically precocious child in different cultural contexts: Wang Yani and Toulouse-Lautrec. *The Journal of Multi-Cultural and Cross-Cultural Research in Art Education, 9/10,* 51–75.

Polasec, J. (1975). *Toulouse-Lautrec drawings.* New York: St. Martin's Press.

Porath, M. (1988). *The intellectual development of gifted children: A neo-Piagetian approach.* Unpublished doctoral dissertation, Ontario Institute for Studies in Education, Toronto.

Rank, O. (1989). *Art and artist: Creative urge and personality development.* New York: Norton.

Robertson, A. (1987). Borrowing and artistic behaviour: A case study of the development of Bruce's spontaneous drawings from 6 to 16. *Studies in Art Education, 29,* 37–51.

Schimmel, D. (Ed.). (1991). *The letters of Henri de Toulouse-Lautrec.* Oxford: Oxford University Press.

Staaller, N. (1986). Early Picasso and the origins of cubism. *Arts Magazine, 61,* 80–90.

Szabad-Smyth, L. (1992). *A longitudinal study of Melissa's spontaneous drawings.* Unpublished master's thesis, Concordia University, Montreal.

Tan, L. (1993). *A case study of an artistically gifted Chinese girl: Wang Yani.* Unpublished master's thesis, Concordia University, Montreal.

Thomson, R. (1981). Henri de Toulouse-Lautrec, drawings from 7 to 18 years. In S. Paine (Ed.), *Six children draw* (pp. 38–48). London: Academic Press.

Visani, M. (1970). *Toulouse-Lautrec* (P. Sanders, Trans.). London: Thames & Hudson.

Wallace, D. (1989). Studying the individual: The case study method and other genres. In D. Wallace & H. Gruber (Eds.), *Creative people at work: 12 cognitive case studies* (pp. 25–43). New York: Oxford University Press.

Walters, J., & Gardner, H. (1986). The crystallization experience. In R. Sternberg & J. Davidson (Eds.), *Conceptions of giftedness* (pp. 306–331). Cambridge: Cambridge University Press.

Warner, M. (1981). John Everett Millais, drawings from 7 to 18 years. In S. Paine (Ed.), *Six children draw* (pp. 9–22). London: Academic Press.

Wattenmaker, R. (1976). *Puvis de Chavannes and the modern tradition* (Rev. Ed.). Toronto: Art Gallery of Ontario.

Wilson, B., & Wilson, M. (1977). An iconoclastic view of the imagery sources in the drawings of young children. *Art Education 30,* 4–13.

Wilson, B., & Wilson, M. (1982). *Teaching children to draw: A guide for teachers and parents.* Englewood Cliffs, NJ: Prentice-Hall.

Winner, E., & Pariser, D. (1985). Giftedness in the visual arts. *Items, 39,* 65–69.

Wolf, D., & Perry, M. (1988). From endpoints to repertoires. New conclusions about drawing development. *Journal of Aesthetic Education, 22,* 17–35.

Zimmerman, E. (1990). *A case study of the childhood art work of an artistically talented young adult.* Paper presented at the 98th annual convention of the American Psychological Association, Boston.

Zolberg, V. (1990). *Constructing a sociology of the arts.* New York: Cambridge University Press.

3

Varda: The Development of a Young Artist

Claire Golomb
University of Massachusetts at Boston

Malka Haas
School of Education of the Kibbutz Movement at Oraniem

The study of gifted child artists is a somewhat neglected topic in the psychology of art and of child development. The paucity of research in this area reflects the difficulty of identifying such children and the scarcity of longitudinal collections.

How do we identify children of special promise in the visual arts, and what signs might predict their future artistic course? A most promising approach might be to begin with the mature works of a famous adult artist, and trace his or her development back to the childhood years in the hope that we might identify significant antecedents. With few exceptions (see Pariser, chapter 2, this volume, on Toulouse-Lautrec) this turns out to be an impossible quest. In the case of most well-known artists, their childhood work has not been preserved, and few examples are known from their early years. In the case of Picasso, the earliest painting dates from age 9, when the skill with which he portrayed his subject met with the approval of his painter father, who was also his mentor. Most commonly, works are only preserved when they show promise in the style valued by the culture. In Western societies, since the Renaissance, this has meant drawing in a realistic style, a relatively rare accomplishment before the middle or late childhood years. Thus, little is known about the childhood work of most of the great masters and questions about their early development, whether it is unique, characterized by a skipping of the typical stages of child art or merely represents an accelerated progression through the same stages, remain unanswered. Stages of graphic development are commonly viewed as progressing from scribble patterns to the typically flat childhood drawings with their disregard for the shape, size, and proportions of a figure, to a more detailed rendering of the object, and within our Western culture, to drawings that provide a realistic view based on perspective projections.

Beyond the question of stages and of precocity, is there something special about the childhood work of artists, is it more original in conception and execution, does it reflect the artist's individuality at an early phase of his or her life, and can we discern some degree of continuity from the childhood years on? The theme of constancy and change in development is of course a central one for psychologists, and, depending on one's orientation, one or the other pole is highlighted. Perhaps change is the most striking characteristic of human development over the life span in both a physiological and psychological sense, although some constancy of self, of an enduring, even if at times illusory, identity is essential for human functioning. Although a single case cannot offer a definitive answer to these questions, its documentation can illuminate developmental issues and provide insight into the creative processes that have long-term projections.

What are our current assumptions of childhood giftedness in the visual arts? In general we find that parents and educators tend to view giftedness in terms of a child's precocious capacity for naturalistic or realistic depiction. This evaluation is not the only one, however, and adults who have honed their appreciation of the arts on the paintings of such 20th-century artists as Dubuffet, Kandinsky, Klee, Malevic, Miro, and Picasso, tend to delight in childish forms that disregard naturalistic shapes and proportions, and make use of bold primary colors. Greater familiarity with primitive, naive, and folk art, and with the writings and illustrations of influential art educators (Cizek, cited in Viola, 1936; Lowenfeld, 1939; Schaefer-Simmern, 1948) also contributed to a reassessment of the aesthetic merits of child art. To these observers, child art with its simple forms, colors, and composition represents an original language that has a direct appeal to the aesthetic sensitivity of the adult viewer. Of course, the precociously realistic child artist (see Golomb, chapter 6, this volume, on Eitan) and the one who fully develops the child art style share a common passion for drawing and painting, and both devote much time and energy in its pursuit.

The case of Varda G., which is presented here, is of interest because we can follow her development from a very early period to her status as an adult artist. She is a young adult whose sculptures have been exhibited in major museums in Israel, usually as part of a group of young promising artists. She has also won awards and thus received the kind of acknowledgment that confirms, however tentatively, the status of "artist." In terms of her early development, we have access to an extensive record that dates from the age of 2 through the flourishing of what we call the *child art style,* which is quite typical of the drawings and paintings of children who have easy access to paper, crayons, brushes, and paints. The course of her development demonstrates the emergence of pictorial-representational characteristics that are universal among children and untrained or naive adults. Beyond these common characteristics, however, we can perceive a visual intelligence at work that creates a meaningful pictorial universe that is at first playful and then increasingly expresses her deepest feelings.

The conditions for Varda's artistic development during the childhood years were propitious: Family and friends showed great respect for her work, enabled her to pursue it, and expected her to be talented in the visual arts. The thoughtful collection of her work by her mother and Malka Haas speaks to the interest shown her work by important adults in her life. Our account of her development rests largely on the material in these collections that comprises more than 500 drawings and paintings that represent the childhood and adolescent years, 30 slides of her more recent sculptures, a fairly large number of etchings, watercolors, and oil pastel portraits. Information about Varda's childhood years was provided by Haas, who is an early childhood and art educator, and the founder of the kibbutz studio, who has closely followed Varda's development from the early years until the present. This account was supplemented by two extensive interviews with Varda, which were conducted by Golomb in the summer of 1991. These conversations were tape-recorded.

Varda is the third of four children in her family, born and raised on an Israeli kibbutz. All her siblings showed a talent for and love of drawing and painting. Varda's older sister developed a special talent for drawing in a naturalistic style from a life model. On her mother's side there are many artists in the family, and there is a general expectation that the children will be talented in the arts. All the children received much emotional support for their artistic endeavors.

Haas has followed Varda's development from the early toddler years through the present time. She perceives Varda's personality as outgoing, warm, and open, but also as a nonconformist determined to find her own ways, a view that Varda amplified in her conversations with Golomb. Drawing and painting were central activities during her childhood and adolescence, activities at which she excelled, although she also enjoyed gymnastics and ballet; she did not show much interest in the academic subjects taught in high school. Growing up in the kibbutz provided Varda with a protective, stable, and caring environment. But life in the kibbutz also presented pressures to fit into a collective that values group norms above individuality, and conveys a communal ethos where art does not have a vital function.

EARLY EXPLORATIONS: THE YEARS FROM 2 TO 4

The earliest drawings in this collection date from the age of 2.0^1 and consist of dots, loops, open circles, continuous and discontinuous lines, and lines drawn almost as parallels. Lines and shapes are dispersed across the page, but even at this early stage they stay within the borders of the paper space, an indication of careful attention to the hand's activity. A little later (2.4) she attends to the open spaces left free by her earlier movements and "fills" them in, usually with parallel scribble lines. We see attempts to differentiate the scribble forms and to experiment with the material, for example, by using the edges of the paper to guide her actions,

---

[1]Ages are represented in years and months: The first numeral indicates age in years, the second one age in months.

choosing a different color for each side and for multiple parallel lines. At 2.7, she discovers the effects of horizontal–vertical crossings and uses different colors for each one of the lines. At 2.8 she draws two vertical scribble patterns and connects them with two horizontal single color lines. She also adds "markings" in the four corners of the paper, and creates a semibalanced configuration. One might see these early efforts as first steps in the organization of pictorial space. At 2.10, Varda draws a red horizontal line across the center axis of the paper and places a tightly formed scribble pattern in its middle, thus creating a symmetrically balanced configuration. At this time she also tries to draw circles and ovals, and attempts to bring the line full circle to its starting point. At 3.0 she creates lattices and dots, and at 3.1 a group of circles, each one drawn separately. From now on, she fills the page with circles, and intersperses them with other forms. She uses color selectively and her color contrasts create, probably unintentionally, three-dimensional effects. On repeated trials one can see how she elaborates on her discoveries and incorporates them into later designs, for example, in her creations of lattices and arcs. Her shapes are now clearly constructed and reflect good visual-motor control. Her awareness of the paper space and her tendency to balance shapes and colors show sensitivity to pictorial effects, and they suggest that even at this early age a visual intelligence is at work.

So far, all her drawings and paintings are nonrepresentational and reflect her pleasure in playing with colors and designs. At 3.2, she surveys a set of disconnected lines and shapes and declares "a man with his face." She organizes her drawings quite deliberately, for example, drawing a crossed square, a circle inside a square, and two arcs connected with a set of vertical lines. She has discovered how lines create two-dimensional shapes, that they can be attached and divided, and that a line can serve two different areas. With this new understanding she creates more complex patterns, that yield clear figure-ground differentiation. She draws triangles, embellishes her squares, and extends structured forms over the whole page. In general, her shapes tend to emerge from a center, often from a set of radials that are at the core of the configuration. Her numerous drawings made in the preschool nursery and at home provide evidence for planning; they reflect visual experience and thought (see Fig. 3.1). At 3.7 she is given oil pastels and experiments with contrasting color patches. When she works with paints and brushes, she employs patterns that are similar to her crayon drawings although the effects can be quite different in this medium, for example, creating droplets and dispersing them selectively across the page. She mixes colors for pleasing effects and creates tonal gradations and colorful patches; a center often guides the construction. At 3.11 she draws her first human, a tadpole, and with but a few trials a fullfledged figure.

So far, the course of her graphic development is in some ways similar to the first steps of young children who have ready access to this medium and are motivated to explore it. What sets her work apart is the care and thoughtfulness with which this preschooler guides her actions, the high interest in its pursuit, and a formal imagination that is strikingly original.

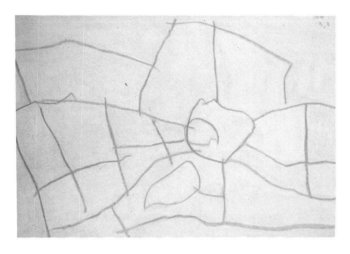

FIG. 3.1. "Early nonfigurative drawing," 33 × 21 cm. Varda, age 3.3.

EARLY REPRESENTATIONAL WORK: AGES 4 TO 6

Varda constantly expands her repertoire of shapes and by now, all her work is multicolored. Although she continues to draw in her preschool, much of her work is now done at home. The drawings have become representational, but not exclusively so. In most of her drawings, decorative elements play a significant role. Humans, animals, and flowers fill the page and compete with ornamental designs for the available space (see Fig. 3.2, on the color panel). This manner of combining decorative and representational elements is specific to Varda. It is rarely seen in drawings of children at this age. Nor does she abandon previously created elements: decorative patches, an abundancy of figures, and the colorful shapes continue to be used.

New elements appear in her drawings, for example, a car and a house, embedded in designs of ladders and lattices that are filled in with circles, colors, and dots. Filling in the lattices is time consuming, and Varda devotes much energy and originality to this pursuit. The first narratives appear, drawn from biblical stories and real life events; they do not replace the purely decorative designs.

Varda tends to divide the picture plane into vertically organized sectors, and to decorate each sector with a different design. The time and effort spent on her designs indicate a seriousness at ages 4 and 5 that sets her apart from most of her contemporaries. The same can be seen in her inventiveness, in the seemingly endless variations in her use of colors and shapes such that she never repeats herself. She tends to create richly decorated borders that frame her pictures, for example, colorful houses that are distributed as abstract shapes along the edges of the paper or a series of trees and flowers that grace its four sides (see Fig. 3.2). Often, these borders consist of different levels and designs. She also develops a new technique

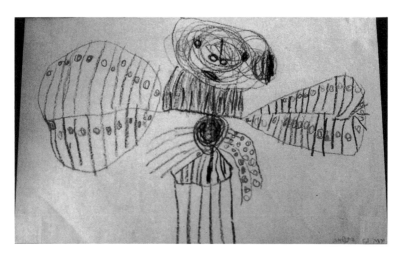

FIG. 3.3. "Dead bird," 33 × 21 cm. Varda, age 5.1

with her crayons, using the broad side of the crayon to create a light and continuous background that unifies the various graphic elements. Her compositions employ symmetry in a lively and dynamic manner.

Different media bring out different pictorial tendencies: Paints and brush yield dramatic creations composed of brilliant colors, bold forms, and broad strokes. In paintings, we find striking color combinations and contrasts, but also examples of fine nuances and gradations. With crayon the tendency is to use detail and embeddedness. The dominance of abstract patterns continues and reflects an aesthetic delight in pure ornamentation. A new design approach is noted: a tendency to divide the paper space into a lower third versus an upper two thirds, or into near halves along the horizontal axis. This division of pictorial space occurs off and on through ages 15 and 16.

During the latter part of her fifth year, her drawings also begin to represent emotionally significant themes, for example, a dead bird and a woman giving birth in an ambulance. The urge to fill the space becomes more pronounced and threatens to overwhelm the usual figure-ground differentiation (see Fig. 3.2). In many drawings from age 5 we see how ornamental designs crowd in on a set of figures that almost disappear in the richly decorated tapestry. But even during this period, Varda can draw upon a varied repertoire, for example, the drawing of a dead bird at age 5.1 (see Fig. 3.3). It is presented in frontal view, in only two colors, black and red–maroon. The lines on the wings are slightly curved, which creates a three-dimensional effect. It is a perfectly balanced creation, that strikes a delicate balance between decorative urge and representational intention.

In many paintings of the 5-year-old we witness this struggle between the desire for representational clarity and the tendency to fill the space with decorative detail. A drawing of two nearly identical figures, perhaps twins, depicts both tendencies, the need to portray separation and connectedness (see Fig. 3.4). The two figures

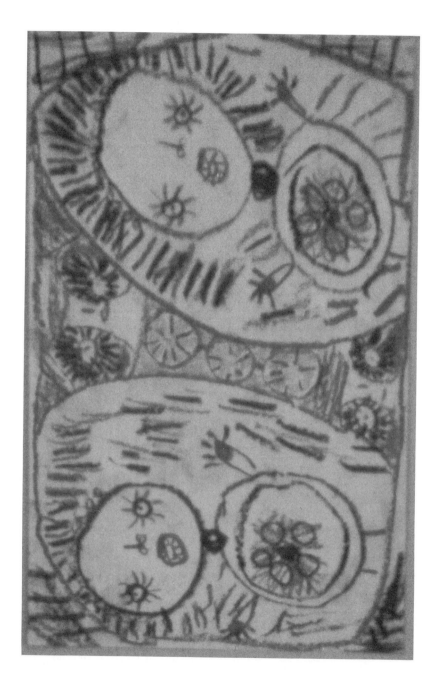

FIG. 3.4. "Twins," 33 × 21 cm. Varda, age 5.11

FIG. 3.5. "Human with masklike face," 33 × 21 cm. Varda, age 5.7

are drawn each within its own orbit, a richly decorated oval that separates the figures. They are, however, linked via the theme, the overall symmetry of the design, and the specific shapes, mostly radials, that connect the two figures. The desire to divide is clearly expressed but also counterbalanced within the unified composition. In this case, she attains differentiation and coordination of figures and theme, allowing each figure its own space and individuality, while also assuring its connectedness.

The themes of the drawings expand to include family affairs, holidays, outings, noting unusual events, Noah's ark, and here and there a mythical landscape. On these thematic representations Varda organizes the pictorial space well and controls her playful decorative tendency. However, in her portraits of humans she gives full reign to her inclination to embellish the figure, especially the prominent heads of her figures. The decorative circles, lines, and dots that comprise the face tend to obliterate its features and to counteract what may have been an original representational intention (see Fig. 3.5). The faces are often dramatic, endowed with unusual colorful features such as red eyes, black mouth, nose and nostrils. The ornamented figures, especially their heads, assume a masklike quality that tends to hide and to distort at the same time that it also embellishes. The expressive power of these faces by far exceeds the usual depiction of 5-year-olds.

FIG. 3.6. "Symmetrical composition of a girl, richly ornamented, against a background of two colors." Decorative and figurative tendencies are well balanced, 33 × 21 cm. Varda, age 6.

THE CHILD ART STYLE BLOSSOMS: AGES 6 TO 9

The work at ages 6 to 7 shows a great deal of continuity in terms of style of painting, color use, and the employment of decorative elements carried over from previous years. There is an increase in the drawings of human figures and their disproportionately large heads. The struggle between expressive features that mask the face and those that merely embellish without submerging it continues and can lead to creative solutions. Figure 3.6 presents an oil pastel painting of a girl against a divided background. In this example, the decorative tendencies find expression in the dotted hair, the elaborate facial features, and the facial design on the dress. The many design features are balanced by a strong central figure that dominates the pictorial space. In this painting, her love for texture and design does not overwhelm the figure that is drawn against a strikingly colored background of half pink and half dark blue. The division of the background into two color fields finds an echo in the repetition or mirror image of the person's face on her dress. However, unlike the dominant face that carries a pleased expression, its representation on the dress is less cheerful; the two faces represent a contrast in mood and feelings.

Themes expand further with paintings on fairy tales, imaginative creatures, themes of birth, pregnancy, and parental relations depicted in a mother hen and her

chicks, a bird cracking a shell, weddings with bride and groom, and more threat-
ening events such as mirage fighter planes chasing her grandmother's airplane.
Abstract geometric designs continue to engage her and are integrated into figural
themes, for example, an animal body with a rich mandala type configuration for
its head that masks the facial features. The heads of Varda's humans tend to grow
in size while the body is frequently omitted or cut short. New themes emerge that
show an interest in feminine attributes depicted in the drawings of a princess or
bride with rosy cheeks, red lips, and heart-shaped decorations. With her rich
inventory of themes, creatures, forms, and colors, Varda creates a fairy-tale world
of animals and humans populating a well-organized pictorial space. Her affinity
for texture and pattern yield beautiful abstracts; the same techniques can be used
when she draws the human figure or an animal.

Around ages 8 to 9, she develops new techniques for her backgrounds and
applies them to clothing as well. She overlays colors and uses a technique of
scratching to reveal delicate and lacy looking patterns that, as background for her
figures, enhance the aesthetic appeal of her composition rather than overwhelming
it. Alongside expressive paintings that deliberately distort the proportions of the
human body, there are also beginning efforts to capture the human face in a more
naturalistic mode, for example, in a portrait of a young man (a prince?) with a
mustache and a carefully trimmed beard, whose ruffled collar and fanciful scarf
represent a new pictorial treatment. She discovers the painterly potentials of her
oil pastels that begin to replace her former emphasis on linear contours. In these
portraits of humans we see a transition out of the child art style as she experiments
with layering of colors and deletions by scratchings that reveal underlying colors
and create new visual effects. In a large painting in gouache done at the kibbutz
studio at 8 years old, she thins the color, uses washes and overlays, and her color
mixtures yield nuances, transparencies, droplets, and runs. With the application of
layers of paint, shapes protrude more prominently. Thus, at the height of her child
art style, marked by figures drawn without regard for their anatomically correct
proportions, colors used expressively rather than naturalistically, and the flatness
of her compositions emphasized, Varda integrates familiar well-practiced patterns
with new techniques.

The tendency to use two different colors as background for her portraits
continues along with other methods for framing her portraits which, with few
exceptions, are of females. She portrays dancers, a harlequin, and a clown (all
performers), and the starving children of Biafra. Her method of depiction changes
according to her theme. The children of Biafra (see Fig. 3.7), painted at 9 years old,
are drawn with huge heads, their pale faces contrast starkly with the large dark-
rimmed eyes, the shrunken bodies with skeleton bones showing through tell of
hunger and impending death. The subdued brown and black colors, and the
relatively sparse design that fill the background, express a somber mood. In this
painting, the child art style, although employed to the fullest, is also transcended
in the self-conscious use of contrasting colors and size relations. From this painting
on, she tends to limit her colors. The Biafra painting might also indicate a turning
point in terms of social concerns.

FIG. 3.7. "The starving children of Biafra," 50 × 35 cm. Varda, age 9.

By contrast with the tragic mood of the Biafra children, Varda's painting of a girl or young woman highlights feminine attributes. The figure is endowed with earrings and a necklace, with large red lips and prominent red finger nails, and a party hat that crowns her head. There is an effort to employ a more naturalistic style although the body remains stiff and ends abruptly above the waist. In her portrait of a clown, Varda presents the head in profile, its nose buried in a fluffy collar composed of layers of gauze, lace, and flowers. She employs color gradients that create the illusion of volume, a fairly recent artistic development of hers. The light yellow background of the clown enhances the theme rather than competes with it, a further sign that her art work is in transition; it foretells the end of the child art style and the birth of a more sophisticated artistic sensibility.

What can we conclude about Varda's artistic development so far? First of all, it is quite striking that her work unfolds according to the same principles that characterize all child art (Arnheim, 1974; Golomb, 1992). By that we mean that her figures are two-dimensional, drawn without regard for the realistic shape, size, and proportions of the model. The objects are drawn in their familiar canonical orientations, mostly in full frontal view, each one occupying its own space in a grid defined by horizontal and vertical directions. We can now answer the question raised earlier in this chapter about the development of gifted children. Varda did not skip any stages; she developed her artistry within the constraints and possibilities of visual thinking in the different phases of its evolution.

This emphasis on the formal characteristics of her child art, which are also found in less gifted children, should not obscure the individuality of her style and conception that single out her work and call attention to an artistic sensibility that is quite special. Despite the constraints that are inherent in child art, Varda's ability to use the pictorial medium effectively is impressive. Thus, for example, she develops a rich and expressive graphic vocabulary, varies the facial features and the shapes of her figures, develops different shapes for the same part, and enhances the subtlety of her background texture. Her sensitivity to color contrasts and gradients is remarkable, and so is her sense of composition, and her ability to create strong centers from which symmetrically organized forms derive. Quite unique to Varda is her early tendency to embed her figures in richly decorated designs so that they threaten to dissolve the common figure-ground differentiation, reminiscent of Klimt's painting style.

Her struggle to deal with a multiplicity of designs and the need to establish thematic and/or figural dominance suggests a deeper source, perhaps a struggle between opposing tendencies of connectedness and independence, of fitting in and striving to assert autonomy. The division of the pictorial space into two horizontally organized sections or vertically organized thirds reflect, undoubtedly, decisions based on artistic design features. However, they also suggest a more personal meaning that can be seen in her later work as well. The divisions are meant to compare, to contrast, and to unite diverse compositional elements, themes, and feelings. A similar tendency of dealing with discordant feelings may well underlie the masklike heads that appear early in her art work. They tend to hide more than they reveal, which recurs at later times as well. Particularly arresting is her inclination to embellish significant parts of her animal figures so that their natural characteristics are completely hidden. The frequently darkened faces of her favorite animal and fairy-tale characters also suggest a duality of feelings and strivings that can be expressed in her paintings. Altogether, her selection of themes reflects mostly an internal drama that, in its expression, overrides naturalism.

Throughout the years discussed so far, and, until Varda entered art school, she was essentially self-taught. True, from the age of 6 on she had access to the kibbutz studio, where children came once or twice weekly with their agemates to draw and paint. However, the philosophy of Malka Haas, the art teacher of the studio, emphasized the virtue of nonintervention, of providing opportunities for work and experimentation without explicit instruction. In her conversations with us, Varda stressed repeatedly how important it was for her development to have gained Malka's attention, support, and respect, and the opportunity to paint in the studio, which allowed her to work without having to cope with outside demands. Varda had a deep-seated need to do her own thing, to receive acknowledgment that did not demand conformity, a lasting tendency that also characterizes her life as an adult artist.

TRANSITIONS: THE YEARS FROM 10 TO 12

The drawings and paintings from this period indicate a conscious effort to represent her figures in a more naturalistic style, and among them are her first attempts to draw from a life model. It is important to note that Varda never copied from a model, and that her repertoire of themes and style of representation are truly her own creation. Even as a child she was a fine observer of the natural and social world, and her drawings reflect the knowledge thus gained. Her artistic efforts developed along the lines we have sketched so far, relatively impervious to the realistic portrayals of book illustrations and photographs. Varda was well aware of her older sister's more naturalistic style of drawing and admired her work. Unlike Varda, her sister created beautiful realistic renderings that Varda knew she could not match, although as a child she valued this style.

The portraits of this transitional period are numerous and reveal Varda's interest in a more naturalistic depiction, in approximating anatomically more realistic body proportions, in paying greater attention to posture and orientation (although most of her portraits are not modeled from life), and in her efforts to capture the mood and thoughts of her subject. Her techniques vary with the medium and include overlays of different colors, application of turpentine to oil pastels, color gradients that yield borderless transitions, mixed media and scratching, shading, modeling, cross hatching, successful overlap of body parts, and the elimination of lines that are hidden from the view of an observer. Her subjects are most commonly portrayed in frontal view, although not invariably so, and attempts to represent the figure in three-quarter view also appear. The major focus is on the head and bust, rarely is the full figure portrayed. At times it appears as if the body is not merely omitted but cut off. When she depicts the body, its posture is stiff and rarely in motion.

Between the ages of 10 and 12, her work comprises many portraits, mostly of girls or young women, with an occasional portrait of a male. She continues to use oil pastels, wax crayons, and various water colors, and experiments for the first time with pencil, charcoal, and India ink. Her compositions become more ambitious as she tries to integrate foreground and background, and grapples with the problem of representing the third dimension. We can see this struggle in several paintings as she tries to discover techniques that will capture both the solidity of the objects and their relative position vis-à-vis each other and the pictorial frame.

Portraits. Paintings done at age 10 highlight some of the transformations of her earlier art style. A portrait of this period depicts the head and bust of a girl composed of colored brush strokes. No longer are the facial features carefully delineated; they are sparse, composed of color splashes, and the product of quick brushwork, a technique not previously seen. The ghostly looking skin color, a mixture of white, green, and yellow, the dark eyes and mouth, the red nose, framed by black hair call attention to the mood of the girl and suggest a brooding state of mind. It is an intriguing, somewhat disturbing portrait that with its theme, technique, and cut-off figure indicates a new concern with psychological intensity. The figure is set against a background noted for its dark-brown color in one half and

FIG. 3.8. "A woman dressed for the carnival," 50 × 35. Varda, age 10.

orange in the other half, a technique Varda has used before. Other themes that suggest a darker side of her emotional life are depicted in the rear view of a girl, painted in black, whose outstretched arms reach upward toward the vague outlines of an apparition.

The dramatic appearance of performers, seen earlier in her work, continues to engage her. In a large colorful gouache from the same year she depicts a woman dressed for a carnival (see Fig. 3.8). The exaggerated size of the hairdo that tends to dominate the portrait represents a deliberate choice and no longer reflects the naivetè of the earlier childhood drawings. Most impressive, however, are the novel features of deftly executed light- and dark-colored brush strokes that create the impression of puffed-up sleeves and of a glittering featherweight blouse and skirt. Color contrasts and borderless transitions endow the figure with roundness, which is further enhanced by the use of overlapping body parts. The dotted background, symmetrically organized, picks up on elements displayed in the figure; it emphasizes the flatness of the two-dimensional space and continues a pictorial tradition that Varda developed earlier on. This treatment of pictorial space enhances the figure's prominence and indicates her lack of interest in creating an illusion of a three-dimensional world.

The theme of birth and infants reappears in a portrait of a nurse with a newborn. The relationship between the highly symmetrical, richly decorated background and the figure of the nurse is less well maintained, and the competition between figural and decorative elements of the composition, which characterizes much of her earlier work, is not resolved. The face of the nurse reflects Varda's new interest in a more naturalistic portrayal, while her hair, headdress, neck, richly ornamented dress, and the baby's blanket emphasize the mythical or fairy-tale character of the dramatic composition, a reflection of Varda's enduring love of design.

Portraits painted a year later continue the theme of self-exploration (see Fig. 3.9 on the color panel). The head and bust of a girl are placed at the center of a colorful and richly decorated background that frames the figure. The head with its hair, facial features, and eyeglasses is carefully drawn in black and white, with lines creating fine textures and facial contours. The neck and clothing are colorful and contrast with the achromatic colors of the face that carries an earnest expression. The two contrasting tendencies of playful ornamentation and the serious, perhaps meditative expression are controlled in a fashion that is quite masterly at her level of development. The polarity between playful sensuality and the expression of deeply held feelings, which has characterized her artwork from an early time, continue to dominate her approach to art. This portrait demonstrates the use of new and more complex techniques, executed in several stages. First a layer of thick oil pastels is applied to the surface; next, the figure is carved with the aid of a special tool, and then covered with ink. After the layer of ink has dried, selective scratchings reveal the lines previously carved out of the colored layer of oil pastels, that are now blackened.

A portrait of a young girl with glasses who is looking into a mirror, drawn at the age of 12, continues this quest for a psychological understanding of the subject, and also explores the potential of the painterly medium (see Fig. 3.10 on the color panel). In this painting, done in oil pastels and watercolor, she applies her newly developed naturalistic conception to the sitter and her background, and captures the individuality and youthfulness of her subject's expression. The girl's dress is richly designed and overpowers or masks the underlying body structure, a feature that has been quite consistent in Varda's paintings, and acquires a special relevance for the adolescent girl. She plays with the decorative elements of the room's partition and repeats them in the mirror, the eyeglasses, the neck, and the sleeves of her dress. Quite striking are the white contours, which display an eerie, negative quality. This painting combines, quite successfully, the older decorative impulse with a desire to depict a visually coherent space. The interior of the room is clearly represented, a function of the effective use of overlapping, some diminution in the size of objects, and color texture.

A series of portraits depicting the heads of two females, perhaps a mother and her child, are painted with delicate pastels. The features are barely suggested by light tonal gradations that do not reveal the identity of the subjects. The figures overlap and tend to merge, conveying tenderness and perhaps a sense of yearning.

The painting is without a border, and, with heads and sides of the body cropped, it represents a novel approach to composition, suggesting, both formally and thematically, that a fantasy world is depicted.

Pencil, Ink, and Charcoal Drawings. It is during this period that Varda, for the first time, employs pencils, ink, and charcoal for landscape sketches, drawings of boys and girls, and somewhat later of portraits that may well have self-referential meaning. Her desire to capture the contours of the human face, its volume, multiple sides and features, is best illustrated in these drawings; they begin with a reliance on lines and quickly progress to techniques where lines fade and contours are suggested by modeling, shading, and techniques of overlap. During this time she makes her first drawings from a model, probably her father.

In a series of drawings she depicts a teenage girl, usually with crossed arms, often with eyes shaded or casting a somewhat troubled look at the viewer. The expression tends to be questioning, probing, and sometimes sad. In one of her drawings with pencil, a girl grasps her neck around which a rope is strung; two hands hover over her head. Her dress is simple and the composition is devoid of extraneous elements. Is the girl choking, contemplating suicide? The picture conveys a sense of oppression, of being hemmed in, of fear. In a conversation years later, Varda offers several explanations, and in the following order. During this period, at age 11, she was interested in mastering the drawing of hands, which she had always found technically difficult. Furthermore, hands are the tools of every human being, especially of the artist, and essential for being effective, to reach out and also to push away. Finally, throughout her childhood she had been preoccupied with thoughts of death and suicide. Reflecting on her childhood work she notes that she had been a sad child who expressed her feelings in her paintings: "Even the drawing of Biafra connects to this personal state. You select your themes, and the themes of sadness and suffering engaged me, for example, the Holocaust with its railroad tracks that in my later work became ladders."

Drawings afforded Varda a very personal voice, a way to express as well as to mask her feelings. This point was brought home when we discussed another painting of the same period, a very large figure of a Black woman with rings around her neck. The size of the paper is 1½ meter long, and 85% of the space is devoted to the central figure. The composition contains a section in the bottom part that puzzled us. Varda explained that the drawing was inspired by a newspaper story about the habits of African Blacks. In this account, the man places rings around his wife's neck; if she sins the rings are pulled over her head so that she suffocates and dies. During the year she read this story, the brother of her girlfriend drowned. This impelled her to draw at the feet of the Black woman a memorial stone on which she wrote the words *yizkor* (remember), and then wiped it out so that nobody would understand. Thus, death is the theme that unites both parts of the painting.

Once again, there appear portraits of two female figures in close contact, faces touching. Their meaning remains obscure, their relationship only vaguely suggested in the adolescent's yearning for closeness. In striking contrast to her paintings, which are richly designed, these pencil-and-ink sketches focus the

FIG. 3.2. "Figural and decorative motifs." They dominate the composition and tend to obliterate the differentiation of figures from their background, 33 × 21 cm. Varda, age 5.7.

FIG. 3.9. "Portrait of a young girl," 33 × 24 cm. Varda, age 11.

FIG. 3.10. "Portrait of a girl with a mirror," 33 × 24 cm. Varda, age 12.

FIG. 3.13. "Woman with a bouquet of flowers facing a man," 30 × 21 cm. Varda, age 17.

FIG. 3.14. "Life cycle." Painting commemorates her parents' silver anniversary, 24 × 18 cm. Varda, age 18.

viewer's attention on the essentials, the person's expression, and background ornamentation is either absent or subdued.

Space.   A number of drawings and paintings from this period reveal Varda's interest in teaching herself some of the projective principles that are useful for the portrayal of three-dimensional space. In a painting of the studio, Varda lays out the room with its assortment of tables at which children work with crayons, and one of the walls that serves the painters. The depiction of the horizontal plane is effective, with Haas, the art teacher of the studio, standing in the foreground handing a child art materials. The tables are presented from various views, some from an aerial perspective, some from ground level.

In another drawing that returns to the theme of childbirth and infants, she depicts a nursery in a maternity ward. The tile floor is well laid out with some indication of texture, although the size of the tiles remains constant; the maternity rooms are depicted in isometric projection, with parallel lines emphasizing the three-dimensions of the surrounding walls. Two sets of bassinets with two infants each (twins?) capture the volumetric property of containers with their outer and inner surfaces. The painting reveals local solutions to the problem of depicting volume and edges receding in space, quite typical of early problem seeing and solving. Not surprisingly, there is no effort to reach a unified presentation and no attempt to introduce converging lines. These studies indicate that Varda perceives new pictorial problems, and that she is developing a broader perspective on art and art making.

This widening of her horizons can be seen in new concerns that stir deeply felt emotions. Themes of human loss and tragedy are portrayed in a painting of a refugee from the Warsaw ghetto, and they gain center stage with the Yom Kippur war and its effects on her community.

ADOLESCENCE: THE YEARS FROM 13 TO 18

At the threshold of adolescence, Varda wrestles with themes of larger social significance. In painting after painting she returns to the theme of the Yom Kippur war, to emotions of bereavement, fear, and consolation. There are images of burials, of waiting for a telephone call from a beloved, of mourners, of a bride receiving bad tidings. The depiction is sparse, devoid of extraneous elements; the colors are muted, and there is very little detail. Her figures are large, mostly in frontal orientation, often faceless, and the dominant mood is conveyed by color, shape, and the grouping of objects. Her compositions are tightly structured, and symbolism is used in an explicit manner. These are narrative paintings whose message is amplified via symbols and metaphors of threat and destruction. They make it abundantly clear that realism is not Varda's intention. Once again the treatment of the background is most commonly flat and two-dimensional, although not consistently so. In these paintings, Varda seems intent on depicting a collective truth, a common fate of grief rather than a psychological portrait of the individual mourner. The tendency to employ a naturalistic style, most noticeable in her pencil-and-ink

FIG. 3.11. "My sister the communications officer," 70 × 50 cm. Varda, age 13.

portraits, is relegated to a subordinate position in paintings that express complex themes of suffering, distilled through her adolescent sensibilities. In these paintings, broad strokes and color patches evoke the theme and its principal characters. Under the pressure of these events, the playful ornamentation disappears; now the theme controls the composition, a mark of her growing artistic maturity.

In a painting of her sister who serves as a communications officer during the Yom Kippur war, 13-year-old Varda depicts her sister in the foreground, parachutists in the background, and an explosion that darkens the sky and dims the colors of the scene (see Fig. 3.11). The contrast between the large, frontal figure talking into a receiver, and the action in the background, imbues this painting with a dynamic tension. The colors are subdued, consisting of blacks and greys, and no attempt is made to portray individual characteristics of the officer. Whatever her feelings, they are subordinate to the general theme of war and threat.

Other paintings from this period depict a faceless woman who is leaning against a barren tree. She embraces a puppy she was given to console her for the death of her beloved. The colors are muted and applied with broad brush strokes. The painting is stripped of all ornament and nothing detracts from a pervasive sense of vulnerability, loss, and emptiness that permeates the scene.

By contrast with the sparse number of elements that comprise the previous painting, Varda creates a highly condensed portrait of the bride who postponed her wedding upon hearing that her brother had been killed on the peak of Mount Hermon. The bride becomes the mountain, her veil turns into the snow that covers the slopes, and red marks punctuate the whiteness of her veil, evoking the image of footsteps and flowers. On top of the bride's head are soldiers encamped in an embankment. Tears descend from the top and mingle with the melting snow; as they fall they turn into daggers and pools of blood. This is a highly complex portrayal for a 13-year-old girl who, out of her need to understand and cope with the experience of death and destruction, generates the symbols that convey the horror and brutality of war.

The experience of the Yom Kippur war sensitizes Varda to sorrow caused by other external forces, by persecution and political oppression. It enlists a whole range of feelings for suffering endured during the Holocaust, the suffering of Jewish refuseniks in Russia, and the lot of refugees from Southeast Asia (the boat people), all of which find expression in the paintings done at ages 13 and 14. The Holocaust attains special meaning for Varda who devotes many paintings to this subject.

The last painting made in the studio at age 15 is an anguished response to the United Nation's declaration that Zionism is racism (see Fig. 3.12). Her painting of gravestones, refugees fleeing, a destroyed village in smoke, a fire in the sky, a river and modern buildings (UN?), express her view that the same antisemitism that led to the Holocaust motivated the declaration. The composition is well structured. It depicts a burning village against a red sky, its buildings transformed into burial stones; railroad tracks and a thick black arrow directed at the fleeing people complete the composition. She uses broad paint strokes of mostly achromatic colors that contrast with the burning sky. Two directional tendencies are clearly marked: a horizontal–vertical organization and a strong diagonal vector from the upper right to the lower left. These two vectors dominate the composition and, although not yet fully integrated, show Varda's growing awareness of compositional dynamics. It is of considerable interest that this painting began as a huge black swastika that covered the large (50×70 cm) surface. As she worked on the various elements of the composition, she covered most parts of the swastika, displaying only the horizontal and vertical vectors that dominate the composition and its underlying theme. In this painting we can see how Varda employs earlier developed structural and dynamic principles, that enable her to express multiple meanings, of a personal and collective nature.

Other paintings from this period show the recurrent theme of masklike faces executed in an artistically striking and original manner. Colorful inserts create the facial features of two centrally placed figures. One of the figures, whose face is partially hidden by a wall, sheds large tears. A third veiled and somewhat mysterious looking head appears in the background. The mood is one of pain and agony, of feelings that are masked and hidden from view.

FIG. 3.12. "UN declaration against Zionism; images of the Holocaust," 70 × 50 cm. Varda, age 15.

The theme of masklike heads and prominent eyes continues to engage her over the next years and leads to densely structured compositions where faces, once again, crowd in on each other, with abstract patterns filling all of the available space. In Varda's words: "Everywhere I turn, there are eyes seeing me, and distorted faces."

A portrait made at 17 depicts its theme more clearly with a man and a woman facing each other (see Fig. 3.13 on the color panel). The woman holds a bouquet of flowers, which serves as the center piece that divides the pictorial space. The hand that holds the offering is large, her veins made prominently visible. It is a complex configuration that emphasizes the segmentation of the faces via colorful and contrasting inserts, a technique of embedding and masking that Varda developed early on, and now uses in an artistically deliberate fashion. The woman's face is softer and somewhat smaller than that of the male, its hues span the yellow–orange spectrum. The male face, by contrast, is painted in dark colors of green, blue, and brown. His facial expression is harsh, perhaps aggressive; his dark fingers touch her head and throat. Both heads, cropped on top and on the sides, tend to merge with their background, diminishing the boundaries that separate the realms of fantasy and reality. The painting exemplifies the tension between the contrasting elements of maleness and femaleness, of closeness and separation, and presents a groping to unify, artistically, a clash of discordant tendencies and emotions. This painting demonstrates both continuity of style and its extensive transformation as the artist shapes, and almost sculpts her images, using more sophisticated techniques, and giving expression to complex and contrasting feelings. In this painting we can see how earlier techniques and motifs are distilled within a more mature compositional framework that reworks its material in innovative ways.

The adolescent paintings represent Varda's continued search for symbolic forms of expression and demonstrate her reliance on color to convey deeply felt emotions; her charcoal and pencil drawings reveal how far she has come in her experimentation with realism. Her portraits show a more assured handling of lines, planes, and views, an indication that she is beginning to master the new techniques. Although her self-portraits tend to carry an anxious and probing expression, her artwork is not limited to the range of topics and feelings described so far. There are also beautiful studies of a male figure and playful experimentation with diverse themes and dimensions.

Paintings made at 17 and 18 are reduced in size, painted with small brushes and opaque water colors. They are dense compositions, with forms and figures, once again, crowding in on each other, but this time in a highly controlled fashion. The graphic linear style contrasts with the gouaches made at 13 and 14. In our interview, Varda affirms that this was an anxious period, that she felt a compelling need to exercise control over her life and the paper space. She deliberately chose small paper and utilized every inch in an effort to exert a magical control over her anxiety and urges. In her words:

> I was beset by conflicts. The eyes look and search, divorce versus love, religion versus discotheque and drugs, kibbutz versus city. These were issues it took years to crystallize and resolve. Most of my paintings during this period were small, I used opaque water colors and tiny brushes. When in a bad mood, I worked till late at night in my room, but showed the paintings to Malka afterwards. ... On some drawings I worked for months, for example with ink. I needed to control every motion, to be precise and exercise mastery over the conditions. It was important to be clear and clean, colorful and symbolic.

A painting in this style (see Fig. 3.14 on the color panel), made at age 18 for the silver anniversary of her parents, is organized into four vertical columns that are divided by a strong diagonal that cuts across the middle of the painting from the lower left to the upper right. The diagonal serves a structural and a thematic function; it counteracts the stability of the vertical registers and endows the painting with tension and suspense.

The painting is a narrative account of her parents' life, a timeline that begins with their childhood represented by toys and ends with old age, symbolized by a mournful looking face and two canes, only one of which is upright, suggesting the death of one of the partners. An all-seeing eye is placed in the top right hand corner. Every inch of the space is filled with old and new symbols, some of which represent closeness and separation, a white and a black figure. The figures are overlaid in complex figure-ground relations that are successfully executed.

This style of painting might be seen as a more structured version of the space-filled drawings of her childhood, and of her earlier tendency to divide pictorial space into sectors. Of course, the differences are also striking in the extensive and thoughtful planning of planes, shapes, colors, and themes, and the exercise of utmost control over every detail. At the end of adolescence, Varda's artwork is a testimony of her genuine talent that has matured largely on its own, that is, with little, if any, explicit instruction or models, but based on her own intensive art work as it developed over the years.

Varda's case provides a clear answer to the question posed earlier about the originality and uniqueness of the gifted child, qualities above and beyond precocious naturalistic drawing skills. Her work, in all of its phases, carries her unique signature in style, composition, and content.

At age 18, Varda enters the army and opts to serve in a unit that deals with the social problems of abused girls.[2] Unfortunately, the paintings made during her military service were lost. After her discharge she returns to the kibbutz and decides to attend the Art Institute of the Teachers Training College of the Kibbutziem at Oraniem, near Haifa. For the first time Varda receives formal art training, and it becomes a turning point in her artistic development. She studies with artists, visits their studios, discovers alternative modes of representation, and gains an understanding of art history. Art making becomes a more informed and disciplined endeavor that reflects her awareness of the styles and concerns of contemporary artists.

Varda discovers new media, etching and sculpture, and selects teachers who respect her individuality and do not force her into their mold. According to Varda, these were art teachers who offered constructive evaluations that benefited her work; the most influential among them was Michael Gross. From this artist she learned the value and power of simplicity, the art to distill experience into concise and simple forms.

Etchings, Lithographs, and Sculpture.   During her student years at the art school, Varda discovers new media that she begins to explore. Her etchings and lithographs made at Oraniem are mostly black and white. They range from delicate engravings that emphasize linear, often abstract elements to a mixture of figural and ornamental designs. A series of etchings in a stylized format represent what appear to be mythical animal creatures, reminiscent of some of the childhood

---

[2]Israel does not have a volunteer army, and women as well as men are called upon to serve as enlisted soldiers in the military. For women the period is 18 months.

themes, and grouping of humans whose relationship remains unstated and somewhat enigmatic.

Varda also begins to experiment with mixed media, using canvas, paint, burlap, wood, iron, plaster, metal, and plastic strings in various, mostly abstract constellations. Sculpture becomes her major focus and remains at the heart of her art after her graduation. When sculpting, the idea is there first, it is a planned construction that changes and develops as the work progresses. One of her earliest sculptures with mixed media was composed of metal, plaster, and a nylon net. It was meant to represent two hands that touch in a gesture of priestly blessing. Others perceived it as two hanged people. Some of the sculptures in plaster are reminiscent of the geometric designs Varda made earlier, as a young child, and reflects a similar pleasure in texture and form, a joy in design and ornamentation. Childhood motifs appear in a series entitled "toys," with two elephants merged into a single unit or attached in other ways. It is a playful, delicate, and lightly colored construction with long transparent tubes that end in pink rounded boxes. Varda made this sculpture after the birth of her son; it represents the womb and also an altar on which offerings are brought.

Varda develops a special technique for working with plaster, clay, and metals, designing her sculptures such that the plaster, which ordinarily is a negative shape, becomes the dominant form. Her sculptures are planned as negatives; when she removes the plaster, it is the cover over the clay construction that constitutes the sculpture (see Fig. 3.15, 3.16, 3.17). In an interesting reversal, the outside is made to represent the inside, it reveals instead of conceals. According to Varda, it

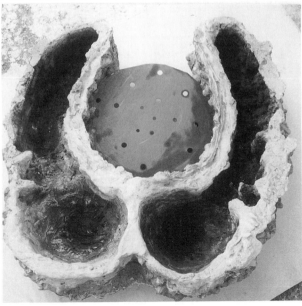

FIG. 3.15. "Womb." Sculpture made of plaster and iron, 60 × 60 × 18 cm.

FIG. 3.16. Untitled. Sculpture made of plaster, metal, and seeds, 65 × 50 × 15 cm.

FIG. 3.17. "Despair." Sculpture made of plaster and wood, 90 × 50 × 30 cm.

happened once by mistake and she continued to develop it. She prides herself on this reversal, it demands much thought and planning. Along with her emphasis on the ideas that need to be worked out in advance, she also stresses the sensuality of this medium, its organic nature, and the sense of immediacy it affords her. She comments on one of her sculptures, made of plaster and iron with holes drilled into its metal base, that it creates a dynamic representation (of a womb) in its use of contrasting materials, of the organic and soft plaster and the metal (see Fig. 3.15). She elaborates on this contrast by listing other polarities: flexible versus inflexible, free versus forceful intrusion, dynamic and womblike versus unnatural and ungiving, fluid and revisable versus relentless immobility. In Varda's view, these contrasts reflect human nature, they create artistic tension but also yield harmony. As these comments show, symbolic meanings come to overlay the intrinsically decorative quality of Varda's work, which is at the core of her artistry. She continues to play with shapes, to create rhythms and patterns in plaster, clay, wood, and metal, materials she finds suitable for the expression of her feelings.

FIG. 3.18. "Conception." Sculpture made of plaster and glass, 80 × 60 × 20 cm.

FIG. 3.19. "Failed conception." Ladder with broken eggs, 200 × 40 cm.

Increasingly, her artistic endeavors center on sculpture and she continues to work in this domain after her graduation from art school. She works with plaster, metals, and wood in various combinations and creates abstract and at times stark looking sculptures. The sculptures express emotions that are intimately tied to her bodily experiences, to being female, to issues of fertility, failed conceptions, gynecological examinations, and birth (see Fig. 3.18 on p. 95). The master theme is the body and its capacity or failure to function in its primary reproductive capacity. Fears of the imperfections of her body are expressed in a controlled and fairly abstract fashion. She looks for simple lines, insists on materials that are unpolished and have a certain roughness that at times borders on violence.

She creates a series of ladderlike structures made of wood and metal that represent the vulnerable and exposed human body. Placed in an elevated position, the figures represent crucifixion, gynecological surgery, and in conjunction with sawdust or a group of smashed eggs, failed conception (see Fig. 3.19). These are titles Varda has supplied. Varda is well aware of the personal relevance these sculptures have. In her words "I always knew that I had a physical defect, even before I tried to get pregnant; deep down I knew. I menstruated late, and before that I suffered from scoliosis and had to wear a halter. That is the reason why I deal with this theme."

Her last sculpture in this series, made during the Gulf War, consists of a ladder and a miniature house (see Fig. 3.20). The wooden frame and the rungs of the ladder

FIG. 3.20. Ladder, 200 × 35 cm; the little house, 40 (W) × 54 (D) × 48 cm (H).

are white and so is the little house. Between the rungs of the ladder are blue glass inserts that effectively cancel the ladder's utility and ascending function, although the last rung is not occupied and holds out some directional promise. The white house, with a picture of her infant son in its front window, is attached midway to the wall, and set apart from the ladder as well as the ground. There is no connection between these two elements of the composition other than their color and relative proximity. Perhaps the ladder represents an expansive vector into the unknown while the house stands for enclosure, safety, home, but also imprisonment; it has windows to peep out from, but no entrance door, and it is detached from the ground. The house and the ladder are disconnected and unreachable, they represent the duality of isolation and the desire for connectedness, and suggest failed contact. This statement is not made with finality; structurally there is a connection between ladder and house, and since the last rung is not blocked, it leaves a possible opening.

Painting.   For her own diversion, and as a more playful and pleasure oriented activity, Varda has continued to paint with water colors and, more recently, she returned to her portraits with oil pastels.

In response to a question, she reflects on her training and what she has gained and perhaps also lost. Her early love was painting, and colors played an essential role in it. With training, and the study of the great colorist Matisse she felt that she could not innovate in painting, that Matisse had said it all.

> I got arrested in my development of painting. I feel that after I studied Matisse I could not contribute. Training gives you a critical eye and also an inferiority. ... In sculpture I look for simplicity and structure and I progressed in small steps; every one of my works is thought out and disciplined. By contrast, in painting the essence is feeling and sensation around color. So I paint only for myself and not for others or exhibits. In terms of the depth of feelings, the abstract sculptures connect more deeply with me.

Varda has drawn a sharp distinction between media, with sculpture giving clear and succinct expression to her thoughts and feelings. She finds comfort in the abstract symbols that embody the meaning she associates with the female body, sensuality, and sexuality. In painting her interest lies in color; it links up with her childhood, is less cognitive, less symbolic and also less constrained. It brings back memories of the studio where she felt happy, free, and valued by Haas. Varda considers the symbolism in painting of a secondary order, subordinate to the direct experience of pleasure. As if to justify the dichotomy she has established, Varda proposes that color has a special role in child art, and that the adult looses this ability and connection with colors.

Varda, however, does not close doors with any finality, and in recent times, after the birth of her son, she has felt a great urge to return to painting, a sign of a happier and more optimistic mood. Before his birth, the mostly black-and-white prints gave expression to somber feelings and so did the sculptures. Her portraits, done in her favorite medium of oil pastels, are striking in their combination of naturalistic techniques that evoke the image of the sitter and the expressionistic use of color that violates realism and is applied in multiple layers. Varda muses about her portraits: "Independent of where I start, the head is cut (cropped). Apparently, I have said the important thing, the central idea, the rest is cosmetics ... the legs are also cut off. It amuses me, it is an escape from a framework. I clearly make my own."

Asked whether her childhood paintings indicate talent, she couches her response in terms of love and fate:

> Some children have this wonderful free line, a chic line [refers to naturalism]. In my case, forms are built up, I use an additive procedure. As a child I loved painting. For the adult to choose art is fate, it's for whom nothing else will do, a necessity, a destiny. It is also a punishment since you can't make a living with it, and it remains just your own experience. Such a choice involves suffering, and if you hesitate, you better choose another vocation.

The need for independence and autonomy that can be clearly seen in her work, also permeates other aspects of her life and motivated her decision, at age 25, to leave, together with her husband, the kibbutz where she grew up. "My reasons are simply that I can't tolerate the collective, the close quarters, a closed in society. I need fresh experiences, novelty, to be responsible for my success and failure. I don't wish to give an account to others and I don't fit into the kibbutz lifestyle."

In regard to the earlier raised question of continuities in the work of the child and the adult artist, the longitudinal data confirm such a trend in terms of the motivation, themes, and even style of Varda's art. From her early work through the present time, we can follow a clear and recognizable pattern of development that carries the stamp of her individuality. Seen over time, there is a continuous enrichment, a restructuring and reintegration of earlier developed forms, themes, and compositional strategies that enhance the expressive power of her work and its aesthetic appeal. Varda's artistic inclinations did not predispose her toward realism as a means of articulating her vision, although she felt a need to master some of its techniques during late childhood, and again in the first years at art school. There is consistency in her adoption of art forms that tend to recast the world in her own image. Her access to the inner world of feelings, and her need to explore them in drawing and painting, present one of the constants in this artist's development, recognizable, despite the transformation its expression undergoes. The need for clarity and order expressed in her small paintings made at ages 17 and 18 finds a new solution in the clear and controlled sculptures that express her deepest feelings in stark and simple terms.

In her art and in her private life, Varda is a nonconformist. But the story is unfinished, it is a life in progress and so is her art. Varda's art was born out of an inner necessity to draw upon her private world, distill it, and cast it into visual forms. Although there are clear continuities between the earlier and later phases of her work, art in adulthood is a different pursuit. The adult no longer lives in the relatively self-contained world of childhood. Personal concerns, aesthetic considerations, training, and economics all converge to create the skilled work of the artist whose audience comprises peers, curators, and art critics. Despite the marked differences between the art of the child and of the adult, and the significant transformations we have chronicled in Varda's work, there is also a remarkable link between the sensibilities and passions of the child and the adult she has become.

REFERENCES

Arnheim, R. (1974). *Art and visual perception.* Berkeley: University of California Press.

Golomb, C. (1992). *The child's creation of a pictorial world.* Berkeley & Los Angeles: University of California Press.

Lowenfeld, V. (1939). *The nature of creative activity.* New York: MacMillan.

Schaefer-Simmern, H. (1948). *The unfolding of artistic activity.* Berkeley: University of California Press.

Viola, W. (1936). *Child art and Franz Cisek.* Vienna: Austrian Red Cross.

4

Germinal Motifs in the Work of a Gifted Child Artist

Constance Milbrath

University of California, San Francisco

The study of gifted and talented children continues to receive attention as educators struggle with defining environments that can optimize the growth of these prized individuals. Formerly, educators were most concerned with identifying highly intelligent children through psychometric testing (Marland, 1972; Terman, 1924). More recently, there has been a growing realization that giftedness does not necessarily reside solely in traditional academic skills and that some high IQ children may not demonstrate any exceptional talent at all, even performing at average levels in school (Robinson, 1977). This has turned the field toward models of multiple intelligence with the acknowledgment that talent is better identified as specific to a domain (Feldman, 1980; Gardner, 1980; Sternberg, 1986). Moreover, in some domains, such as mathematics, music, or chess, talent appears dependent on special instruction (Feldman, 1980) and therefore unlikely to be identified by general tests of intelligence. The necessity for instruction, however, calls attention to the advantage these domains have of a clearly defined knowledge base that makes explicit what constitutes skillful performance. By using the skill levels defined for the domain as a yardstick, child prodigies are more easily identified (Feldman & Benjamin, 1986; Feldman & Goldsmith, 1986).

In a field such as the visual arts, defining what constitutes excellence has been difficult and most researchers report that gifted child visual artists are rare (Feldman & Goldsmith, 1986; Goodenough, 1926; Lark-Horovitz, Lewis, & Luca, 1973). Some are of the opinion that it is the less coherent definition of the domain's knowledge base that has led to difficulties in identifying excellence in the visual arts. Csikszentmihalyi and Robinson (1986) pointed out that in fields such as music or mathematics, a near unanimous agreement in Western culture as to what constitutes the domain has led to clear criteria for what comprises excellence and facilitated the recognition of superior performance. In contrast what constitutes good art in the visual arts is more often determined by changing tastes of a culture (Csikszentmihalyi & Robinson, 1986; Feldman & Benjamin, 1986). Further, it could be argued that given an ill-defined knowledge base and poorly established criteria, it is difficult for children themselves to be motivated toward excellence because they are unsure what skills need to be mastered. In that sense rarity of excellence in the visual arts is a function of poorly defined goals based on the absence of a clear and coherent understanding of what constitutes the domain's knowledge base.

Csikszentmihalyi and Robinson (1986) also emphasized the importance of social and historical context to talent development. During the Renaissance a young child who could draw realistic pictures was highly prized, whereas in the middle part of the 20th century such children were overlooked in favor of children who were spontaneous and emotionally expressive in their drawings. Talent always occurs in the context of culturally defined values. If a culture fails to value a specific skill within a talent domain, then it is judged as irrelevant to the domain and is either ignored by the culture or remains underdeveloped. In addition, the investment that a society is willing to make in supporting development of the domain of talent itself can determine its appearance (Tannenbaum, 1986). For example, school districts may have well-developed music and math programs in grammar school but little of substance to offer in the visual arts. Society, therefore, in large part determines both the valued skills within a domain and the kinds of talent domains that develop. Csikszentmihalyi and Robinson took this argument even further by suggesting that when a culture supports talent within a given domain it is not so much that talent can then be recognized, as that a child with such talent can recognize the possibility of excelling within the domain. Rarity of excellence, from this perspective, is a function of societal supports.

If we accept that the definition of talent in the visual arts is susceptible to changing cultural tastes and that it has a less rigorous and formally defined knowledge base than for example music or mathematics, it leads to the interconnected problems of not only what constitutes an adequate definition of talent in the visual arts but also of how to describe its development. Both depend heavily on how the visual arts itself is defined, on what knowledge base constitutes the core of the domain. If, as in the middle part of this century, expressiveness and spontaneity are forefronted while realism is relegated to the background, then a child who masters veridical forms and spatial relationships may go unidentified as talented. Moreover, many more children will be thought of as talented, since development of these artistic aspects appear early in many children's work (Gardner, 1980; Luquet, 1935). Indeed, one visual arts teacher told me that most of the children aged 3 to 6 attending her art school were talented. The developmental trajectory associated with artistic talent also varies depending on what constitutes the core of the domain. For example, the appreciation and production of expressive and spontaneous art usually declines after early childhood, giving way to latency age desires to conform to realistic depiction (Gardner, 1980; Gebotys & Cupchik, 1989; Golomb, 1992) but also to a typical overall cognitive concern for literalness, concreteness, and conformity to rules that marks middle childhood and early adolescence (Flavell, 1986; Piaget, 1932; 1981; Turiel, 1969). In some individuals, expressiveness and spontaneity reappear in late adolescence or adulthood and these individuals may again be recognized according to cultural values as exceptionally talented. In this case, then, with core skills defined in terms of expressivity and spontaneity, development in talented individuals follows a U-shaped course (Gardner, 1980; Winner, 1982).

IDENTIFYING TALENT IN THE VISUAL ARTS

One criterion that has been invoked to identify child prodigies is performing "at or near the level of an adult professional in an intellectually demanding field" (Feldman & Benjamin, 1986, p. 299). Tannenbaum (1986) argued, however, that childhood precocity leading to adult giftedness and adult giftedness should not be conflated. In reality gifted children are identified by comparisons with other children and not with the standards by which a mature adult is evaluated. If held to standards used with adults, few if any children would be identified. Tannenbaum proposed a criterion for selection that emphasizes a child's *potential* for excellence within a given domain when an adult.

Moreover, imposing a culturally defined adult standard does little to acknowledge the years needed to master the fundamental skills of a domain. Retrospective studies of the development of what is recognized as exceptional talent in adults usually does lead to acknowledging the mastery of a defined set of skills even in the visual arts where a formal definition of the knowledge base is apparently lacking. Realistic drawing was mastered early by Renaissance artists (Vasari, 1979) and Pariser (1991) pointed to the ease and fluidity of line with which some of this centuries great artists could draw realistic images as youngsters. Mastering basic technical skills such as realistic drawing, therefore, may be necessary for success in the visual arts, even if the exceptional works of a mature artist are essentially abstract and even if what is currently prized is not realism. Although it is important to note that not every artist of great merit need to have mastered such basic skills as a young child (see Golomb, 1992; Lark-Horovitz et al., 1973, for counterexamples), it is probable that at some point prior to attaining recognition, an artist did have to go through an apprenticeship in which this skill was mastered. One criterion, therefore, for identifying gifted children in the visual arts might be early mastery of realism because it indicates a certain level of technical mastery and because it is a skill most children who draw are likely to find motivating. That is, many observers of children's art report that school-age children are strongly motivated toward obtaining a faithful likeness of reality (Freeman, 1980; Luquet, 1935; Thomas & Silk, 1990).

Technical Mastery. Why insist on this criterion when it could well be irrelevant? One reason might be that a skillful artist does not wait on a happy accident, but is able to fully translate intentions to product. In this light, drawing accurately what one sees represents technical mastery over line and form. As such it indicates an ability to attend to one's own perceptual processes and to regulate production of a work. The former has been identified as an important sign of artistry in adults along with attention to higher order properties of organization that lead to sophisticated and dynamic compositions (Cupchik & Winston, in press). The ability to regulate production of a drawing or painting insures that an artist's intention can be translated to the work. By this I do not mean simply slavish adherence to a prior concept but also the ability to interact with a work of art during its production and evolve the piece through this interaction process. In the film *Le Mystere de Picasso* by the French director Clouzot, Picasso is shown at work on a painting. As he continues work on the painting the piece evolves, constantly changing until it finally assumes a stable end form.

Is technical mastery a sufficient condition for recognition of talent? In a discussion of genius and talent, Langer (1953) distinguished between talent as technical mastery and genius as "the power of conception." She pointed out that more often than not children who are recognized early for their technical mastery become professional adult artists of little distinction. Genius is unlikely to be found in the work of a child. More likely it "grows and deepens from work to work ... long after technical mastery has reached its height" (p. 409). Life experiences as inspiration and an artists' progressive development of techniques and concepts through the process of creating are additional and equally necessary ingredients to produce works of genius.

Creativity.   A second criterion might be creativity. Some researchers consider creativity synonymous with giftedness and judge it by the extent and quality of an innovation (Tannenbaum, 1986). Others stress individuality and a highly personalized pursuit of interests, preference for complexity, and the theoretical and aesthetic aspects of problems, in describing the creative person (see Albert & Runco, 1986). In a study aimed at predicting artistic success, Getzels and Csikszentmihalyi (1976) showed that being able to find or pose an artistic problem was more highly related to later success than solving an artistic problem. Developing artists who manipulated more objects prior to deciding on an arrangement to draw and who delayed closure during the drawing process were those who 7 years later were judged more successful and who 20 years later were more likely to have received recognition for their art (Csikszentmihalyi & Robinson, 1986). According to these authors problem finding is related to creativity. A similar construct appears elsewhere as divergent thinking (Getzels & Jackson, 1962), but when put in the context of a psychometric test, divergent thinking has only shown modest relationships with creativity (Guilford, 1967; Torrance, 1970) and has not been validated against real-life criteria (Jordan, 1975; Renzulli, 1986). Difficulties in validating measures of creativity notwithstanding, creativity, or an ability to generate something novel, to go beyond an existing frame of reference, may still be a valid harbinger of giftedness in children when applied to a specific domain of talent.

Commitment.   In addition to technical mastery and creativity as potential identifiers of talent in children, a third criterion added by most in the field, is motivation or task commitment (Csikszentmihalyi, Rathunde, & Whalen, 1993;

Renzulli, 1986). Eitan, a highly gifted child studied by Golomb (see chapter 6, this volume), spent 15 to 20 minutes a day drawing even as a 2-year-old. Other examples for the visual arts abound in the literature (Gardner, 1980; Goldsmith & Feldman, 1989; Richardson, 1991; Winner & Martino, 1993). In a study by Csikszentmihalyi et al. (1993) of talented teenagers in five talent domains, including the visual arts, music, athletics, math, and science, subjective commitment and the highest level course taken in a talent area were significantly related and judged the best measures of commitment to a talent area. These measures were especially predicted by factors such as being open and cheerful when engaged in a talent area and by reporting flow experiences related to a talent area. As defined operationally, flow experiences are those in which a person's concentration is so intense, their attention so undivided and wrapped up in what they are doing, that they are unaware of things of which they normally would be aware. The authors emphasized that the relationship between flow experiences and commitment is not a trivial one, because at its foundation is the exhilaration of creating and the profound enjoyment of the activity that makes the likelihood high that an individual will continue to develop their talent. The relationship of an academic measure such as highest level course taken to subjective commitment and flow experiences underscores the compatibility of serious goal-directedness and task enjoyment. Flow experiences have also been linked to creativity in accomplished scientists suggesting that complete engagement in an area is highly related to success (Klein, 1990, cited in Csikszentmihalyi et al., 1993).

The Role of Development. Are we to use an adult standard when applying these indices of talent? As indicated earlier, an approach that looks for adult performance, ignores the time talent takes to develop. It also fails to take into account universal stages of cognitive and emotional development. Does the expert child use the same processes as the expert adult? The delightfully expressive and spontaneous forms of a 4-year-old artist, as read by the aesthetic eyes of an adult, do not necessarily match the child's intention. Instead the adult takes the felicitous accident and gives it meaning. Most researchers agree that what young children are primarily trying to achieve in a drawing are recognizable forms (Freeman, 1980; Luquet, 1935; Thomas & Silk, 1990) so even if sensitive to expressive aspects of art (Geboyts & Cupchik, 1989, but see Gardner, 1982) children's intentions are most likely not centered on producing it. Additionally, an adult achieves expressiveness and spontaneity using quite a different and more highly elaborated set of techniques that, although evocative of the childish simplicity adults find pleasing, are quite different in their etiology. When Max Ernst first saw the work of Paul Klee at the Sturm gallery, he was struck by its affinity to the art of a child or naive artist. But he was also quick to recognize that this was a conscious construct, fashioned by a child who had looked at and studied well his Picasso, Delaunay, and Macke (Temkin, 1987). Although such questions as how precocious children accomplish remarkable performance have received little research attention (but see Bamberger, 1982; Chi, 1978; Milbrath, 1987), they are the crux of a developmental stance toward giftedness and its identification.

A potential answer to questions about how gifted children accomplish remark-able performances comes from recognizing that younger gifted children perform very well when they can capitalize on memory and perceptual processes but often expose their limitations when more advanced cognitive processes are demanded. In Bamberger's (1982) study of gifted child musicians, it was found that excellence at earlier stages of development did not always transfer to subsequent stages. Two aspects of musicianship were explored; the figural in which musical representation is tied to grouped motor patterns executed on an instrument, and the formal in which fixed referent structures such as scales are used, and notes are represented as individual elements in relation to these referent structures allowing comparisons of elements across different pieces of music. Mature artistry, is an integration of both figural and formal strategies of representation. Bamberger argued further that the child musical prodigy has an extraordinarily developed ability to use figural strategies in representing music. Formal strategies remain impoverished and can even interrupt well-practiced figural strategies when they develop (i.e., reflection on automatic procedures serves to interrupt their smooth functioning; Posner, 1978; Stroop, 1935). But as the child matures and takes on the developmental tasks of adolescence, figural knowledge is questioned. Bamberger referred to this period as the midlife crisis in the development of a child prodigy. Many musical prodigies are unable to build formal strategies reciprocal to the well-developed figural procedures and effect an integration of the two types of representational strategies. Several points emerge from her work. One is that the young child prodigy relies on different strategies than an adult to effect a sophisticated performance. A second point is that young child prodigies do not always become talented teenagers or adults.

In my studies of artistically gifted children related phenomena were noted (Milbrath, 1987, in preparation). Talented children were able to realistically depict forms as two dimensional shapes and achieve accurate proportions between their third and sixth year. Inclusion of realistic projected depth relations, however, occurred much later and could be observed in the longitudinal study to emerge from a period of protracted practice; a period in which the child appeared to pose increasingly more demanding problems to be solved within a drawing, therefore allowing for the development of flexible representational strategies that culminated in true perspective drawings by early adolescence. It was argued that later devel-oping representational strategies were dependent on the appearance of universal spatial operations characteristic of later stages in cognitive development, whereas early representational strategies were evidence of highly developed visually guided motor procedures.

A CASE STUDY

The case study approach to understanding development of gifted individuals is safest when applied retrospectively from the vantage of society's confirmation that the specimen has been "bagged." Prospective long-term case studies involve a risk; the gifted child may grow up to do ordinary things and never realize his or her potential. Elements of luck (Getzels, 1979; Tannebaum, 1986), as well as harsh economic realities associated with the life of an artist, play into a young person's decision to press forward with a career in the arts. In Getzels' (1979) sample of student artists, one third had abandoned a career in the visual arts 5 years after graduation and another third were only peripherally involved with the arts. In my longitudinal study of seven talented children first identified between 10 and 11 years of age and now 2 years past college graduation, only three young people still have a strong commitment to their art (Milbrath, 1987). The case presented here is one of these strongly commited young people who despite the odds has chosen to define himself as a visual artist. This chapter focuses on the development of two major themes elaborated by this artist as a child and on the disciplined strategies he used to perfect his representational style.

I was introduced to Joel Rivers in 1980 by a mutual acquaintance who knew I was recruiting children to be part of a longitudinal study of gifted children artists. Joel was 11 when I first interviewed him and his mother. Even at this first meeting it was unmistakable that I had stumbled onto someone quite singular. My aim was to sample spontaneous drawings or those from a child's imagination rather than from a model. I was more than gratified to find that Joel not only did not draw from models, but there also was little indication that his drawings were influenced by the crazes of his day (i.e., Batman, Superman, Star Wars, etc.). In addition, he was then, as he is now, an exceptionally articulate, well-informed, and personable young man. Much of what follows is taken from a series of nine interviews beginning when Joel was 11 with the most recent occurring in the winter of 1994 when Joel was 24.

The Developing Artist

At our first meeting, Joel and I spent several hours pouring through his notebooks and drawings dating back to his fifth year. He stopped at almost every drawing telling me in great detail about the drawing, its significance and even the circumstance around its origins. His mother added that many of the drawings represented more than what I saw because they often accompanied a story. Then, as now, Joel had a very clear style with bold sure lines and a wonderful comic sense.

Joel began drawing early; seated in his father's lap at the age of 2, father and son spent time drawing together. Neither of his parents, however, was particularly noteworthy in the visual arts. Joel's mother had graduated from college with a degree in English and had aspirations to become a writer. She was employed doing office work and later by a hospital as administrative personnel. Joel's father is half Cherokee and during these early years was an unemployed musician. Both parents had come from Oklahoma and had been raised rurally. Later in describing this influence Joel stated that, "I was raised in a very rural way … even in the middle of the city [we had] chickens and rabbits."

Before Joel was 3 years old he was already drawing recognizable forms. His mother recollects teaching Joel the difference between the fins and tails of sharks and dolphins when he was 3. The next morning when she awoke and went into his room she found he had used a magic marker to cover the walls as high as he could reach with sharks and dolphins. They all had wonderful expressions. Neighbors came in to see the wall and added their own graphic commentaries and his mother remembers the fun they had with the wall before it was finally painted over. Joel's mother suggested that magic markers were an important innovation in allowing very young children to achieve control over form. She noted that with markers, Joel could make a result that was satisfying, whereas crayons were more difficult to control. She also described obtaining rolls of newspaper ends from the local newspaper when Joel was 3 and rolling the paper out on a long table for Joel to draw on. Joel drew and narrated active companion stories; his mother recalls this activity as both play and social because their household was always filled with people who would sit with Joel as he drew, adding to his stories and pictures. She estimated that this activity might last 30 minutes or more at a time.

When Joel was 4, he had a serious fall and was in a coma for 2½ days. While in the hospital recovering, his mother showed him a book about dinosaurs, one that was really meant for an adult reader. The detailed pictures in the book provided the stimulus for Joel's most pervasive early theme and his mother reported that it was after that incident that he began to draw dinosaurs. At around this time, Joel's parents separated and Joel and his mother and younger brother moved to a new home (one consequence was the loss of Joel's earlier drawings). At the age of 6, Joel was introduced to the second theme that also dominated his drawings until late adolescence. A friend who lived nearby showed Joel his extensive collection of old Disney comics and Joel began to draw his own cartoon characters that shared some of the Disney features.

Drawing was always a part of Joel's identity. His mother reports that he drew constantly at home, involving others around him as much as possible; "he drew every day of his life." He drew while he watched television, while he chatted with his mother, in the school yard, and his mother recalls once even during a medical exam. She also remembered that when he was young, he would look at a pattern and "see" figures and objects in its undefined lines and shapes. Similar childhood phenomena were recalled by both Ernst and Klee (Temkin, 1987). Ernst saw human forms in the patterning of the fake mahogany foot board of his bed, whereas Klee picked out grotesques human forms from the polished marble table tops at his uncles restaurant and drew them.

In first grade Joel began drawing in notebooks. His mother gave him small (5 × 7 inch) black bound notebooks to carry so he could draw at school. He never went anywhere without a drawing notebook. Joel remembered sometimes being taunted in grammar school because he preferred drawing to playing sports but he also reported that the other children were often intrigued and would crowd around to watch him draw. Later, in grammar school, he and his brother and friends created games based on his drawing skills. He drew the characters and the children would make clay figures from the drawings, wooden game boards, and villages out of clay and sticks. Of this period, Joel recently said, "I realized early on that school was not where I was going to be happy ... that I would have to find another way of compensating. We had friends at school but we'd go home after school and we had our own little worlds ... [we played] real elaborate imaginative games sometimes inside sometimes outside … me and my brother and our friend, Taj … we had a real rich childhood." Joel's relationship with his younger brother was an important one. The two brothers spent a lot of time together, playing their own games, drawing, and watching television. They continued these close pastimes throughout Joel's high school years.

Joel's mother reported that Joel needed very little instruction in drawing. Once he was shown a technique he would spend hours practicing it until he was able to successfully incorporate it into his drawings. Joel began to draw in notebooks at about the age of 7 and, therefore, kept an ordered record of his exercises in technique. He continued the practice of keeping notebooks through high school and college. The family had several friends who influenced Joel in his early years. One friend, Dominic, although not an artist, occasionally showed Joel different techniques. When Joel was 6, Dominic introduced him to shading and shadow, however, no consistent use of these techniques appear in his work until the following year. He showed Joel how to cross-hatch when the child was 7. Prior to that, Joel's drawings were single line drawings, but once he was shown this technique he began to use it for backgrounds, stating at 13 that it had a nice effect. Reflecting on that period recently, Joel recalled that if he was shown something linear like cross-hatching, "I could sink my teeth into [it]."

When Joel was 9, artist John Kolliq instructed him in perspective and several sketches of cubes encasing a three-dimensional form and drawn in perspective appear in his notebooks for that year. But Joel was not comfortable with geometric perspective and preferred to use "the tricks" of perspectives such as diminished size and foreshortening. Buildings rarely appear in his work until high school and he confesses that even today he "still can't draw buildings." The tricks of perspective, however, were not shown to Joel. Recently he recalled that he understood that size differences and distance were related at an early age and that when he tried to draw a front view of a dinosaur "something was wrong but I didn't know what it was." Joel began to use diminishing size to indicate distance at age 7 and was consistently successful with foreshortening by age 8.

Joel also credits John with introducing him to the life of an artist, showing him "what a situation was like, [that] it was serious." John suggested Joel draw from life at age 9 and introduced him to color the following year, encouraging him to experiment with its use. Up until that time Joel had hardly ever used color working primarily with black magic marker and later pen; but he spent the summer following John's instruction, experimenting with color and producing many exciting and brightly colored drawings. Although color was used more frequently by Joel in subsequent years, black pen drawings continued to dominate his notebooks throughout his early adolescence. These were sometimes colored in with ink washes or watercolor. In addition to drawing, during his younger years, Joel made puppets, cardboard constructions such as a doll house and its furnishings, figurines, and other three-dimensional constructed scenes.

It was not until Joel went to a public arts magnet high school that he received formal instruction in drawing and painting. Even so, he continued to refine his pen technique, concentrating on inking in with a brush fine pen-point drawings, expanding a bold broad stroke pen technique, and spending increasingly more time working with color. Some of Joel's notebooks during this period are in pencil as well. It was in high school that his teachers suggested he start working on a bigger scale. Up until this time most drawings were done in notebooks that varied in size from 5 × 8 inches to 11 × 14 inches. In high school he began to work on canvases as large as 20 X 24 inches and some of his drawings were done on sheets of 14 × 18-inch paper. Under the instruction and stimulation of the arts high school Joel developed an interest in new media. He acquired an air brush, began to paint in acrylic and water colors, and developed a layered crayon technique upon which a drawing was etched. His teachers also demanded that he draw from life, a practice he had not previously pursued with any regularity. In addition, Joel made an animated film and acted in and directed another film he wrote. When he graduated he received an award for his artistic merit. This high school period is marked by development of bolder lines, much more use of color and rather than doing a single drawing per page, each notebook page was filled with drawings

After high school, Joel obtained a scholarship to study art at a state college. He was able to take good classes in color theory in college, studying with Marie Thiebaud, and learning the transparent layered technique of water colors from Mark Johnson, a student of Josef Albers, one of the pioneers in the Bauhaus movement. This was "a big breakthrough for me." He also learned fresco technique, which he remains excited about, and printmaking combining lithography with water color by coloring in his prints. In college he had several one-man shows in the local town and entered two juried school shows in his senior year. He was active in political organizations, particularly multicultural activities and acted, worked as a stage-hand, and did performance pieces as well as painting. In his last year at college he taught drawing and painting, which he enjoyed and which he entertains as a potential future direction. He graduated in 1991 with honors and was strongly committed to a career as an artist.

In considering his main influences, Joel named the following individuals: his mother, who raised him and always encouraged and supported his artistic interests; his brother, "We drew all the time together. We influenced each other. He was more of a colorist … he was geometric too. He did patterns"; his father, who although having relatively little to do with raising Joel, he describes as a "pretty creative person … he drew a lot, real abstract things … more design than anything else"; John Kolliq the artist and family friend; and Dominic, the family friend, who provided some early instruction. Other influences he named were M. C. Escher, Tin Tin, Gustav Klimt, John Audubon, the dinosaur drawers like Gregory Paul, Zap comix, and other comic book artists like Griffin and Crumb. Of Paul's book, "Predatory Dinosaurs of the World," Joel said "that would have been my book if I had been born 10 years earlier."

The Developing Themes

Between his fifth and seventh year, Joel's drawings showed many repetitions of a single theme. Roughly 50 drawings were saved by his mother that showed variations on the theme of animals, usually in family groupings (it is during this period that his parents separated); turtles, birds, bats, and dinosaurs among others. Figure 4.1, a tyrannosaurus family, was done at age 6 and is representative of this family theme series in which forms were confidently rendered with an almost continuous line. The control Joel had already achieved even at this young age over the two-dimensional form is evident. Joel rarely drew people until adolescence and then usually only in the context of his cartoon or fantasy creations. Animals remained the most dominant theme in his work until high school. Their importance Joel ascribes to "what my father instilled in me early on," and their Native American heritage. One significant animal theme that was specifically influenced by his father was birds (not presented here). Because he was part Native American, his father was very interested in birds and collected and mounted their feathers. Joel spent 3 months with his father in Arizona prior to adolescence, a period he particularly remembered, and had numerous trips to the Nevada desert with his mother and a friend of hers who had land there. In addition and perhaps as important was the fact that the family always kept animals, "we always had animals ... [they] have always been in my life. ... I was the kind of kid who would save mice from cats." Recently, when I asked him about the preference he had for drawing animals as opposed to people he said, "people didn't interest me, at least most of the ones I met and a lot of people I knew around me were interested in animals."

FIG. 4.1. A tyrannosaurus family, age 6.

Dinosaurs. The most pervasive theme to emerge from Joel's interest in animals, was that of dinosaurs. By his own account, a serious preoccupation with dinosaurs started when he was 5. At first, Joel often merged realism with cartooning. In Fig. 4.2, done at age 5, Joel has drawn a diplodocus in his early realism style. In Fig. 4.3, done at age 7, Joel has mixed realism and cartooning and imbued the allosaurus family with comic elements by using their facial expressions and gestures to suggest that papa saur has "overstepped" some boundaries. These two aspects in his drawings began to separate and evolve on their own with the dinosaurs becoming increasingly realistic after age 8 but crossover themes such as a dinosaur chasing a cartoon character were always apparent.

Joel generally executed only one drawing per page in his notebooks until he was 14. A rather detailed record appears in his sketchbooks for these and subsequent years as he gained increasing mastery over the dinosaur theme. In Fig. 4.4, drawn at age 9, a parasaurolophus wades in a delightfully elaborated scene of a swamp, while an allosaurus looks on. Joel described this drawing when interviewed at 13, "it was the second one I really tried with backgrounds … it was strange, you couldn't really make everything out but it … the trees and plants and all...in that respect it was okay but. … I didn't really master the technique of outlining the main subject so it sort of blends in with everything else and … gives it a strange effect." This can be contrasted with Fig. 4.5, a lambeosaurus, done at age 12, in which Joel clearly separates the main subject from the background; as he says at 13, "I made

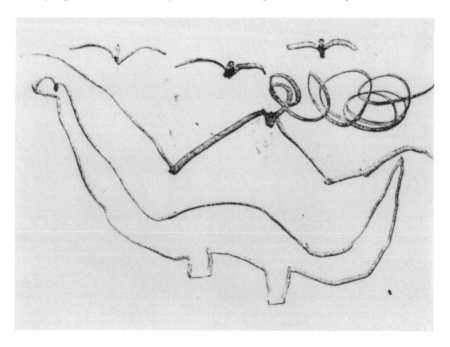

FIG. 4.2. Diplodocus, age 5.

FIG. 4.3. Allosaurus family, age 7.

FIG. 4.4. Wading parasaurolophus, age 9.

FIG. 4.5. Lambeosaurus, age 12.

the subject really profound. You could tell it was there and the background, you don't really look at that first, you look at the front and that's the main effect I wanted to get." This drawing is also noteworthy for its pleasing composition and because of the manner in which Joel has skillfully implied the surface of the water by using ripples yet still preserved the water's transparency by suggesting the animals partially hidden legs under the water. Joel stated that he specifically practiced dinosaurs from many points of view and in different orientations, often varying the position of the same animal and starting the drawing from a different part of the body, for example, the tail or feet instead of the head. Such a practice was also recorded in Picasso's biography (Richardson, 1991). Picasso's cousins and sister would request drawings beginning from different parts of a figure. Figure 4.6, done by Joel at age 10, shows a dinosaurlike creature with a mammalian head in three different orientations. Practicing rotation was a conscious exercise for Joel. In order to get away from developing drawing formulas, Joel varied the orientation of his figures. At 13, he was asked if it was hard to think of animals in different positions. He replied, "no I just know basically what the design is and then I do it. ... I know where the femur is, the pelvis is, the skull, how long the neck is."

Varying the rotation of a figure is not typical of most children's drawings. Both children and adults tend to draw the human figure in front view, whereas most animals are drawn in profile (Ives & Rovet, 1979). Variations that use three-quarter orientations are much less frequent, particularly in spontaneous drawings. Three-quarter views were not seen until the age of 9 in the studies of children at the Cleveland Art Museum and were always rare and limited to a small number of

FIG. 4.6. Rotation exercise, age 10.

talented children (Lark-Horovitz & Norton, 1959; Munro, Lark-Horovitz, & Barnhart, 1942). In my study of the human figure in spontaneous drawings of children ages 3 to 14, three-quarter rotations only appeared in the drawings of approximately 15% of the children ages 11 to 14, who were not particularly talented in the visual arts (Milbrath, in preparation). In contrast, at least 25% to 50% of the talented children, sampled cross-sectionally or followed longitudinally, showed three-quarter rotations of a figure or figure parts (e.g., head or torso) by age 6, and percentages increased with age up to 68% at 13 and 14 in the cross-sectional sample and 100% by 11 and 12 in the longitudinal sample. Although Joel rarely drew the human figure before adolescence, he did begin rotating the heads, torsos, or entire bodies of animals quite young. During his sixth year, half ($n = 4$) of the drawings randomly sampled from a much larger collection of Joel's drawings showed three-quarter rotated views. By 7, all ($n = 5$) of the sampled drawings contained some figures drawn in three-quarters orientation. These included left- and right-facing three-quarter front views, mixed left- and right-facing three-quarter front views, and, although rarer, back views and three-quarter back views.

This dramatic transition during the period between years 6 and 7 was also marked by the development of effective means to convey movement. When first interviewed at age 11, Joel stated that he was most concerned with depicting form and action in his drawings. He reported using his imagination instead of models as guides for his drawings and specifically to make his subjects three dimensional and in action. At 13, Joel reflected that an artist should not have to use the convention

FIG. 4.7. Flying pteranodons, age 11.

of action lines to depict movement but should be able to use position, perspective, and certain expressions. In a beautifully composed drawing (Fig. 4.7, age 11, flying pteranodons and sauropods in water), Joel captures a dynamic sense of flight by creating tension between the oblique position of the bodies and wings of a group of flying pteranodons. Such a sophisticated compositional technique is reminiscent of the techniques used to effect the flight of angels by early masters of religious art. One example is the anguished sense of flight achieved by Giotto in his painting "Lamentations" (Arnheim, 1964).

Although partially based on hours of practice, the early success Joel had with rotation and movement was in large part likely due to his use of a visualized image and developmental changes in the mental representation of the image. An analysis of the appearance of movement and rotation in his drawings shows that both abruptly appear between his sixth and seventh year, a time when children move from preoperational to concrete operational thought. The striking contrast between the drawings from the "family" themes done at age 6 and the drawings done in the subsequent year suggest that such a precipitous change could not be the result of practice alone. In Fig. 4.1, a clear two-dimensional depiction of the larger and smaller dinosaur indicates Joel already had good control over the depiction of forms. In these drawings, however, the figures seem static and lack the solidity and roundness that would mark their volume projected in depth. In Fig. 4.3, the following year, the dinosaurs seem infused with a sense of motion, solidity, and roundness. The third dimension is clearly portrayed by the near successful fore-shortened distortions of father allosoraus' tail and snout and of mother allosaurus' snout as well as by the inclusion of a background, a ground line, and a ground plane. If Joel relied primarily on a visualized mental image as a guide in drawing, this transition could be explained by parallel structural changes in cognition that support a transition from static to rotated moving views.

A critical mental process necessary for dynamic representations of movement and rotation proposed by Piaget and Inhelder (1971) includes the ability to think about displacements (movement) and transformations (rotation) by linking static states together in succession. This mental process has its analogy in Winsor McKay's historical first animation, "Gertie the Dinosaur," which he made by temporally linking together many drawings, each representing a slightly different static state of the figures. Crucial in this process is the ability to place images in a given order of succession and to anticipate and make deductions about relationships as they undergo transformations. It is after this transition in children's thinking that they are first able to demonstrate, by correctly identifying pictures of rotated views or by simple drawings, the successive transformations simple objects undergo during rotation (Piaget & Inhelder, 1971). This same mental process (transitivity) allows children to give serial order to weights and lengths and to understand the idea of hierarchical inclusion in classifying plants and animals (Inhelder & Piaget, 1964). It should be stated, however, that even though the mental image seems to have played a strong role in Joel's drawing other talented children in my longitudinal study did not show this same ability. That is in most other cases, rotation was accomplished by a more laborious process of amalgamating front views and profile views to achieve a rotated appearance and only gradually accomplishing the distortions necessary for true rotation. These observations are the subject of another work (Milbrath, in preparation).

Joel's fascination with dinosaurs did not seem to be rooted in them solely as symbols of power although they were at times portrayed as powerful. More salient was a scientific fascination that intensified as he reached early adolescence. The following examples of Joel's preoccupation with paleontology and evolutionary theory are taken from discussions we had over a 7-year period. In his first interview at age 11, Joel told me that he was particularly interested in science and had seized on the jurassic to cretaceous periods during the reign of the dinosaurs as a focus. About this period, he hypothesized a near collision or cosmic disturbance as the probable cause of the dinosaurs' demise. Such a disturbance, he said, would have led to changes in the tropical habitat and to the disappearance of the dinosaurs' food as new plants replaced the old. He informed me that prior to this disturbance there were no seasons, the world was only hot. On another visit when he was 15, we discussed the expanding and contracting theory of the universe. He showed me a drawing in his notebook of an object going into hyperspace; the receding part of the object was in red and then gradually changed to blue as it entered new space. On a final interview the summer before college, he reported a new find in Wyoming that showed CroMagnon man was on this continent. He also told me about a theory that holds modern man to be a blend of CroMagnon and Neanderthal. In Asia, for example, man was pure CroMagnon but in other places he was mixed to a greater or lesser extent. He cited the occurrence of blonde aborigines in Australia as an example of such a mix. Other topics were estrus differences in man and ape and the relatively recent appearance of knuckle walking in the great apes.

Joel did not learn to read until age 10 when he began reading paleontology books because, by his own account, he "was very interested in that stuff. Dinosaur information was changing and I was voracious trying to find out the new information. Once I was able to read that opened a whole new door." He had been labeled dyslexic in public school but frequent changes of address and a series of public and private schools meant that no one attempted to work with his difficulties. Hard work on his own allowed him to "rewire" his brain but even in college he reported having a problem with abstract symbols. He could understand concepts but they had to be of a certain type, "something I can make an image for" Joel reports recasting concepts into cartoon diagrams to improve his retention of abstract material. Difficulties with written language, such as Joel's, have been reported in other studies of young artists (Frith, 1980; Phillips, 1987; Winner, Casey, Da Silva, & Hayes, 1991) and are often associated with dominance of visuospatial areas of the brain over language areas (Geschwind, 1984). On the other hand, superiority in visual imagination (Hermelin & O'Conner, 1986; O'Conner & Hermelin, 1983) and visual memory (Rosenblatt & Winner, 1988) are reported for artistically talented children.

At the age of 12, Joel brought home paleontology books with skeletons of dinosaurs and stated that he wished to be a paleontologist. It is at this point that more formal studies begin to appear in his notebooks and some of these are detailed and labeled skeletons of dinosaurs. The books helped him with the accuracy of his drawings and he reported that at times he traced the anatomical drawings to learn how they went. Using the anatomical drawings of dinosaur bones as a guide, Joel also reported intentionally distorting the poses to different positions in order to put action into a figure and draping the skeleton with skin. His drawings from that period reflect these processes as mental activities instead of production activities since rather than commencing with a skeleton armature, the process appears already completed in a drawing. When asked about this process recently, Joel stated that although he had done those types of drawings (e.g., sketching the skeletal structure first) as school assignments, he did not use an armature for the image, "but more often that not [I] start with the front and go all the way to the back." In addition, when interviewed at 13, Joel reported that descriptions accompanying the anatomical drawings served as useful information in draping the flesh of the animal. For example, when it was surmised that pteranodon had scaly skin rather than feathers he changed the way he drew it. If the animal was thought to have a "wattle" he drew it with a "baggy throat." This addition of detail also extended to including vegetation that matched the animals' diet, for example lambeosaurus in Fig. 4.5 appears anatomically correct and surrounded by appropriate habitat and vegetation.

Although Joel became less preoccupied with dinosaurs after he entered the arts magnet high school, this theme continued to be elaborated. A beautiful drawing done with brown crayon that was taken from his notebooks in his senior year shows his fluid style and ability to use shading and texture techniques (see Fig. 4.8, tryannosaurus, age 18). Expansions of his interest to a broader paleontology during

FIG. 4.8. Tryannosaurus, age 18.

high school led Joel to draw other related themes, such as early man, varieties of monkeys and apes, and reptiles. The theme of dinosaurs eventually merged once again with his cartoon themes to create a series of fantasy and science fiction characters that are described here.

Cartoons. Joel began cartooning at age 7, using his favorite theme of dinosaurs but also immediately developing his own cartoon characters. In Fig. 4.9, when Joel was age 7, the central character, Little Foot, makes his first appearance struggling up a hillside trail. It is evident that Joel was immediately able to achieve the comic by both facial and bodily expressiveness. At our first interview, when I asked him why he chose cartoons he said because they were funny and expressive. The figures in this section bear testament to the truth of that statement in the hands of this talented child. They also belie the common wisdom in the literature that children draw cartoons because they are less successful with realism. As Joel's

FIG. 4.9. Little Foot, age 7.

drawings suggest and as stated by his mother, Joel could go from realistic drawings to cartoons in the same sitting with absolutely no difficulty.

In developing a cartoon character, Joel reported that at times he used a picture from a book as a model for a drawing of a realistic animal. Once he understood the basic shape, it became the basis for a cartoon. For example, an owl was used for Miwis, a character that begins to appear in Joel's cartoons at around age 9 (see Fig. 4.11, figure on the right with long bill). Some of Joel's cartoons were influenced by existing cartoon characters. In Fig. 4.10, done at age 10, the cast of Saturday morning cartoons fills a page. Often such drawings were done while watching television and indicate the speed and flexibility with which Joel was able to draw. By his own account, Donald Duck and Scrooge were particularly influential in developing one of his most important cartoon characters, the Geeples. In Fig. 4.11, done at age 14, Joel traces the evolution of the Geeples starting with its appearance when he was 10 years old. When Joel was 12, he added a snout making the Geeple less insectlike and by his 13th year he had incorporated the Disney duck's eyes. The Geeples continued to be featured in his cartoons throughout high school but further evolution was in store for them (described later).

When Joel was 13 and 14 he went to considerable effort to chronicle not only the development of the Geeple but also different aspects of the cartoon. Character sheets appear depicting the principle Geeple, other Geeples, and related characters such as Miwis, Freez, and others. One shows a Geeple expressing all the basic emotions and a significant number are panels that depict Geeples' exploits. Joel

FIG. 4.10. Saturday morning cartoons, age 10.

FIG. 4.11. Evolution of the Geeples, age 14.

also developed an elaborate game based on the Geeples. Starting with cardboard cutouts, he and his brother moved the Geeple characters around in action sequences but following their introduction to Dungeons and Dragons, Joel had the idea of switching to a role-play game. In the context of this game, Joel combined his cartoon and realistic styles to create a haunting and powerful assemblage of supernatural characters whose adventures he illustrated for the players as the game was played. The Geeples evolved to Progees as well as assuming other more human forms. Alter egos began to develop as Joel expanded the characters for his game. He developed several for himself, his brother, and his best friend. Some of Joel's most superb pen-and-ink washes were drawn as character profile sheets for the players. Under the illustration of each character were the vital statistics about its powers and abilities.

The game was a very important social focus for Joel and an outlet for an active mental life in which he was beginning to take on the idealistic sociopolitical interests of adolescence. Joel played the game with his brother and with friends at high school although recently he reflected that others besides his best friend and brother were never enthusiastic. Joel was always the game master, and drew all the characters for the players and all of the action sequences. The scenarios often contained adult themes of a political and social nature such as divisions among species with a dominant and unjust ruler species, and individuals taking on the battles of their people and often winning against tremendous odds. Joel reflected that once they realized that their inspirations were their own fears based on current political realities "it stopped being fun." Nevertheless, the three boys continued throughout high school and even for a few years into college playing the game.

Joel's graphic inventiveness was at a peak during this period of tremendous productivity in relation to the game. Joel developed a particular identification with his game characters. In describing the genesis of the different characters, Joel stated that at one time there were the descendants of the Geeples. A nuclear blast caused mutations such that a variety of types emerged including the Progees, a green Geeple who preyed on the Goregons, centaurlike beings with horse faces whose planet had been destroyed and who were victims of genocide. Saxton Gander, the character played by Joel's brother was a Progee but the last of his clan and considered an outlaw; he was also hunted by the Progees. In Fig. 4.12, from Joel's notebooks at 15, a Progee sentinel patrols the city. This page fairly represents the care with which Joel composed the pages of his notebooks so that almost every page is a delight to the eye. At this point, Joel's notebooks became less of a chronicle of his exercises and practice of drawing and more of a catalogue of his creative graphic ideas that were almost always presented as finished compositions.

Joel stated that Goregons were lower middle class. In addition there were Spigelis, polymorphs, who were the original inhabitants of earth while human beings were an experiment gone awry, and Ibyons, red creatures who were a cross between a dog and a bear with green cat eyes. Joel played both a Goregon and a Spigeli. Spigelis were like "Gods," they lived to be very very old and contained all the genetic information of everyone who ever lived. Therefore, they could assume the shape and identity of any creature who had ever lived. This combined with their

FIG. 4.12. Progee sentinel, age 15.

advanced age made it difficult sometimes for a Spigeli to remember who he was. Ibyons were considered the "bad guys" and retrogressive. Freezes (example in lower portion of Fig. 4.11), another creature that reproduced like a plant but had the choice of taking in food or light, and an elaboration of on insect with features that included "respiration apparatus," "eight eyes," and a "central hole with filters," were some of the other figures Joel developed in conjunction with the game. Examples of this pantheon dominated Joel's notebooks from the age of 14 into college.

Ed, an 8-foot tall Goregon, became one of Joel's principle alter egos in the game. In examining cartoons done by Joel prior to these developments in the game, it was evident that precursor equine creatures had already made their appearance in his notebooks during his 13th year. Often they were depicted as female as well as a male. In its incarnation as a Goregon, however, the centaur becomes a clearly masculine and powerful figure. In Fig. 4.13, done at age 15, Ed sits at an

FIG. 4.13. "Ed," a Goregon, age 15.

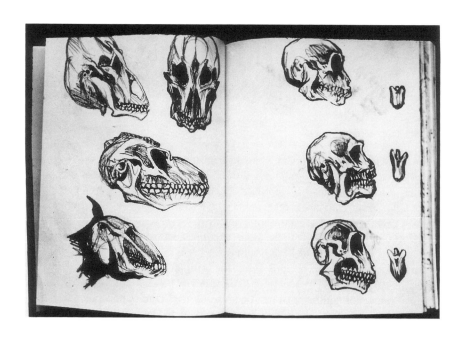

FIG. 4.14. Anatomy drawing, age 16–17.

intergalactic bar with a glass of "wine." Joel achieves a brooding strength in this haunting portrayal by facial expression, body posture, and color. The background color, not visible in this black-and-white photo, is rendered in purple water color while the figure is a combination of black water color and pen. In this drawing, as in most of his drawings, Joel shows a concern for anatomical features. Figure 4.14, taken from the pages of his notebooks during his junior year in high school, is a fine example of the anatomical drawings Joel did as he worked out the skulls for some of these different characters including Goregons (center left).

In Fig. 4.15, a heavily armed Goregon is regrouping after impaling a victim. This drawing in pen and ink, done when Joel was 16, shows his superb draftsmanship and also conveys the dark and bleak mood associated with war. In that respect, this drawing brings to mind the Gothic and German expressionists art which both

FIG. 4.15. Armed Goregon, age 16.

FIG. 4.16. Saxton Gander, age 21–22.

expressed "pathos with similar convulsive distortions, [and] with the same relentless realism" (Read, 1963, p. 66). In Fig. 4.16, taken from the notebooks of his 21st
to 22nd year, Joel has used a variety of textures created by line alone to depict the
strength and force of a battle between Saxton Gander, his brother's character, and
a dragon. Joel creates light by leaving the space as blank paper and shade by a range
of line textures. It is this striking contrast between the white space of the paper and
the heavily textured and shaded space that greatly enhances the communicated
power of this drawing.

Recently I asked Joel where his ideas came from and how he thought of a
subject to draw. In some instances his dreams supplied him with new fantasy
figures. He might have a dream and either wake up to make a quick sketch of
the idea or wait until the next morning. He described some monsters that came
"into" his dream once called "skasses, big scarlet things with big disjointed
limbs and they live in the desert. I can still draw those things and it was just
from one dream." More often, however, Joel said that he discovered what he is
going to draw by drawing. First he "warms up" by drawing and then like
"discovering what's in the clay" when sculpting, he finds what he will draw.
When I pointed out that a blank piece of white paper provided less of a stimulus
than clay or stone, he acknowledged that although this seemed true, "you have
whatever you have drawn before," and that is likely to suggest itself. You at
least "know where you could start … and maybe that's where [drawing] formula
is … a familiar way of moving the pencil around the paper."

DEVELOPMENTAL RATE

Most literature is consistent in reporting that artistically talented children go through the same stages of artistic development but accelerated and always several years in advance of their less talented peers (Winner & Martino, 1993). They begin representational drawing earlier, and reach each milestone 1 to 3 years before other children. Joel also began drawing early and reached the milestones of representational drawing several years in advance of expectations for artistic development. Table 4.1 shows a comparison of Joel, the group of talented children sampled longitudinally of which he was a part, and a cross-sectionally sampled less talented group of children. The values for Joel and the talented children sampled longitudinally are the mean proportions of drawings at a given age that were judged as having a category, whereas the values for the children in the less talented cross-sectional sample are the proportion of children; in most cases only one drawing was obtained from each child in that sample. The categories presented are three types of figure rotations or orientations and six different pictorial devices for each of five age blocks, from 5 to 14 years of age. (Although there is data for younger children in each of the groups, Joel's drawings prior to 5 were not available.) Interrater reliabilities for these categories ranged from a Kappa = .67 for indicators of perspective in the longitudinal study (K = .88 for cross-sectional study) such as foreshortenng, modeling, shadow, and shading to Kappa = .90 for figure rotations. All other Kappas were above .80.

If the less talented children are compared with the talented children, it is evident that profile figure orientations have a somewhat similar developmental course despite differences in the type of data. Between the ages of 5 and 10 approximately the same percentage of drawings contain profiles in the talented group as there are children who use profiles in the less talented group. After that, the use of profiles decreases in the less talented group largely as a result of an increased interest in drawing portraits using front views. The two groups are also similar in the use of a ground plane. Talented and less talented children are beginning to construct a ground plane between their fifth and sixth years, discarding the use of a single line or horizontal alignment of figures to indicate the ground in favor of coloring in a bounded space or using other devices to indicate a plane. Although not in the table, a ground plane was constructed in only 9% of the drawings of the talented 3- and 4-year-olds and by none of the less talented children at 3 and 4 years of age.

Generally, linear perspective drawings were rarely sampled in this study. Drawings were only judged to be in linear perspective if a child depicted the apparent projection of a geometric object with one face parallel to the picture plane and its two parallel sides orthogonal to the picture plane and converging to a vanishing point on the picture plane. (Other types of projection devices were also rated but are not included here.) Surprisingly, linear perspective drawings did appear in both samples but much earlier in the talented children. Although all the talented children had at least one linear perspective drawing by the age of 13, they were frequently produced by less than half of these children. Many of the children appeared to prefer drawing figures rather than geometric objects. Similarly, in the less talented group,

TABLE 4.1
Percentages for Figure Rotation or Pictorial Devices

	5 and 6 years	7 and 8 years	9 and 10 years	11 and 12 years	13 and 14 years
*Joel**	*(N = 6)*	*(N = 5)*	*(N = 6)*	*(N = 6)*	*(N = 6)*
Figure Rotation					
Profile	86	100	78	83	57
Three quarter	29	86	78	50	57
Mixed three quarter	29	43	33	33	43
Pictorial Devices					
Ground plane	43	100	89	67	86
Overlap	29	100	100	100	100
Perspective	0	0	0	17	14
Foreshortening	14	57	89	33	57
Modeling	14	71	89	100	71
Shade and shadow	14	43	78	67	86
*Talented**	*(N = 61)*	*(N = 53)*	*(N = 50)*	*(N = 58)*	*(N = 37)*
Figure Rotation					
Profile	49	54	54	48	26
Three quarter	12	33	44	55	59
Mixed three quarter	10	20	30	33	32
Pictorial Devices					
Ground Plane	45	72	76	89	74
Overlap	46	98	96	97	84
Perspective	0	4	2	16	17
Foreshortening	3	33	55	44	53
Modeling	4	43	56	66	78
Shade and Shadow	4	14	24	37	58
*Less Talented***	*(N = 12)*	*(N = 11)*	*(N = 14)*	*(N = 13)*	*(N = 12)*
Figure Rotation					
Profile	46	46	50	15	8
Three quarter	0	0	7	0	17
Mixed three quarter	0	0	14	15	8
Pictorial devices					
Ground plane	46	77	71	77	92
Overlap	18	31	57	77	100
Perspective	0	0	0	0	8
Foreshortening	0	0	7	15	17
Modeling	0	0	0	23	50
Shade and shadow	0	0	7	23	17

*N = total drawings; percentage of drawings were figured for each child and then averaged.
**N = children; percentage of children.

figurative rather than geometric subjects were increasingly favored as children became adolescents and in fact only two children, one in each age group, actually did produce a perspective drawing.

In other respects, the two groups are quite dissimilar. This is particularly apparent in the use of three-quarter orientations for figures (human or animal). Talented children began using three-quarter figure rotations by ages 5 and 6, showing consistent use in a little less than half their drawings by 9 and 10 years of age. This group also began to use mixed three-quarter orientations at about the same time. These views include drawings such as a torso drawn in three-quarter view and a face rendered in profile, or a torso drawn in a three-quarter right facing view with the face depicted in a three-quarter left facing view. Clearly, these are more complicated views to produce even for the talented children. The use of three-quarter orientations for figures in the less talented children was rare. Only a very small percentage of the 75 children studied ever produced these types of drawings and then not until 9 or 10 years old, 4 years later than for the talented children.

Differences in pictorial devices were marked as well. The use of overlap to occlude a far object by a near object was much more frequent and at younger ages in the talented group. By 13 and 14 years of age, however, the levels in the less talented children were comparable to the talented children. A more striking difference appears in the use of pictorial devices that are most often applied to figures to indicate perspective. Foreshortening was used consistently by the talented children in a third of their drawings by 7 and 8 years of age, whereas levels in the less talented children were not comparable even by 13 or 14 years of age. Modeling, by shading or using curved full lines to indicate volume or rounded surfaces of figures and objects, was also more frequent in the talented children and had roughly the same developmental course as foreshortening. In the less talented children it appeared in children 2 years older than the children first using foreshortening but by 13 and 14 years of age half the children employed modeling. The use of shading and shadow to indicate a light source was generally less frequent but again the talented children began experimenting with this pictorial device early and by 13 and 14 it appeared in about half their drawings. The less talented children used shade and shadow much less frequently; only six children in all ever used this device. It is possible that observations of older children in this population might show further increases in these types of perspective indicators, although, generally, in studies of less talented children up through high school such indicators are reported as relatively rare (Lark-Horovitz & Norton,1959; Munro et al., 1942).

Joel's development was similar to the talented group's as a whole but there were several distinctive features that support the qualitative analysis of his drawings. As noted, Joel concentrated on figures, and particularly on putting motion and movement into his figures. In the quantitative analysis all of the dimensions relative to figural depiction are accelerated even in relation to his talented peers. Joel developed a consistent use of three-quarter and mixed three-quarter orientations by 7 and 8 years of age. The higher proportion of drawings showing all three types of figure orientations, also indicated his great flexibility in figure rotation. As examination of the presented drawings demonstrates, there was almost always more than one figure in Joel's drawings and each figure was in a different orientation. He also abruptly began using foreshortening and modeling in most of his drawings by 7 and 8 years of age and shade and shadow in a little less than half. This marked increase in foreshortening has already been discussed in relation to Joel's use of a visual image. Overall, Joel makes more consistent use of all the perspective indicators and shows acceleration in their development relative to his talented peers.

A final developmental aspect is the emergence of style in a young artist's work. As children and young adults, some of this centuries great artists were able to imitate a variety of artistic styles demonstrating their flexibility and mastery over form. Pariser (1991) noted that both Picasso and Lautrec imitated and assimilated the styles of the great artists they studied. Even adult artists often experiment with many different styles and continually evolve new styles as they mature (e.g., Richardson, 1991; Temkin, 1987). Joel did not appear to attempt imitation of other artistic styles, but he did evolve several unique styles quite early and although there is evidence of change in his style, the drawings presented here also testify to its continuity. In the most recent interview, Joel commented on his style.

> I have had different styles from time to time. I would consciously go into a cartoon style ... and I would draw things as realistically as I could. Now I paint pretty ... I don't know what the word is ... not in an expressionistic sort of way. ... Very interior psychological paintings that have no figures in them ... just furniture and things. I also do cartoon work. I draw from life. All the styles I've ever had are still with me, it's just a question if they are relevant to something I'm thinking about.

RECENT DEVELOPMENTS

While in college, Joel turned increasingly toward painting. After graduation, he continued to paint and over the 2-year period of 1991 and 1992 produced a number of very intriguing mixed medium pieces. Two bodies of work engaged Joel at that time. One was a series about chairs in which he explored the theme of the empty chair. The theme was inspired by his thoughts about an audience for his paintings; who are they and why would they want to look at his paintings? During this period Joel was also ruminating about his future and in particular trying to decide whether or not he would paint for the galleries. He decided against such a direction. The chairs also carried with them the symbolism of the theater, an aspect of Joel's high school and college life that he very much enjoyed. Chairs, he said recently, are the basic prop of a theater set as well as symbolic of its audience. The second body of work revolved around his interest in cartooning and using paintings as a vehicle for a storyboard. In this series of paintings animal themes were prominent, appearing in small inset squares that unfold a story as would a cartoon panel. Joel notes that when he invented this device his teachers did not approve and attempted to discourage it. The two genres of work are united by the appearance of human hands and fingers, which play a part in some of both types of paintings. Several paintings from these genres are described here.

"Green Chair" is part of the chair series begun in 1991. It is an acrylic on masonite and measures 24 × 24 inches. This is an abstract painting and although some figurative elements can be read, Joel appeared more concerned with working the surface of the painting. He uses a layering technique in which paint and a jelled medium might be mixed and applied with a pallet knife. A larger chair painted in white is on the left and two smaller chairs, one in red and one in white and browns are on the right. The chairs are empty and face the viewer at a diagonal. Dominating the center of the painting is the suggestion of a rectangle made by building up and texturing the paint. In its center is an inverted fan shape in red. Joel worked many colors into the surface of this painting, browns that move toward green, bright blue and red, white and dark browns to black. When I commented that the color scheme and feel appeared inspired by Gustav Klimt, Joel agreed that it had that appearance.

"Rocket Chair" is also part of the series about chairs but done later, in 1992, during a week at his mothers. The painting measures 30×16 inches and is a highly abstract acrylic collage painting. Its scale is intentionally distorted so that the viewer is seeing in the foreground, at close range, the ski or curved part of an old rocking chair in his mother's home painted in a green tinged white and orange. It is overlapped with torn paper on which the painting continues, and which creates the three-dimensional effect of being draped over the rocker. A domed building painted in white occupies the upper right quadrant. It is seen as if through a veil or film of orange to smoky green giving the effect of a parted curtain of a window through which one sees the building. Joel took the building from a photograph in his mother's home. The negative space in the painting is either a dark black which reads as outside the putative window or an orange to green with dark hues for the inside. Joel also uses a layering technique to build up the paint but the surface is less worked in this painting.

"Fireside Chat" belongs to the second genre of painting and was done in 1992. It measures 30×20 inches and is a water color lithograph on paper. Joel did several versions of this painting. It has a shamanistic theme, perhaps a death ceremony Joel suggests. It appears more figurative than the works in acrylic and there are many levels to this painting. Two hands are interlaced. One rising vertically in the center of the painting is colored a brown green with blue lines that define a face and vein type structure. The second hand is largely two fingers in black and brown tones and comes in horizontally from the lower right side of the painting. It overlaps the vertical hand but remains transparent so that the vertical hand shows through as continuous. Behind the hands on the left and above are what appear to be a vertical fencepost and three horizontal fenceposts. In reality these are a continuous series of inset squares that Joel uses as a storytelling format. The ones above are inset as diamonds rather than aligned as squares. The insets contain birds and people dancing. On the vertical storyboard is a larger cartooned bird head or skull with open beak. Again Joel uses a layering technique to build up the color but the theme and story appear as more important than the surface of the painting.

Although these paintings were done 1 to 2 years ago, Joel remains interested in painting. He would like to have more time to paint and perhaps attend the Chicago Art Institute, where one of his college teachers went. Economic realities, however, have forced him to assume a "day job" that leaves little time for serious concentration. He also has been sharing a home with several other people his age, making it difficult to find the proper space. Right now he is in the process of moving to a more private situation. He has continued to draw almost every day. Primarily working on cartoon storyboards that appear to give vent to some of the frustrations Joel experiences regarding political and social aspects of U.S. life. A new gallery of characters have made their appearance but like much of what Joel has done in the past, the germ for these new characters and themes is evident in his earlier forms.

ACKNOWLEDGMENTS

This chapter was based on a talk given as part of a symposium chaired by Delmont Morrison on "The Roots of Creativity: Childhood Imagination and Cognition," given at the annual meeting of the American Psychological Association, Toronto, Canada, August 1993. I also acknowledge the important contributions of Tom Houston, who took the photographs and Ana Caminos, who collaborated on analysis of drawings for the studies presented in this chapter.

REFERENCES

Albert, R. S., & Runco, M. A. (1986). The achievement of eminence: A model based on a longitudinal study of exceptionally gifted boys and their families. In R. J. Sternberg & J. E. Davidson (Eds.), *Conceptions of giftedness* (pp. 332–360). New York: Cambridge University Press.

Arnheim, R. (1964). *Art and visual perception.* Berkeley: University of California Press.

Bamberger, J. (1982). Growing up prodigies: The midlife crisis. In D. H. Feldman (Ed.), *Developmental approaches to giftedness and creativity* (pp. 61–78). San Francisco: Jossey-Bass.

Chi, M. T. H. (1978). Knowledge structures and memory development. In R.S. Siegler (Ed.), *Children's thinking: What develops?* (pp. 73–96). Hillsdale, NJ: Lawrence Erlbaum Associates.

Csikszentmihalyi, M., Rathunde, K., & Whalen, S. (1993). *Talented teenagers: The roots of success and failure.* New York: Cambridge University Press.

Csikszentmihalyi, M., & Robinson, R. E. (1986). Culture, time and the development of talent. In R. J. Sternberg & J. E. Davidson (Eds.), *Conceptions of giftedness* (pp. 264–284). New York: Cambridge University Press.

Cupchik, G.C., & Winston, A.S. (in press). Confluence and divergence in empirical aesthetics, philosophy, and mainstream psychology. In E.C. Carterette & M.P. Friedman (Eds.), *Handbook of perception & cognition, Vol. 16, Perceptual ecology.* San Diego, CA: Academic Press.

Feldman, D. H. (1980). *Beyond universal in cognitive development.* Norwood, NJ: Ablex.

Feldman, D. H., & Benjamin, A. (1986). Giftedness as a developmentalist sees it. In R. J. Sternberg & J. E. Davidson (Eds.), *Conceptions of giftedness* (pp. 285–305). New York: Cambridge University Press.

Feldman, D. H., & Goldsmith, L. (1986). *Nature's gambit.* New York: Basic Books.

Flavell, J. (1986). *Cognitive development* (2nd ed.). Englewood, NJ: Prentice-Hall.

Freeman, N. H. (1980). *Strategies of representation in young children.* London: Academic Press.

Frith, U. (1980). *Cognitive processes in spelling.* New York: Academic Press.

Gardner, H. (1980). *Artful scribbles: The significance of children's drawings.* New York: Basic Books.

Gardner, H. (1982). *Art mind and brain: A cognitive approach to creativity.* New York: Basic Books.

Gebotys, R.J., & Cupchik, G.C. (1989). Perception and production in children's art. *Visual Arts Research, 15,* 55–67.

Geschwind, N. (1984). The biology of cerebral dominance: Implications for cognition. *Cognition, 17,* 193–208.

Getzels, J. (1979). From art student to fine artist: Potential problem finding and performance. In A.H. Passow (Ed.), *The gifted and the talented: Their education and development* (pp. 372–387). Chicago: University of Chicago Press.

Getzels, J. W., & Csikszentmihalyi, M. (1976). *The creative vision: A longitudinal study of problem finding in art.* New York: Wiley.

Getzels J. W., & Jackson, P. W. (1962). *Creativity and intelligence: Explorations with gifted students.* New York: Wiley.

Goldsmith L., & Feldman, D. (1989). Wang Yani: Gifts well given. In W. C. Ho (Ed.), *Wang Yani: The brush of innocence* (pp. 59–62). New York: Hudson Hills Press.

Golomb, C. (1992). *The creation of a pictorial world.* Berkeley: University of California Press.

Goodenough F. (1926). *Measurement of intelligence in drawings.* New York: World.

Guilford, J. P. (1967). *The nature of human intelligence.* New York: McGraw-Hill.

Hermelin B., & O'Conner, N. (1986). Spatial representation in mathematically and in artistically gifted children. *British Journal of Educational Psychology, 56,* 150–157.

Jordan, L. A. (1975). Use of canonical analysis in Cropley's "A five-year longitudinal study of the validity of creativity tests." *Developmental Psychology, 11*(1), 1–3.

Inhelder, B., & Piaget, J. (1964). *The early growth of logic in the child.* New York: Basic Books.

Ives, W., & Rovet, J. (1979). The role of graphic orientations in children's drawings of familiar and novel objects at rest and in motion. *Merril-Palmer Quarterly, 24*(4), 281–292.

Langer, S. (1953). *Feeling and form: A theory of art.* New York: Scribner.

Lark-Horovitz, B., Lewis, H., & Luca, M. (1973). *Understanding children's art for better teaching.* Columbus, OH: Charles F. Merrill.

Lark-Horovitz, B., & Norton, J. (1959). Children's art abilities: developmental trends of art characteristics. *Child Development, 30,* 433–452.

Luquet, G. H. (1935). *Le dessin enfantin* [Children's drawings]. Paris: Alcan.

Marland, S.P. (1972). *Education of the gifted and talented: Report to the Congress of the United States by the U.S. Commissioner of Education.* Washington, DC: U.S. Government Printing Office.

Milbrath, C. (1987). Spatial representations of artistically gifted children: A case of universal or domain specific development? *Genetic Epistomologist, 15,* 3–4.

Milbrath, C. (in preparation). *Patterns of artistic development.* New York: Cambridge University Press.

Munro, T., Lark-Horovitz, B., & Barnhart, E.N. (1942). Children's art abilities: Studies at the Cleveland Museum of Art. *Journal of Experimental Education, 11*(2), 97–155.

O'Conner, N., & Hermelin, B. (1983). The role of general and specific talents in information processing. *British Journal of Developmental Psychology, 1,* 389–403.

Pariser, D. (1991). Normal and unusual aspects of juvenile artistic development in Klee, Lautrec, and Picasso. *Creativity Research Journal, 4*(1), 51–65.

Phillips, I. (1987). *Word recognition and spelling strategies in good and poor readers.* Unpublished doctoral dissertation, Harvard Graduate School of Education, Cambridge, MA.

Piaget, J. (1932). *The moral judgment of the child.* London: Routledge & Kegan Paul.

Piaget, J. (1981). *Intelligence and affectivity: Their relationship during child development* (T.A. Brown & C. E. Kaegi, Eds. and Trans.). Palo Alto, CA: Annual Reviews.

Piaget, J., & Inhelder, B. (1971). *Mental imagery in the child.* New York: Basic Books.

Posner, M. I. (1978). *Chronometric explorations of mind.* New York: Oxford University Press.

Read, H. (1963). *A concise history of modern painting.* New York: Praeger.

Renzulli, J. S. (1986). The three-ring conception of giftedness: A developmental model for creative productivity. In R. J. Sternberg & J. E. Davidson (Eds.), *Conceptions of giftedness* (pp. 53–92). New York: Cambridge University Press.

Richardson, J. (1991). *A life of Picasso.* New York: Random House.

Robinson, H. B. (1977). Current myths concerning gifted children. *Gifted and talented brief no. 5* (pp.1–11). Ventura, CA: National/State Leadership Training Institute.

Rosenblatt E., & Winner, E. (1988). Is superior visual memory a component of superior drawing ability? In L. Ober & D. Fein (Eds.), *The exceptional brain: Neuropsychology of talent and superior abilities* (pp. 341–363). New York: Guilford.

Sternberg, R. (1986). A triarchic theory of intellectual giftedness. In R. J. Sternberg & J. E. Davidson (Eds.), *Conceptions of giftedness* (pp. 223–246). New York: Cambridge University Press.

Stroop, J.R. (1935). Studies of interference in serial verbal reactions. *Journal of Experimental Psychology, 19,* 643–662.

Tannenbaum, A. J. (1986). Giftedness: A psychosocial approach. In R. J. Sternberg & J. E. Davidson (Eds.), *Conceptions of giftedness* (pp. 21–52). New York: Cambridge University Press.

Temkin, A. (1987). Klee and avant-garde 1912–1940. In C. Lanchner (Ed.), *Paul Klee* (pp. 13–37). New York: Museum of Modern Art.

Terman, L. M. (1924). *Genetic studies of genius: The gifted group at mid-life.* Stanford, CA: Stanford University Press.

Thomas, G.V., & Silk, A. M. J. (1990). *An introduction to the psychology of children's drawings.* New York: New York University Press.

Torrance, E. (1970). *Encouraging creativity in the classroom.* Dubuque, IA: Brown.

Turiel, E. (1969). Developmental processes in the child's moral thinking. In P. Mussen, J. Langer, & M. Covington (Eds.), *Trends and issues in developmental psychology* (pp. 92–133). New York: Holt.

Vasari, G. (1979). *Artists of the Renaissance* (G. Bull, Trans.). New York: Viking.

Winner, E. (1982) *Invented worlds. The psychology of the arts.* Cambridge, MA: Harvard University Press.

Winner, E., & Martino, G. (1993). Giftedness in the visual arts and music. In K. Heller, F. Monks, & A.H. Passow (Eds.), *International handbook of research and development of giftedness and talent* (pp. 253–281). Elmsford, NY: Pergamon.

Winner, E., Casey, M. B., Da Silva, D., & Hayes, R. (1991). Spatial abilities and reading deficits in visual arts students. *Empirical Studies of the Arts, 9,* 51–63.

5

It Was an Incredible Experience: The Impact of Educational Opportunities on a Talented Student's Art Development

Enid Zimmerman
Indiana University

There have been a number of recent case studies about work of talented young artists who evidenced precocious abilities in visual arts (Gardner, 1980; Goldsmith, 1992; Golomb, 1992a, 1992b; Wilson & Wilson, 1980; Zimmerman, 1992b). All of these studies emphasized spontaneous artwork done by precocious youngsters from their early childhood through their adolescence or emphasized separate time periods during the development of these young artists. Only a few case studies have highlighted schooling and effects of differential programming opportunities and options on the development of art talent (Clark & Zimmerman, 1987; Nelson & Janzen, 1990). It is an underlying assumption of this case study that early formal educational opportunities in art can enhance and accelerate, rather than inhibit, the art development of talented young artists.

In *Artful Scribbles*, Gardner (1980) presented a case study of spontaneous drawings of a 16-year-old artistically talented adolescent, Gabriel Foreman, who was able to discuss drawings he did over a 12-year period and relate the experiences that lay behind their creation, techniques he used, reactions to his work by others at the time they were created, and current critiques of his past and present art work. This talented young artist grew up in an environment that was very supportive of the arts. Both his parents are painters who exhibit their work and earn their livings as graphic artists. Gabriel was recognized at an early age for his graphic skills and Gardner reported that he passed through traditional stages of art development at an accelerated pace. Gabriel was influenced by popular culture, copied artists' and cartoonists' works with great accuracy, and had many interests other than creating visual art. Gardner discussed Gabriel's cautious reaction to formal art lessons and stated that he preferred to "feel out his artistic destiny on his own" because many of his teachers were "of indifferent quality and may have discouraged rather than enlightened him" (p. 245). An informal art education was gained at home, however, under the tutelage of his parents. Going to museums and being immersed in the world of art was not of primary concern to Gabriel. Although Gardner did not find formal art instruction to have much impact on Gabriel's art development, he concluded that a person needs more than a supportive environment to be successful in art; he or she needs "tenacity, willingness to overcome obstacles, [and] the desire to succeed" (p. 251).

Robertson (1987) reported a case study of her son Bruce's spontaneous drawings from ages 6 to 16. In this study, she intimated that formal art instruction, rather than supporting Bruce's art development, might have been an inhibiting factor. As an art teacher and researcher, she was in a unique position to observe and have conversations with her son about how and why he created his drawings. This case study was focused on his graphic images that emerged at puberty in the form of human figures drawn in a cartoonlike style. This form of expression met Bruce's need to express central themes of importance to him such as power, violence, family, and teenage subculture including sex, drugs, and rock and roll. His drawing sources included rendering scenes from memory and borrowing images, styles, or techniques that resulted in graphic problem solving, restructuring images, and metaphoric thinking. Continuity of drawing practice, motivation to sustain such practice, personality characteristics, and environmental and family support were credited as factors that influenced Bruce to continue drawing into his adolescent years. "Although aesthetic quality of fine arts models" (p. 44) may be valued by art educators, Robertson warned that teaching techniques without engaging ado-lescents in meaningful expression through popular culture may result in "mediocre and trivial art work" (p. 44).

In case studies reported by Goldsmith (1992) and Golomb (1992a, 1992b), formal art lessons or directed art experiences were viewed by a parent and a teacher as inhibiting the visual art development of artistically gifted and talented students and corroborate findings by Gardner (1980) and Robertson (1987). Goldsmith discussed style development in the work of Wang Yani, a Chinese painting prodigy, from the time she was 3 to 8 years old and from the time she was 8 to 12 years old. Wang Yani's early work was characterized as unique, spontaneous, and playful. Her later works were less individualistic and more focused on formal relationships between elements and principles of design. Yani was greatly influenced in her art development by her father, a painter, who acted as her guide and mentor. His stated position was that Yani should have no formal art lessons, either privately or in school, but he appears to have guided her development to a significant degree. He encouraged her budding art talent and gave her free reign of his art studio to experiment and paint. At the time Goldsmith studied Yani's stylistic development, Yani had yet to integrate her more formal development and acquired technical skills with her evolving, more mature, thoughts and feelings.

In *The Child's Conception of a Pictorial World*, Golomb (1992a) described three case studies of Israeli children who she considered gifted child artists. Golomb contended that these students, who exhibited high abilities in the visual arts, had "guided their own graphic development" (p. 252). Golomb's sources of data were interviews with the students when they were in late adolescence, longitudinal studies of the students' drawings from early childhood to young adulthood, and interviews with parents and a teacher. The art teacher of two of the children, Malka Haas, condemned what she referred to as mindless copying and felt that directive instruction hindered normal art development and individual expression. Haas also believed that the purpose of teaching art was to help students have healthy personalities and be well adjusted, and that their development in the visual arts would proceed best without directive instruction until they were young adults.

In the book, *Developing Talent in Young People*, Bloom (1985) and his associates reported case studies of talented individuals, who before the age of 35, had reached extremely high levels of accomplishment in their respective fields. In one case study in this book, Sloane and Sosniak (1985) studied 20 sculptors and concluded that the absence of formal art education before college did not appear to have a negative effect on their art development and eventual success as practicing artists. These sculptors' program opportunities during their elementary school years included a variety of out-of-school options. One educational option conspicuously absent, however, was regularly scheduled art classes. Sloane and Sosniak speculated that this absence of out-of-school art classes had to do with lack of availability, because private art instruction was not easily accessible. All the sculptors remembered their elementary schools' art classes as noninstructional and without any direct relationship to the world of art and artists. Those who recalled secondary classes remembered that art was not considered an academic subject and that their art teachers were not artists and treated art making only as "crafts."

Wilson and Wilson (1980) studied the graphic art work of a 15-year-old, John Scott, and his ability to construct symbols through graphic narratives that took the form of a 10-part epic saga. They credit John's teacher with encouraging and nurturing his talents by stressing the value of popular, narrative models rather than only emphasizing fine art models of instruction. John's art work was derived from graphic images found in comic books. Borrowing, combining, and extending these images allowed John to master processes he used in creating his own visual narratives. Wilson and Wilson contended that young people who have mastered cultural conventions are most inventive and able to generate new graphic discoveries when working on their own graphic images. They concluded that "the act of generating visual images and the process of recording them graphically deserves more attention than art teachers give it" (p. 24). The visual narrative, for some students, is recommended as a way to build insights about themselves, what is important to them, and how they can understand the world in which they live.

Few researchers have studied the positive effects of accelerated or enriched art learning experiences on a student with high abilities in the visual arts or advocated these types of experiences after studying a student who possessed art ability and talent. Nelson and Janzen (1990) used case study methodology to study "Diane" and the positive effects of art education opportunities that were offered to her. Diane was described as having personality characteristics associated with students with high abilities in the visual arts, such as creativity, independence, nonconformity, tenacity, love of solitude, and low tolerance for boredom. Her elementary art classes were predominately cut-and-paste activities and Diane's reaction was to be bored. Important factors that the researchers believed helped Diane succeed in her rural environment was appropriate, formal educational options offered by mentors in her junior high school art program and encouragement by the school psychologist and gifted-and-talented coordinator. Other factors were the teaching she received in college, strong family support, and her own personality, that was described as stubborn with integrity and having a spirit of independence.

Although they had parents who were talented in art and encouraged their early art interests, formal art education did not play a significant role in Gabriel Foremen's (Gardner, 1980), Bruce Robertson's (Robertson, 1987), or Wang Yani's (Goldsmith, 1992) art development. The students in Wilson and Wilson's (1980) and Golomb's (1992a) studies had teachers in their schools who encouraged their art talents. Diane (Nelson & Janzen, 1990) profited from a variety of enriched and accelerated formal art education experiences, although she did not have parents with art interests or abilities or school art teachers who supported her art development. In the case study that follows, I describe my son Eric Zimmerman's [1] early art experiences that began in elementary school, continued through high school, and ultimately influenced his later interests and abilities in studying art at the university level. For Eric, like Diane, formal art education experiences, through accelerated and enriched educational opportunities, played a major part in his art development. Unlike Diane and similar to the young people in Gardner's (1980), Robertson's (1987), and Goldsmith's (1992) case studies, Eric's parents had interests and abilities in the visual arts and nutured his talents in this area. In addition, like the students in Wilson and Wilson's (1986) and Golomb's (1992a) studies, Eric had encouragement and support from a number of his school teachers in developing his art talents.

In this case study, I discuss Eric's spontaneous art work, created from ages 3 to high school, in respect to perceptual qualities such as expression and skill with media and conceptual qualities including themes, puns, paradoxes, and metaphors. I also consider the impact of accelerated and enriched art experiences on Eric's development, from elementary through high school, through accounts of his

---

[1]In 1992, I published an article about factors influencing the graphic development of my son, Eric Zimmerman, through retrospective accounts and reactions to his spontaneous artwork created from preschool until he was in Grade 10. I found that family background and preferred subject matter contributed, to a great extent, to the form and content of Eric's graphic representations. His desire to master skills, including copying and borrowing of images from a variety of sources, and personal dispositional factors all found expression in his drawings. Some of Eric's accelerated and enriched educational opportunities were described previously (Clark & Zimmerman, 1987). In that article we suggested that just as alternatives in educational planning to accelerate the education of mathematically precocious youth were successful (Stanley, 1977) so might enriched and accelerated education opportunitites for artistically talented students be of value.

reactions to his art work created in situations of formal art instruction produced for and in specific schooling contexts. The sources for this study included audiotapes of more than 15 hours of conversation between Eric and me that took place in 1989, 1990, and 1991 and over 350 artworks including paintings, drawings, ceramics, sculptures, games, and school projects; slides and photographs of art works, school notebooks, and written classwork.

Content analysis was used to discover themes and their meanings and comparative analysis was used to interrelate themes through Eric's discussion and reactions to his art works. Gordon (1978) described this research process as steps in which the researcher listens and reads collected data critically, tries to discover the meaning in the data, looks for significant relationships, synthesizes, and arrives at conclusions based on the data. A case study approach to the data was emphasized in which implications will be drawn from themes that emerge from the data. In their studies related to the development of artistically talented young children, a number of researchers used personal reminiscences, autobiographical statements from which they gleaned valuable insights about art development (Beck 1928; Bloom, 1985; Chetelat, 1982; Gardner, 1980; Pariser, 1985; Robertson, 1987; Wilson, 1976; Wilson & Wilson, 1980). I hypothesized that graphic development may be best understood by interviewing artistically talented young adults who are old enough to be insightful when discussing their past art work, yet are not adult artists several steps removed from their childhood creations (Zimmerman, 1992b).

FAMILY BACKGROUND AND THE CULTURE OF SCHOOLING

Eric's biological father and I both were artistically talented as children and adults. His father died when Eric was 5 years old. I was identified as an academically and artistically gifted-and-talented student and attended Music and Art High School in New York City. I majored in fine arts in college and completed a master of fine arts degree, after which as an art specialist, I taught art in elementary schools in New York City for a decade. I completed my doctorate in art education at Indiana University in 1979 and have been teaching at this same institution ever since. I met my present husband, Gilbert Clark, when Eric was 7 years old. We both teach in the Art Education Program, in the School of Education, at Indiana University.

Eric is the youngest of two children, his sister is 3 years his senior. She writes poetry, is interested in crafts, and presently is studying to be an elementary school teacher. From the earliest age, Eric has been exposed to his parents creating art, talking about art, and discussing art education theory and practice, often with a focus on artistically talented students. With his family, Eric was a frequent visitor to art museums. Dinner conversations often involved discussions about art, prompting Eric at one time to beg us not to mention Art Nouveau or the National Art Education Association one more time. In Eric's early years, there was much art-making activity at home. I painted and created soft sculptures and, influenced by his background as a landscape architect, Gil sketched and took photographs of wild flowers. We both exhibited our work locally, but as we became more involved in writing professionally our art production activities diminished. At home, Eric's artwork received much encouragement and criticism that he always welcomed with enthusiasm and often demanded on his own. Being art educators, we were aware of his "burning desire" to create art and were able to help him make decisions about what educational opportunities might help him develop his art interests and abilities. Given Eric's initiative and desire to study art, I was able, both financially and through my own interest in art education, to provide instructional contexts in which his talents could flourish.

Eric's first encounter with special art classes was in the fourth grade when he attended a class for students with high interests and abilities in the visual arts. After a few months, he stopped attending this class because he did not want to miss his regular class, which he found more interesting and challenging.

Eric's introductory extra-school opportunity in art was to attend the Indiana University Summer Arts Institute, a residential program for students entering Grades 7 through 10 who were identified as gifted and talented in the visual arts. Eric began attending this program the summer before he entered the sixth grade and continued for 5 years until the summer before he was a sophomore in high school. His stepfather and I were directors of this Institute and Eric's attendance not only aided him in his art education, but also provided a place for Eric to study while we were engaged in coordinating this program. Principle goals set for the Institute were to extend knowledge, skills, and understandings about all aspects of the visual arts and provide opportunities for students to interact with others with similar and differing backgrounds, interests, and abilities as well as with professionals in the arts. At the Institute, emphasis was on studio arts and enrichment in other art disciplines. When Eric attended the Institute, he enrolled in classes that emphasized developing skills and expression in drawing and painting, photography, computer graphics, visual narrative illustration, dance, and mime.

In the sixth and seventh grades, Eric also attended evening art classes for adults held at Indiana University. In these evening classes, he learned about drawing the human figure and how to handle a variety of media such as conté crayon, charcoal, and pastels. The summer before his junior year, Eric attended a college-credit painting course for high school seniors at Indiana University. During his junior year, he took advanced drawing and painting classes in his high school where he excelled and was rewarded by winning several local and state art competitions. Eric was academically advanced and attended accelerated classes in subjects such as calculus and advanced physics that were taught at his high school. Eric's interest in the arts also included music. He was active in his high school's music program and was selected to play in an all-state orchestra and performed regularly as a member of a Baroque recorder quartet.

The summer before his senior year, Eric received a scholarship to study at the Interlochen Center for the Arts summer camp in Michigan. At this camp, Eric pursued his interest in music and the visual arts; he played a variety of recorders in a Baroque music ensemble and took art classes stressing several different media. In his senior year in high school, Eric attended fine arts classes at Indiana University in the afternoons in painting, drawing, and ceramics, and attended high school courses in the mornings. When he was a senior in high school, Eric was awarded state and national gold keys in the Scholastic art competition. At the same time, he was selected as one of several state-level science fair winners for his research about perception and organization of colors.

The summer before college, Eric, once again attended the Interlochen summer art camp on a scholarship. He then attended the University of Pennsylvania (Penn) and received a bachelor of fine arts degree. In his junior and senior years, he was awarded a teaching assistantship and taught color theory to graduate and undergraduate students in the Fine Arts Department at Penn. At Penn, he was officially a painting major, but by the time he graduated he had studied many media and art forms including sculpture, printmaking, drawing, photography, filmmaking, fiction writing, performance art, and multimedia installations. Eric's diverse interests in the arts were rewarded when he received a Rose Award for a performance art script he wrote. After graduation, Eric was an employee of The Painted Bride Art Center, a performance space and gallery in Philadelphia. At present, Eric is 24 years old and attends the Ohio State University where he is a graduate student in a special program at the Advanced Computer Center for Arts and Design. He also writes role-playing game scenarios for a small game company.

ERIC'S ASSESSMENT OF INFLUENCE OF TEACHERS

Eric's teachers in elementary and secondary school as well as teachers in his other art program options influenced him and his art making in both positive and negative ways. Eric remembers fondly working with his stepfather and creating posters, books, and other school-related projects. Looking at a poster he made in the fourth grade about whales, he remembered that Gil helped him make letters and whales that looked three dimensional.

Reminiscing about a game he created in the fifth grade, he recalled how his science teacher really liked the game. In elementary school, he felt he was in an environment that supported his interests, especially expressing ideas and concepts visually. His teachers had senses of humor and appreciated his humorous individual responses to situations. He did not comment about his elementary and junior high school art teachers except in respect to specific assignments and how he completed them. These teachers did not appear to make any deep impressions in terms of his studying art, nor did teachers he studied with at the IU Summer Arts Institute.

He did not have art courses during his first 2 years of high school. During his junior year, he enrolled in an advanced drawing class, but his art teacher was not viewed as creating a positive experience. Eric remembered that his teacher was not at all creative in the type of assignments he gave to students and was not supportive in giving advice or encouraging students in their work. This teacher would sit in his office and did not care if students were engaged in art work. Eric considered him "an unintelligent, poor teacher." The other students in this class were not involved or interested in doing art work and usually "goofed off." When some assignments were structured, although results might be attractive, none of the students knew the purpose of the assignments. Usually when Eric showed the art teacher his work, the teacher didn't have anything to say or offer any suggestions or criticisms for improvement. Eric often demonstrated individual initiative working on projects of his own design. Eric remembered asking this teacher what to put in the background of one of his paintings. This art teacher replied, in a sarcastic tone, "why don't you put inverting sausages and clocks behind them, that's what Dali does." This response demonstrated, for Eric, the teacher's ignorance and lack of strategies for critiquing students' works.

His teacher at the College Credit for High School Students Program did influence him a great deal. At this college credit program, Eric had what he referred to as his first "big breakthrough." Eric related this incident with the same fervor as if it happened the day before and not 6 years before. At this time he felt he was struggling to reach some goal, and this struggle was accompanied by:

> a real kind of frustration. I knew something was out there but I didn't know what it was. I was extremely dissatisfied. Then I was working on a drawing of a model and she corrected it, ruining it by drawing on it with a palette knife ... I was furious, she had violated my drawing ... I started painting just to spite her, exaggerating what she suggested by making the drawing more geometric with places for the hips and shoulders. Suddenly an intense feeling unfolded out of me. It was an incredible experience. I felt like my hand was moving and my eye and my whole body was involved in my art work in a way I had never known before ... I remember thinking that if I became an artist it will be because of this experience.

This art teacher also was remembered as taking her art class to the University's art museum and having all the students critique, with the teacher's guidance, art works in the museum. Eric liked this approach because it helped him see that creating art required intelligence and how Picasso's art work was "intelligent in a visual way." Before this experience, Eric was not aware that art making entailed planning, working through problems, and finding solutions, all of which require cognitive ability as well as technical facility. After having this incredible breakthrough experience during the summer at the college-credit program, he felt returning to high school art classes would be entering the art teacher's "cave of cliches."

Unlike his high school art teacher, an English teacher encouraged an intellectual and creative approach to learning in which visual as well as verbal responses to assignments were encouraged. This is evident in a visual narrative, without words, Eric did of Scene III from Shakespeare's *MacBeth* in response to one of his English assignments. In this assignment Eric was able, in a limited number of frames, to capture the essence of this scene using his technical skills and cognitive abilities. This English teacher was viewed as a "great teacher who taught him how to write and read critically." Her class was one of the best classes Eric had in high school, but he admitted he did not realize how valuable this class was until he attended college and was required to critique his art work publicly and in written form.

In his senior year, when he was able to study half a day in the Fine Arts Department at Indiana University as part of Indiana's gifted-and-talented student waiver option, he found most of his teachers to be more knowledgeable and inspiring than his high school art teacher. He reported that he did not have any trouble fitting into the class, either socially or intellectually. In fact, he stated, "I never felt over my head." One teacher, who was a fine arts faculty member, was remembered as being an outstanding mentor. This teacher challenged students to think about space in sophisticated ways and encouraged them to find their own directions. He pushed students from being purely perceptual to thinking about what they were doing and why. According to Eric, this teacher would say, "'don't use such loose marks. Think about where you are going and the form and light you're making. Don't be so random in your work.' Then I would tighten up and he said, 'don't lose your freshness and freeness.' I would say, 'yesterday you told me not to be so free.' He replied, 'well, I see you do one thing, one day, and I think one thing. Then on another day I think another.'" This teacher helped Eric see that there are no absolute right solutions to art problems and that criticism always is subject to interpretation. As these comments suggest, Eric was eager for instruction and open to the assistance teachers could provide. Although intolerant of teachers he did not respect, he admired those who had technical competence and were able to communicate with their students and carry on a critical dialogue with them about their artwork.

SCHOOL PROJECTS

Eric's elementary school served many graduate students' children because the school district included a number of large dormitories that housed married students and their families. This elementary school had been a university laboratory demonstration school until two decades before when, due to political and monetary constraints, this designation ended. At the time Eric attended elementary school, innovative teaching strategies and individualized curricula models dominated the educational policies of this school, a legacy of its laboratory school designation. Teaching was theme oriented and students' individual projects usually were related to specific themes. Student projects were displayed publicly, especially at the end of each school year when a schoolwide "learning festival" became the culminating activity for most classes.

In kindergarten, Eric did a visual narrative of the life cycle of a caterpillar that eventually burst forth as a butterfly. He also did a detailed drawing of a crossing guard directing traffic for a safety poster assignment. Beginning at the first grade, Eric incorporated the idea of combat into his artwork whenever he could. This inclusion of battle scenes with monsters also can be seen in his spontaneous art work beginning at the same age. For dental health month, he created a humorous drawing, "that's really a visual narrative battle of good guys and bad guys" that included plaque bullets, a plaque person being lassoed by floss, toothpaste squirting the plaque and destroying it, a wanted poster for the plaque, and an image of plaque sitting on a tooth that is brown and decayed.

FIG. 5.1. Crayon drawing of whales (Grade 3).

A theme about whales dominated both his third-grade spontaneous artwork done at home and his school-oriented artwork (Fig. 5.1). Two whale posters about the theme "save the whales," indicated Eric's knowledge of whale anatomy and other physical features of whales. Eric was drawing whales for several months at home and knew how to draw their tails so that they looked three dimensional. His stepfather helped him with lettering for these posters and even though Eric wanted him to draw the letters, he always made Eric draw them himself. Other themes, done at the same time, were a winter collage in which Eric created a detailed image of a cardinal he often observed in his backyard and a drawing of a corner of his room based on a movie about a boy who did not have a room of his own. Eric's own image of a corner of an imaginary room contained a tree with furniture made of boxes and crates, a cat, a hamster, a squirrel, and snakes all twisting and turning in front and behind tree limbs (Fig. 5.2).

At his elementary school, many options were given for students to meet the requirements for book reports. Eric often chose to do visual interpretations rather than written book reports. Eric reminisced about reading many books in elementary school and making detailed illustrations of scenes from these books. He often made drawings that he termed his own "tongue-in-cheek" interpretations of original plot lines of the stories. In the fourth grade, for each of five books in a series, he made cutouts that illustrated a scene from each book. Eric had to make the same characters in each scene and have them age from one scene to the other. The characters drawn in colored pencils and black ink, were rendered realistically with much attention to detail. The books were fantasy tales and his book report was, according to Eric, "a filmic kind of thing, a kind of epic, in scope" (Fig. 5.3).

FIG. 5.2. Corner of an imaginary room (Grade 3).

FIG. 5.3. Cut out illustrations for scenes from a book series (Grade 4).

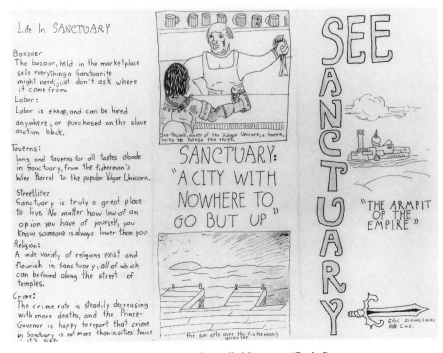

FIG. 5.4. Illustrated book report about a place called Sanctuary (Grade 5).

Eric had many opportunities to use his imagination in response to book report requirements. A book report, made in the fifth grade, about a place called Sanctuary; took the form of a travel brochure that advertised life in a fantasy kingdom. Illustrations included a bazaar held in the marketplace, taverns, street life, religion, and crime. Written materials about the history of Sanctuary and a map also were included as part of the brochure (Fig. 5.4). In the sixth grade, a poster was Eric's preferred form for reporting about a book, *The Monster of Loch Ness*. These book reports are evidence of Eric's interest in visual narratives and his ability to plan an assignment, organize many different elements, employ humor and puns, and create an organized, attractive product that is informative and engaging.

In the fifth grade, students had to write and illustrate their own stories. Eric wanted to be original. He had been exposed to a collection of illustrated children's books at home and was aware of many options available to him. Eric remembered that other students' ideas for illustrated stories appeared "naive" to him. For this assignment Eric created a "balancing book" of the ABCs that included, for each letter of the alphabet, different things that began with an appropriate first letter. For example, there is a zig-zag line on a zipper, zipping up a zebra, flying on a zooming zoo, and so on. Eric remembered the surreal quality and humor found in images in the book he created, such as a zebra, cut in half, being zipped up.

For a fourth-grade social studies project, Eric created a very detailed "Black History Time Line." He was influenced by a dinosaur timeline in one of his children's books. This interest in timelines parallels his interest in visual narratives, evidenced in his spontaneous art work. According to Eric, he "loved the progression, the temporal progress, and the representation of it." For an English project in the sixth grade, he did a detailed drawing of the poem, "Jabberwocky," that was a visual interpretation of nonsense words and all the creatures that inhabited the Jabberwocky world. In his sixth-grade social studies class, humor, coupled with serious subjects, took the form of political cartoons. For example, one cartoon about nuclear and solar power as alternatives to using oil, was illustrated by the theme, "Don't beg for oil, use the good old American know-how." In one part, Uncle Sam is giving money to the Arabs and in the other he is dancing in front of a nuclear reactor and the sun.

The flexibility of teachers in Eric's elementary school allowed him to express himself and his ideas, both discursively and nondiscursively. Many of the projects he created were specific options offered to all students, whereas others were open-ended assignments in which students could design their own projects. In junior high school, in Grades 7 and 8, the same flexibility found in elementary school persisted in science, social studies, and English classes, and Eric was encouraged to express his ideas through images as well as words. For a seventh-grade unit about Greek mythology, he found different illustrations of the gods and adapted them. For this project, he drew the planets in relative sizes and the Greek god associated with each one. Echoing his fifth-grade Sanctuary project, in seventh grade, Eric made a brochure with the theme of an amusement park for visiting Olympus with a map that included Hall of Gods, Temple of Gods, Aphrodite's house of love, Minerva's brain-shaped house, Hades' horror house, Poseidon's aquarium, and so on. Creating political cartoons remained a popular form of expression for Eric in the eighth grade where he could demonstrate his growing sense of humor. One, for example, had to do with 18th-century America, the colonists, the crown, and the Stamp Act. Colonists are depicted as destroying stamps from the Tea Tax and the Boston Tea Party is shown tossing little Ts, instead of tea, into the harbor. For an eighth-grade science class, Eric created a number of visuals including a poster that explained a wind powered machine he created for a science project, an illustration for a solar nuclear energy report that included superheros in combat scenes, and a detailed drawing of a dissected rat with appropriately labeled parts. Eric enjoyed drawing this rat so much that at this time he considered medical illustration as a career. In high school, classes were more compartmentalized and the flexibility of doing artwork along with written responses to class assignments, an option he enjoyed in elementary and junior high school, was no longer available.

GAMES

Another category of school projects that elicited Eric's interest and response to school assignments was games. Since he was in the first grade, Eric displayed a keen interest in the process of gaming and creating games. This interest continued through college and persists until the present. In the fifth grade, Eric created "The Digestive Game," as a response to an assignment for science class, that combined his scientific curiosity, humor, writing and research skills, and ability to depict ideas graphically. This game was a teaching tool about how the human body digests food, the object of which was for food to leave the body as waste. It began with players being either a fat, carbohydrate, or protein particle. A twirl on a spinner began the ride down the esophagus. The game board is a large chart on which Eric's stepfather traced an outline of Eric's head and body and Eric drew the internal organs. It took much research to provide accurate information for each move through the digestive system.

In the fifth grade, Eric studied with a private teacher who was an artist who published his own comic book-type stories. Under the guidance of this teacher, he made a board game that featured a battle between two medieval fantasy armies. This game was very complex visually and conceptually and was influenced by Dungeon and Dragons games he began to play at that time. There were a variety of game characters of different classes including archers, foot soldiers, horsemen, a king, spearman, warriors, gnomes, pixies, and a wizard. This game had rules and contained complex combat tables and many detailed illustrations of scenes with 25 different figures in a variety of battle contexts.

In the seventh grade, on his own, he made a Mother's Day board game for me that was based on our family life. In this game, Eric demonstrated his ability to view situations and derive meaning and humor from his observations. His drawings for this game contained small detailed accurate drawings for the different places on which players landed or were obligated to go. The Mother's Day game, based on everyday ordeals a mother encounters, could result in good or bad consequences. For example, "drive the kids to music lessons," "the students are yelling at you," "do the dishes," and "go back to the office" all caused the player to go back a variable number of spaces. "Have friends over," "go to a museum," and "sell pet gerbils" all resulted in progressing several spaces and eventually to the end of the game that was "a vacation for two." Another board game, Zero Population, created in response to a seventh-grade social studies project, required researching a topic in depth. The goal was zero population growth; for instance, if your piece landed on "earthquake" that was a positive move because the population was reduced.

VISUAL NARRATIVES

Eric also spent a great amount of time at home doing spontaneous visual narratives with very complex story lines. These visual narratives were a favorite drawing mode in which movement and action were depicted as taking place over time in one scene or in a number of separate scenes. The visual narratives he created demonstrated his early technical ability to depict figures and animals in action as well as his conceptual ability to combine many different visual elements in coherent and complete scenarios.

When I noticed his first interest in telling stories visually, I provided Eric with long rolls of paper to facilitate his favored mode of expression. A visual narrative, created when he was 5, included Santa Claus, Rudolph, the other reindeer, a tree, smoke, and the roof of a house. Spaceships he drew at the same age represented his interest in movement and flight and he often would erase spaceships that were destroyed during the duration of a story. At age 6, a narrative that proceeds from left to right about Native Americans hunting and killing a deer and a whale was created on a long sheet of paper and contained many detailed visual narrative elements including individually decorated tepees, a dozen Native Americans who are hunting a deer, a canoe with several Native Americans killing a whale, tomahawks and arrows flying, and water coming from the whale's spout announcing "The End." The deer is frowning because he is hit by an arrow and the feathers on all the Native Americans' costumes are a certain number and length.

Another detailed visual narrative, made when he was 7, was titled "All About Archeology"; it included an archeologist in an underground cave, broken artifacts, tools, a notebook, rock walls, a man shoveling at an excavation site, a close-up of an artifact that was unearthed, the bottom of the ocean, people in wet suits, and fish that were working as archaeologists (Fig. 5.5). When he was in Grades 3 and 4

FIG. 5.5. Detail from a visual narrative, "All About Archaeology" (Grade 1).

Eric's visual narratives were principally about space wars in which he would imagine events happening and then draw them. Narratives he created in Grades 5 and 6 ran a gamut from how ice cream cones are made to complex compositions of knights from the Middle Ages fighting 20th-century army men. Eric's interest and past experiences with visual narratives were evident in an Epics and Sagas class he took at the Indiana Summer Arts Institute when he was in sixth grade. His teacher at the Institute was an artist who taught students to use comic book conventions to create narratives that were visually interesting and exciting.

Creating games and drawing visual narratives with superheroes also were dominant themes during Eric's junior high school years and in the first year of high school. A "Prince Parthan" series, drawn when he was in the sixth grade, was a visual narrative with a very complicated story line and many characters who represented good and evil forces. "Nukeman" and "Icarus" were seventh- and eighth-grade superheroes Eric continued to draw into his high school years (Fig. 5.6). At this same time, Eric created "Xenn" and "Nexx," two brothers depicted in

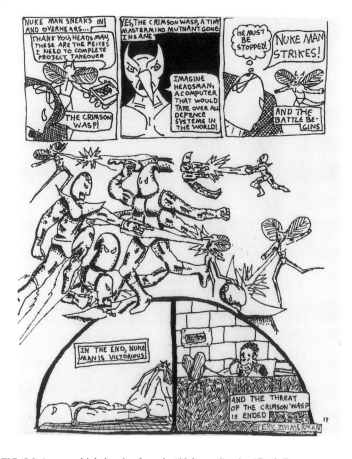

FIG. 5.6. A pen-and-ink drawing from the "Nukeman" series (Grade 7).

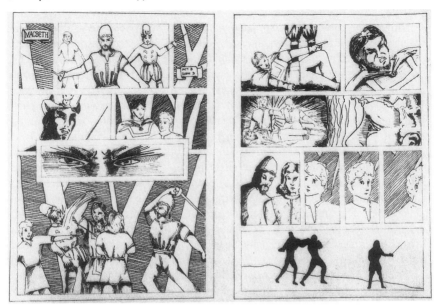

FIG. 5.7. A pen-and-ink drawing of a scene from *MacBeth* (Grade 9).

an epic story that consumed numerous pages of written narrative accompanied by drawings of many other characters. In his first year in high school, in response to an assignment about Shakespeare, Eric created a visual narrative of a scene from MacBeth (Fig. 5.7). Gore became a prevalent theme in many drawings done in junior high and high school, for example the depiction of a man cutting off a woman monster's head that Eric described as a "typical adolescent drawing." Brainia was the only woman superhero Eric created and this lack of female characters was later explained as his identification with the male characters he drew and the male culture he experienced as an adolescent.

SUBJECTS IN ARTWORK

The subject matter of Eric's artwork, done spontaneously in school and in extra-school contexts, through various art program opportunities, varied both according to his own interests and to specific assignments given by teachers in different classes. Content of Eric's drawings varied from preschool through the first year of high school, although some themes remained constant. Beginning at ages 3 to 4, subjects he depicted most frequently included animals, members of his immediate family, houses, trees, mazes, trucks, underwater submarines, and self-portraits. Additional subjects created at age 5 included ghosts, monsters, solar systems, sunflowers, Native Americans, and policemen. At the same age, Eric also was interested in creating books with characters, such as the Dills, a family of pickles he invented, in addition to his continued interest in drawing himself and his family members.

Through the third grade, to supplement the themes described, new subjects were added such as war themes, airplanes, archeological scenes, and fish. In the fourth grade, his repertoire of subjects expanded to include whales and spaceships. In his drawings at this age, whales were shown either as classified into different categories or being attacked in violent battle scenes. In fourth grade, when he was assigned to draw an emotion, he chose to portray evilness as a portrait of a man with a spider web coming out of his nose, scars on his face, and a distorted mouth and beard. By the fifth grade, additional themes made their appearance including Star Wars figures, superheroes, and medieval fantasies. In the sixth grade, Eric studied privately with the same artist who taught his Epics and Sagas class for the IU Summer Arts Institute and he learned to draw visual narratives using techniques such as framing, close-ups, and drawing objects and people from a variety of perspectives. The subjects of these visual narratives were battles with men fighting and a variety of other characters and monsters. During the time he studied with this artist, Eric created a complex game based on one of the visual narratives he had created previously. In his seventh-grade art class, Eric drew a model, who posed for the entire class wearing a gas mask. He remembered that he was more interested in drawing the gas mask than he was in drawing the girl. When he took drawing and painting classes in his junior year of high school, subjects he usually chose were still lifes, drawings of family members, someone in the act of fencing, and a lighthouse copied from a magazine. The subjects of art projects he did the following summer at the Interlochen Art Academy were more challenging than those done in his regular art classes. In a ceramics class, he created a chess set with fantastic figures and a monster head derived from many drawings of skulls. Student dancers and musicians performing for their arts classes and a number of surreal landscapes also were themes found in his paintings and drawings done at this time (Fig. 5.8).

When he was a senior in high school, in the afternoons Eric attended art classes at Indiana University. In his painting classes, he mostly worked from nude models, although landscapes and interiors were other subject matters he painted. He was aware of his own awakening sexuality when he was painting these nudes and associated these feelings with Picasso's experiences of being aware of sexual elements when he created his art works. He did many portraits in oil pastels of female friends who he thought were attractive. He reported that painting them was an occasion to flirt and tell them how "interesting looking" he found them (Fig. 5.9). At this time, Eric's interests changed from an emphasis on imaginative and fantastic subject matter to an interest in aesthetics, with a focus on what Eric expressed at age 24 as "not emotion or psychology, but upon what is art and how is it perceived and created."

Portrait subjects were not confined to those of his women friends. For a sixth-grade science class project about inventions, Eric researched and wrote about the invention of the rocket and created an oil crayon portrait of Robert Goddard that he drew from a photograph. Self-portraits, which were to become a dominant theme in Eric's art work through college, began in art class in the seventh grade with self-portrait drawings that closely resembled him and were carefully done with details and shading (Fig. 5.10). One reason he later gave for his interest in creating

FIG. 5.8. Painting of a student playing the cello (Grade 11).

FIG. 5.9. Portrait of a friend (Grade 11).

153

FIG. 5.10. Self-portrait pencil drawing (Grade 7).

self-portraits in high school was that he had "control over the model and situation. I was always there. I put in a lot of time outside of class. The relationship with the viewer became apparent as I strove to confront the viewer ... I wanted this relationship to be ambiguous. Am I shouting? Am I calling out? Is that a look of surprise?"

SELF-CONFIDENCE AND COMPETITIVENESS

Eric always set high standards and he was very competitive both with himself and his own goals and with the achievements of others. Looking at the oil portrait he made in the sixth grade of Robert Goddard, he remembered that he was proud that it was displayed in the school library, but he was not satisfied with it, although his mother, father, and teachers thought it was well done. By the time he was a junior in high school, Eric explained that he remembered he was "a virtuoso and had excellent skills. I always looked for an opportunity to be really flashy, to demonstrate my rendering ability. This showing off stuff grew thin after a year." In high school he liked drawing out of doors and was pleased at being recognized as an artist. He enjoyed having people watch him work and claimed, in retrospect, that this was the "theatrical part of me."

The first time he went to Interlochen on a scholarship, when he was 16, he was concerned at first that he would be "shown up," but he stated he was mistaken and was a "superstar" there and received the top visual art award and won a scholarship to attend Interlochen next summer and the following academic year. He did go during the summer, although he decided to remain at home for his senior year and attend IU part time. At Interlochen, he was very involved in his artwork and always was confident that, with hard work, the high goals that he set for himself could be achieved. He would get up early in the morning and spend the entire day in the studio. He was able and determined to use his studio time efficiently. At the same time, he also participated in an advanced Baroque Music Ensemble and attended many concerts and recitals of professional and student groups. Looking back, 6 years later, on this first summer at Interlochen, Eric did not think that he was conscious of how competitive he was and that this competition was a critical force in his art-making activities.

At this same time, he felt he was advancing as an artist, quickly making progress in his own work. Competition, in respect to surpassing his peers, was very important to him. He wanted to be the best and this goal lingered more than halfway through college. He also enjoyed pushing rules and stretching parameters that others set for him. Like many talented young people, he at times was overly self-confident and not always sensitive to others' points of view. In his senior year in high school when he went to IU, he remembered feeling like "an intellectual missionary making people question their beliefs." Although he was the only high school student among art majors at Indiana University, he reported that at the time he never felt over his head, "I still wanted to be one of the best students in the class."

In junior high and high school, Eric sometimes was critical of his works, both at the time he created them and looking at them retrospectively; at other times he was enthusiastic about his past works and appreciated what he had accomplished. An example of his positive reactions to an art work created in high school took place in a conversation with me when he was 20:

> the colors are really nice, I like that … I loved this drawing, I thought it was successful, that's why I still have it; that's a nice arrangement on the page; I won a prize for this one, I like the way I put the shapes together, it came easily; this painting has a lot of motion in it. I think it really works. (see Fig. 5.11)

FIG. 5.11. Drawing of a friend (Grade 12).

In the same conversation, some of his work elicited negative responses from Eric such as one that received a National Scholastic Gold Key. A painting, done in his senior year of high school, of a young women seated in a chair and looking down pensively, was rejected by Eric as stiff, formless, and overworked (Fig. 5.9).

ISSUES ABOUT ART MAKING

In other conversations with Eric, a number of issues related to creating art recurred at numerous times. These concerned the act of drawing and painting, formal issues, technical issues, and the role of copying.

Act of Drawing and Painting

Eric explained that the act of looking at his artwork, created several years before, could only be subjective in terms of the present lens from which he was viewing the past when he was deeply involved in the act of painting. Reminiscing about a painting he created in the seventh grade, he noted that he was getting the entire painting "down all at once" and that he didn't "labor over it and repaint parts, it has a freshness about it."

Since junior high school, Eric has been the popular, central figure in organizing social activities for a group of a dozen friends. In high school, six male members of this group met regularly to engage in role-playing games and were still close friends when Eric was interviewed in 1990. Nonetheless, when he was in high school, creating artwork sometimes served his needs to express himself and his feelings that were not met by relationships with his friends. Part of the summer he was in his junior year in high school he remembered, for the first time, being somewhat depressed and wanting attention. Drawings and paintings created at this time were a reflection of his need "to be secure from the outside world and build a brick wall around myself so that I didn't have to deal with anybody." He drew clowns and used their images to pretend to be someone else: "to put on make-up and be another person, that's the best way to interact with others."

Breakthrough transformational experiences were salient in his art development. Starting in the Grade 7, Eric remembered a number of these experiences as beginning with dissatisfaction with his work, followed by a vibrating feeling that was "tense and dramatic," and finally something broke through. He credited dissatisfaction as a motivating factor that leads to higher levels of achievement in any field. He also reported that he enjoyed watching his own progress, realizing he had taken great leaps forward, and exploring multiple possibilities and solutions to problems.

He found pleasure in the act of painting more than drawing and viewed the paintbrush as an extension of his arm; paint was more fluid than drawing in charcoal or pastel. Sometimes, however, he was aware that painting could be very frustrating. Drawing from memory was difficult for him, he preferred to have objects and people in front of him, although he always altered what he saw.

Attending college classes at Indiana University when he was in high school helped him maximize his learning experiences. He questioned why people would go to college and not want to learn. When he was in IU art classes he was focused and always had limitless energy, was never tired, and was continuously challenged. In retrospect, he found it "ridiculous that some people would come to class and not immerse themselves totally and try to do the best that they could." Coming from an academic family, with both parents continuously engaged in a myriad of interesting and challenging activities, it is not surprising that Eric did not suffer the grass to grow under his feet. Eric's motivation for what he called "bouncing off the walls," was acknowledged as emanating both from his competitive spirit and his feelings of uneasiness about being idle.

Formal Issues

Eric at 20 years, viewing work he did when he was 4 years old, remembered that it was always important for him to get the "details right." People always had five toes and fingers, two eyes with eyelashes, all other facial details, and clothing with belts, buttons, and zippers. Including all these elements, when he was 4 years old, is evidence of his keen observation of the world about him and his ability to make order of that world two-dimensionally. Drawings of animals done at this same age demonstrate his ability to capture the essence of these animals through observation and depiction of colors, lines, and shapes.

His interest in showing as many details as possible continued through elementary school. In reference to a portrait of me he made for a Mother's Day gift, when he was in first grade, Eric remembered during our conversations that he really observed in great detail how my lips, hair, and eyelids were made and how he tried to render all these individual parts so that they would eventually fit together to create a portrait that resembled me. Eric's renderings of whales, in the fourth and fifth grades, received the same attention to details and sensitivity to color, line, shape, and texture, and unity of form that he gave to his earlier animal drawings and his later, more mature, paintings of people and landscapes.

Beginning in the fifth grade, he became interested in perspective drawing. The spaceships he was drawing were becoming more and more complicated and he felt a need to make them appear more three dimensional. It was not until the seventh grade, however, that he learned about a formal system of perspective. Beginning in the sixth and seventh grades, drama and action were Eric's primary concerns. A visual narrative drawing done when he was in sixth grade depicted close-ups of different scenarios such as an axe going into someone's back, someone getting stabbed in the back, a spear entering someone's head, and someone running into battle. Eric remembered he purposefully mixed proportions, angles, and sizes to result in what he termed a "mixed-up effect" that dramatized the action taking place and made the drawing appear to include more people than it actually did. Artworks done at the Indiana University Summer Arts Institute, when he was in sixth grade, were interpreted by Eric as having a few basic shapes to create strong images and loose, graphic, bold, and free lines to create dramatic effects. In his seventh-grade art class, he enjoyed learning systems of drawing in Western perspective for the

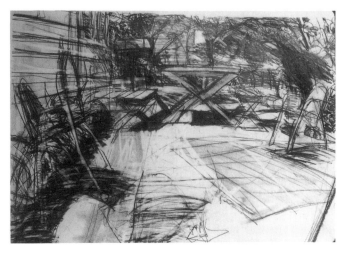

FIG. 5.12. Drawing of an outdoor scene (Grade 12).

first time and then going off on his own to explore perspective as a tool for his own paintings and drawings. In a drawing of a city, with cars traveling down a street, Eric used his newly learned knowledge of perspective to create a feeling of three-dimensionality.

In his junior year in high school, when he was taking a drawing and painting class, he was experimenting and developing a drawing style that continued into college, in which he outlined simplified forms in flat thick lines that gave an abstract, graphic quality to his work. A painting of a tuba he did at this time shows a loose, expressionistic way of applying paint to a surface so that the form of the instrument becomes dissolved in swirls of paint. In his paintings of figures done at the same time, he had similar concerns about applying paint freely and using his paint brush as if it were a chisel, carving into the planes depicted in two dimensions on the canvas. This act of carving up space and chiseling art forms, was, for Eric, a metaphor for a viewer's relationship to a painting and the way he or she might negotiate visually and physically through the painting. By the time he attended Interlochen, the summer before his senior year in high school, Eric remembered he was "into formal issues" involving the use of line, color, and space and "using loose brushstrokes that eventually became quite formulaic." He used these brushstrokes without paying much attention to the form and space surrounding the figures he was painting. In high school, when he attended Indiana University, Eric had aesthetic concerns about carving out space when he did figure drawings. Even though he was attempting to be expressive, he wanted to create solid forms that appeared to be carved out of a background and had the potential to move through time and space (Fig. 5.12). He was interested, at that time, in how Degas used ground planes as means for the viewer to feel as if he or she were entering the context of a painting or drawing and how Degas painted his figures as if they were about to dance through space.

Techniques

Technical challenges of making art often frustrated Eric. His early artworks, beginning with those done in second grade, elicited responses from the now adult Eric about his interest in how things fit together. He reflected about his frustration when drawing a tree, that he was not able to depict the complexity of the interlocking branches, the way the leaves were attached to the branches, and how to mix colors to make the tree look realistic. Eric remembered that beginning with fourth grade, the discipline of keeping his work neat and free from smudges and fingerprints became an important issue. Looking at his artwork created at this time, it is evident that Eric would get so involved in the process of making art and rendering forms all at once on the whole page, that he sometimes neglected to worry about neatness or even correct proportion or perspective.

His first encounter with photography was in the seventh grade when he attended the Indiana University Summer Arts Institute. Eric recalled liking the magical quality of developing images in a chemical stew and coming out with surprising results. These earlier experiences with photography prompted him to study photography again in college. In his regular art classes in high school, he experimented with different ways of making textures, creating linear effects, and experimenting with a variety of media. Filmmaking influenced drawings done in his senior year of high school when he attended Indiana University, in respect to the idea of carving out forms. As Eric later stated, "the viewer could roam about the drawing and move through time and space." This is evident in a drawing he did of the interior of the IU Art Museum in which the viewer could choose where he or she would gaze, beginning with winding a line of vision down the stairs and then going off to the left or right in or out of multiple doorways. To create this drawing he used graphite sticks making quick, thick marks as if he were cutting through the two dimensional page to create three-dimensional space (Fig. 5.13, see p. 160). Eric described artwork done at this time, as a "filmmaking idea about drawing" that contained the seeds of what was to germinate into Eric's current interest in technology and multimedia that involves the viewer as a participant in an artwork.

Copying

Discussions about copying involved issues of plagiarism in terms of borrowing ideas and images from his own previous artworks, reproducing and reinterpreting art works by well-known artists, and using images from popular media. Modeling his own images after the images of others was a salient factor in the development of Eric's spontaneous drawings. Gil and I encouraged him to copy images telling him that this was a beneficial way to learn to draw. We also informed him that copying was a traditional way that many artists in the past used to develop their drawing skills. From first to fifth grade, Eric adapted images from Ed Emberly's drawing books. He remembered that creating these drawings gave him confidence and helped him develop his drawing skills. From fourth grade through junior high school, Eric copied images such as spaceships, whales, and knights in armor from

FIG. 5.13. Drawing of the interior of the IU Art Museum (Grade 12).

encyclopedias and illustrated fantasy and science fiction books. In seventh grade, he began to be greatly influenced by illustrations in comic books and he learned to render people by drawing images of popular culture heros they depicted. By ninth grade, books such as the *Avengers*, *Thor*, and *New Mutants* were sources of images for spontaneous drawings of comic booklike portraits and figures of people.

His art, created in formal educational contexts, evidenced similar concerns about copying, plagiarism, borrowing images, and reinterpreting works of art. His fifth-grade "Balancing Book of the ABCs" could be viewed as Eric plagiarizing himself because it was based on a book he did in the third grade on the same theme. At the Summer Arts Institute, in the Epics and Sagas class, he borrowed the story line and comic booklike images and concepts he had previously employed when he was working on a similar visual narrative at home. He also made a travel brochure about Olympus in the seventh grade, and repeated a similar theme as a brochure in the ninth grade. Eric remembered learning to draw at home by copying

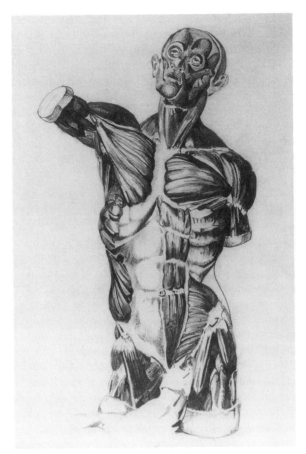

FIG. 5.14. A copy of an anatomical drawing of the human body (Grade 11).

characters from comic books. He enjoyed assignments at the Summer Arts Institute that involved making drawings and paintings based on well-known artworks. In his seventh-grade art class, an assignment was to copy a masterwork and he made a likeness, from a reproduction, of a Utrillo landscape painting. In our conversations, Eric reported that even now he does not mind reproducing someone else's work, in fact he explained that this was a good way to learn about art making.

An accurate, technically advanced copy of an anatomical drawing of part of a human body was chosen for an assignment by Eric, in his junior year in high school, because it was so difficult to reproduce. He made a grid and copied this drawing from a book, although anatomy, as a subject was never discussed in this class. He lamented in retrospect, "we just did mindless copying. I spent a long time doing this drawing, including all the little shapes and different textures of the layers of skin and muscle. I remember how boring it was to do" (Fig. 5.14). At the College Credit for High School Seniors workshop that he attended after his junior year in high school, students were required to do paintings based on artists' works. Eric thought his interpretation of a Rubens painting was well done when he created it, although in retrospect he thought it looked a bit disjointed and not very unified. While studying at Indiana University in his senior year, he had opportunities to copy artworks in the Indiana University Art Museum. Eric's painting teacher at Indiana University suggested he copy a Picasso. While he painted, he later reported, he began to understand how space unfolds and how Picasso established picture planes from different perspectives and carved space in a variety of directions. Thus, copying artworks provided an important means for understanding pictorial space and for acquiring technical skills.

CULTURE

Eric grew up in a home where, from an early age, he was exposed to artworks and was able to observe his parents looking and talking about and creating art. His art making also was greatly influenced by the middle-class culture and academic environment in which he developed interests and motivation to do art work. From ages 4 to 8, Eric, at age 20, recounted how he was influenced by Richard Scary's children's books, especially Scary's drawings of trucks at construction sites, and Saturday cartoons on television. Commencing at the fourth grade, and throughout high school, established popular culture genres, including fantasy and science fiction genres, had a great impact on the content of his artwork. A number of popular cultural influences became important, in the fourth through sixth grades, including books about dinosaurs and spaceships, Micronauts and Shogun warrior play figures, and Star Wars movies. Godzilla, King Kong, and other popular monsters from movies and television series also were remembered as influencing both the themes and styles of his artwork done in elementary school. Other popular culture phenomena that were used as sources of images and ideas were movies such as *Close Encounters of the Third Kind*, Dungeons and Dragons fantasy games, and Tolkien's *The Lord of the Rings*. Eric went through phases where one week he would draw one subject and the next week another.

The summer he turned 13, and throughout the seventh grade, Eric's artwork was influenced by comic books, the rock group Kiss, and Heavy Metal magazines. The following year other influences also became important such as the movies *Flash Gordon* and *Conan the Barbarian*, video games, and the book *The Flight of Dragons*. By the ninth grade, influences in addition to those already mentioned included Doré's illustrations for Milton's *Paradise Lost*. By his junior year in high school, he had abandoned using popular culture images and began to do more academically oriented subject matters such as landscapes, still lifes, and portraits.

CONCEPTUAL ISSUES

A number of conceptual issues about being a young artist, related to the processes and products of art making, recurred throughout conversations between Eric and me. Three salient conceptual issues surfaced: the influence of academic training, formalism versus expressivism, and the role of the viewer in respect to an artwork.

In the seventh grade, Eric viewed traditional, academic art training as both dangerous and helpful. Speaking from a more adult voice than he might in the seventh grade, Eric explained that any paradigm taught as the truth may be dangerous and that was why he often rejected academic ways of teaching art that are prominent in many university art departments. In the seventh grade, he started to grapple seriously with certain formal issues and relegated expressive and imaginative issues to a less important place in his art work. He now thinks that concentrating only on formal design issues can be ultimately damaging to a young artist and result in artwork that is "dry and purely visual" and not connected to the world of the artist's imagination.

In the seventh grade, he began to understand the effect of his artwork and what kind of emotive quality it would have on a viewer. In a drawing about "tension," he drew a person with the focal point of stress between his eyes right above his nose. What Eric achieved, however, was an illustration of tension rather than creating it formally or conceptually. Although he had some notions about the role of a viewer confronting a work of art, he was not yet able to bring these ideas to fruition. These ideas would only resurface in his senior year of high school.

As a junior in high school, he liked the idea of meta-level presentation of ideas, such as manipulating the frame of a drawing so that the content becomes a drawing about a drawing. For example, he drew the corner of his sketchbook leaning against a window. There is, in this drawing, an interplay of the drawing on the sketchbook, the window, and the frame of the drawing itself. Implicit relationships between the act of painting, the viewer, and the subject became of primary importance to Eric when he was 16, the summer before his senior year in high school, when he was painting portraits at Interlochen. In his senior year, when he studied at Indiana University, the process of painting, the role of viewer, and the content of the artwork dominated his art making. Reconstructing his motives in creating a self-portrait at this time, Eric remembered he was:

> sizing up the viewer as if I'm painting the viewer but of course it's a portrait of me wearing yellow gloves and a mask thrusting my left hand forward ... I was grappling with the relationship between the artist, viewer, and subject. Especially when the artist and viewer are the same and different. I was interested in a bifurcation of myself in relation to other people, which is the basic issue I'm now dealing with in my artwork. (see Fig. 5.15, p. 164)

This issue is nowhere more apparent than in Eric's description, 5 years later, of a painting done when he was studying at Indiana University. He related how he created an abstraction of Goya's painting, "October 14." The assignment was to do an abstract rendering of a famous artwork. According to Eric, most people in his class created what he termed "wimpy, flippant kind of abstractions." The other students, he felt in retrospect, were unimaginative in their approaches to their work and did not really engage themselves in problem solving in relation to the assignment. His, he felt, was "very conceptual and well thought out." He reported that his teacher was very impressed by the thought he put into his abstraction. Eric

FIG. 5.15. Self-portrait painting (Grade 12).

changed the point of view, and instead of looking across the picture plane horizontally, the viewer is seeing the soldier's point of view and becomes, metaphorically, the soldier who is next in line to fire. Eric intensified the Christlike image of the victim; the entire point of view is changed from a somewhat static horizontal composition to one that is more dynamic. Eric also emphasized the source of light that emanated from a lantern in the original painting and changed the configuration of the buildings depicting them at a "weird" angle that made them look "horrific," as if they were falling down flat against the landscape. Eric's remembered that he "rotated the figures from their original positions in my head. It was challenging. I also loved the dark shapes of the soldiers. I homogenized them to emphasize their fascist conformity" (see Fig. 5.16).

The summer before Eric entered Penn, when he was 17, he studied at Interlochen Arts Camp and had a one-person show of his work at the end of the summer session. At that time, he wrote about his intentions and the focus of his work that consisted of a series of self-portraits, portraits, small still lifes, interiors, and landscapes:

FIG. 5.16. Abstract of Goya's painting, "October 14" (Grade 12).

As with many two-dimensional artists, the concept of space is perhaps most important in my work. The paradox of distance with the flat plane of the canvas continues to fascinate me. To this end, I make use of aggressive marks. These not only reveal the energy of the process, remind the viewer of the flatness of the rectangle, and speak about the medium, but also attempt to literally carve elusive form and space out of flatness. Color continues to be a struggle but is progressing steadily in my work. I am trying to make use of intensity and temperature of color rather than simply tone.

The psychology of art is also a growing concern of mine. In many of my most recent pieces, the viewer enters through a large wide floor plane into an environment that is often jammed with forms and yet also hidden spaces into which the viewer may investigate. In my portraits, and especially my self-portraits, I explore the relationship between the artist, the subject in the work, and the viewer. It is very important to me that the viewer interact with my art in some way.

ERIC'S REFLECTIONS ON THIS STUDY

In 1991, when Eric was 24 and in his first year of a master's degree program in multimedia arts at the Ohio State University, he read this case study and reflected on the interview process and ideas and concerns posed by my interpretations of his work. He asked me to make some minor factual changes in the text and discussed his reactions with me. Eric views his own artistic development not in terms of his development of style, but in terms of his conceptual development. The concepts found in his artwork have always interested him more than the graphic style through which they are expressed. It is conceptual issues that he feels unified his artworks.

The interview process, and reading the case study allowed him to view changes that took place in his art development over a period of about two decades. He began to notice how themes that appeared in art done in his early childhood still are relevant in his artwork today. He is empathetic with Picasso who as early as age 4 drew bulls and continued to be obsessed with that image to his last days of productive artwork.

The enriched and accelerated art education opportunities Eric received supplied him with experiences that enabled his art work to change and mature. They also provided him with contexts, teachers, materials, and other students to nurture his growth as a young artist. He often thought, throughout his art development, about what was considered art and what was not; what was considered high art and what was viewed as popular art. Today he enjoys breaking down these distinctions as they exist in Western culture and confronting viewers with his or her own culturally constructed dichotomies between high art and popular art.

In Eric's adolescent years, the educational contexts in which he studied art were demanding and competitive and challenged him not only to do what was expected, but allowed him to go well beyond those expectations. Those educational experiences, described in this study, were, according to Eric, critical to his development as an artist. Being in those educational settings exposed him to new points of view and accelerated his art learning. At present, his tendency is to study with as many professors and about as many different subjects as is possible in order to be exposed to different areas of knowledge. He described this learning style as eclectic and incorporating many different perspectives. If left to learn on his own, he claims he would not have enough stimulation to be challenged and move forward.

As he looked back at his artwork, created over time, he could easily discern how his style and interests varied and changed. "Cultural production," he told me, "is contextual. It is not about a genius unfolding him or herself in isolation. Therefore changing and growing contexts aid an artist's entire development."

Education always helped him question what he learned previously and to accept some things and subsequently reject others. As a college undergraduate, this evolution in his art classes was paralleled by his intellectual growth in academic classes. Eric's tendency to question what he had learned in the past lead to what he described as his "rejection of painting and drawing as a viable means of primary expression in contemporary art making." The contemporary expression, "the canvas is dead," summarizes Eric's disenchantment with drawing or painting on two-dimensional surfaces and his current interest in using new technologies and alternative media to express his ideas visually. In graduate school, he continues to experiment with a variety of means of expression, such as performance art, installations, computer graphics, and public art projects that incorporate recent art developments with more historic art forms. Eric concluded:

> I'm finally making my own art forms, combining my diverse interests in theory, game design, visual art, performance art, story telling, and social construction of art. This all is a result of critical self-consciousness that was nurtured by my institutional education and my home life.

DISCUSSIONS AND CONCLUSIONS

In this study, Eric's positive reports about the benefits of accelerated and enriched art program opportunities for study in the visual arts echoes Van Tassel-Baska's (1986, 1987) defense of acceleration for high-ability students as a very effective intervention technique that improves motivation, confidence, scholarship, prevents habits of laziness, and allows for earlier completion of professional education. Stanley (1977) reiterated similar justifications and claimed that acceleration programs tend to reduce educational arrogance and resistance to learning, allow more time to explore careers, create better preparation for advanced study in college, and benefit society by providing more years in a chosen profession and by creating better citizens with improved education. Benhow and Stanley (1983) also asserted that acceleration opportunities for high-ability students provide greater opportunities for these students to interact with professionals in fields in which they have particular interests.

There is, however, a commonly expressed concern by many educators that acceleration may have detrimental effects on a student's social development, although research has failed to justify such criticism (Clark & Zimmerman, 1994; Daurio, 1979). Eric was fortunate to have parents who could guide his acceleration decisions and encourage him to pursue his interests in a number of different arts enrichment and acceleration options.

Sculptors in Bloom's (1985) study reported that at the secondary level, although they had some formal art experiences, they did not feel that they had been engaged in professional study in the world of art and regretted this omission. Although Gabriel Foreman (Gardner, 1980), Bruce Robertson (Robertson, 1987), and Wang Yani (Goldsmith, 1992) did not appear to have positive experiences with formal art education, their talent was nurtured by artist parents. The two students in Golomb's (1992a) study who lived on a kibbutz had an art teacher who encouraged experimentation and supplied materials and encouragement for their emerging talents. It was fortunate that John Scott (Wilson & Wilson, 1980) had a teacher who encouraged his visual narratives and allowed him to use subject matter in his art projects that was of interest to him, thus fostering his involvement with art.

Diane, in Nelson and Janzen's (1990) case study, was a student with high ability in visual art, who like Eric, profited from enriched and accelerated visual art programs. Feldman (1980) studied children who were prodigious in many different areas and is convinced that all progress in learning is the result of intensive and prolonged instruction. Successful teachers of highly able students who are knowledgeable about their subject matter, and able to communicate instruction effectively, select important learning experiences that lead their students to attain mastery level achievements. In *Nature's Gambit: Child Prodigies and the Development of Talent*, Feldman and Goldsmith (1986) reported their study of six boy prodigies, aged 3½ to 9 years, using observations and interviews with their parents and teachers. These children possessed outstanding abilities in areas of chess, musical performance, music composition, writing, and foreign languages. Such talent, they contended, does not develop without an enormous amount of work, practice, and study, coupled with a great deal of direct assistance, guidance, and encouragement. Although there is much discussion about whether outstanding visual art ability manifests itself at an early age, as do talents studied by Feldman and Goldsmith (Clark & Zimmerman, 1992), their conclusion that an individual's talent within a culture involves the interplay of many forces, including education, has great relevance for the education of high-ability visual arts students.

Teacher encouragement and flexibility were relevant to Eric's feelings of being successful and challenged. When his teachers were insensitive to his needs and unable to communicate their insights, his feelings were of frustration and not being supported in his art-making activities. Those art teachers Eric viewed positively possessed important characteristics such as their emphasis on art skills, general knowledge about art, empathy with students, ability to make classes challenging, and a readiness to help students become aware of the contexts in which they make art and examine their reasons for creating art. These characteristics are similar to those of successful teachers of talented adolescents I studied at the Indiana University Summer Arts Institute (Zimmerman, 1991, 1992a). Eric also was fortunate in his elementary and junior high schools in that most of his teachers were flexible and taught enriched, theme-oriented classes in which students could complete assignments according to their interests, in a variety of modes, including combinations of visual and verbal problem solving. In many of Eric's classes, study of the arts was interrelated with other subjects. Gardner (1980) and Wilson and Wilson (1980) also recommend that teachers encourage talented art students to incorporate subject matter that has meaning for them into their art projects and assignments. These kinds of curriculum adaptations allowed Eric to express his skills, values, and understandings in a variety of discursive and nondiscursive contexts.

Many themes and subject matters such as games, visual narratives, self-portraits, and political cartoons, evidenced in Eric's elementary and junior high projects, persist in his present artwork. He had high expectations for himself and the artwork he created. He worked hard and from an early age was committed to making art. Eric enjoyed showing off his skills, was competitive with himself and others, and pushed boundaries whenever it was possible. His limitless energy and feelings of needing to be challenged made him dependent on the approval of those teachers he respected, who offered him encouragement and criticism that kept him interested and committed to creating art. Eric described a number of transformational experiences that allowed him to view himself as a young artist achieving his own predetermined goals, rather than being a student creating art in isolation from the world of art.

Taylor (1987) described students talented in art as having "illuminating experiences" that changed their lives through encounters with original works of art. Eric described how assignments to copy or reinterpret works by well-known artists made him look carefully at art works with an understanding of how they were created and what the artists might have intended. Without the accelerated and enriched art program options in which Eric participated, he probably would not have had those frustrating experiences that eventually led to illuminating insights and transformations from which he was able to grow intellectually, emotionally, and in his art making. Although as a young adult Eric cautioned that formal academic art training might be dangerous, he did acknowledge his need to learn skills and techniques, and balance both formal and expressive concerns in his own art work. His interest in relationships between the act of painting, the viewer, and the subject, that began in high school, is one of primary concern for him today. The accelerated and enriched art program options offered him throughout his elementary through high school years provided impetus for him to continue his art study and become a practicing artist, using technology today to solve the same problems he grappled with as a talented adolescent.

Studies by Gardner (1980), Goldsmith (1992), Golomb (1992a), Robertson (1987), and Wilson and Wilson (1980) presented cases that might lead to a conclusion, that children can develop best in art if left to their own devices provided they have plenty of art materials and emotional support from the teacher. This view of teaching art was described by Eisner (1974) as one of seven myths about art education that pervaded the field two decades ago. The myth of a student with art talent being allowed to develop on his or her own has become even more prevalent in the gifted and talented literature than in writings about art education for the general school population (Clark & Zimmerman, 1984, 1987, 1994). Eisner, like Feldman (1980), stressed the importance of realizing that artistic development is not an automatic consequence of maturation. It is instead, a learned set of abilities that to a large extent are greatly influenced by the culture or cultures in which a person lives, studies, and works and the kinds of educational opportunities that are available.

REFERENCES

Beck, D. W. (1928). *Self-development in drawing: As interpreted by the genius of Rommo Dazzi and other children*. New York: Knickerbocker Press.

Benhow, C., & Stanley, J. C. (1983). Constructing educational bridges between high school and college. *The Gifted Child Quarterly, 27*(3), 11–13.

Bloom, B. (Ed.). (1985). *Developing talent in young people*. New York: Ballantine.

Chetelet, F. J. (1982). *A preliminary investigation into the life situations and environments which nurture the artistically gifted and talented child*. Unpublished doctoral dissertation, Pennsylvania State University, College Park.

Clark, G., & Zimmerman, E. (1984). *Educating artistically talented students*. Syracuse, NY: Syracuse University Press.

Clark, G. A., & Zimmerman, E. (1987). Tending the special spark: Accelerated and enriched curriculum for highly talented art students. *Roeper Review, 14*(1), 31–36.

Clark, G. A., & Zimmerman, E. (1992). *Issues and practices related to identification of gifted and talented students in the visual arts*. Storrs, CT: The National Research Center on the Gifted and Talented.

Clark, G., & Zimmerman, E. (1994). *Programming opportunities for students in talented in the visual arts*. Storrs, CT: The National Research Center on the Gifted and Talented.

Daurio, S. P. (1979). Educational enrichment versus acceleration: A review of the literature. In W. C. George, S. J. Cohn, & J. C. Stanley (Eds.), *Educating the gifted: Acceleration and enrichment* (pp. 13–63). Baltimore, MD: The Johns Hopkins University Press.

Eisner, E. (1974). Examining some myths in art education. *Studies in Art Education, 15*(3), 7–6.

Feldman, D. H. (1980). *Beyond universals in cognitive development*. Norwood, NJ: Ablex.

Feldman, D. H., & Goldsmith, L. (1986). *Nature's gambit*. New York: Basic Books.

Gardner, H. (1980). *Artful scribbles: The significance of children's drawings*. New York: Basic Books.

Goldsmith, L. T. (1992). Wang Yani: Stylistic development of a Chinese painting prodigy. *Creativity Research Journal, 5*(3), 281–293.

Golomb, C. (1992a). *The child's creation of a pictorial world*. Berkeley: University of California Press.

Golomb, C. (1992b). Eytan: The early development of a gifted child artist. *Creativity Research Journal, 5*(3), 265–279.

Gordon, W. I. (1978). *Communication: Personal and public*. New York: Alfred.

Nelson, K. C., & Janzen, P. (1990). Diane: The dilemma of the artistically talented in rural America. *Gifted Child Quarterly, 13*(1), 12–15.

Pariser, D. (1985). The juvenilia of Klee, Toulouse-Lautrec, and Picasso; A report on the initial stages of research into the development of exceptional graphic artistry. In B. Wilson & H. Hoffa (Eds.), *The history of art education: Program proceedings from the Penn State Conference* (pp. 192–202). College Park: Pennsylvania State University College of Arts and Architecture.

Robertson, A. (1987). Borrowing and artistic behavior: A case study of the development of Bruce's spontaneous drawings from six to sixteen. *Studies in Art Education, 29*(1), 37–51.

Sloane, K. D., & Sosniak, L. A. (1985). The development of accomplished sculptors. In B. Bloom (Ed.), *Developing talent in young people* (pp. 90–138). New York: Ballantine Books.

Stanley, J. C. (1977). Rationale of the study of mathematically precocious youth (SMPY) during the first five years of promoting educational acceleration. In J. C. Stanley, W. C. George, & C. H. Solano (Eds.), *The gifted and the creative: A fifty-year perspective* (pp. 75–112). Baltimore, MD: The Johns Hopkins University Press.

Taylor, R. (1987). *Educating for art*. London, England: Longman.

Van Tassel-Baska, J. (1986). Acceleration. In C. J. Maker (Ed.), *Critical issues in gifted education: Defensible programs for the gifted* (pp. 179–196). Rockville, MD: Aspen.

Van Tassel-Baska, J. (1987). The ineffectiveness of the pull-out program model in gifted education: A minority perspective. *Journal of Education of the Gifted, 10*(4), 255–264.

Wilson, B. (1976). Little Julian's impure drawings: Why children make art. *Studies in Art Education, 17*(2), 45–61.

Wilson, B., & Wilson, M. (1980). Beyond marvelous: Conventions and inventions in John Scott's Gemini. *School Arts, 80*(2), 19–26.

Zimmerman, E. (1991). Rembrandt to Rembrandt: A case study of a memorable painting teacher. *Roeper Review, 13*(2), 76–81.

Zimmerman, E. (1992a). A comparative study of two painting teachers of talented adolescents. *Studies in Art Education, 33*(3), 174–185.

Zimmerman, E. (1992b). Factors influencing the graphic development of a talented young artist. *Creativity Research Journal, 5*(3), 295–311.

6

Eitan: The Artistic Development of a Child Prodigy

Claire Golomb

University of Massachusetts at Boston

The literature on children who show a precocious talent for the naturalistic rendering of objects and scenes is extremely sparse and seems to confirm Goodenough's (1926) assertion that there is little evidence for such talent in children. Her extensive search for child artists able to represent the world in an adultlike realistic style led to her conclusion that such talent in the visual arts is either absent or exceedingly rare. Kerschensteiner (1905), who initiated a massive study of the drawings of public school children at the beginning of this century, seems to have shared this opinion. Thus, when Selfe (1977) published her findings on the stunning drawings of Nadia, an autistic child, her graphic virtuosity was generally taken as a mark of her pathology (autism) rather than a sign of an extraordinary talent pursued with intense dedication (see Selfe, chapter 7, this volume).

The claim that there are no precociously talented children in the visual arts stands in sharp contrast to the achievements of youngsters in the domains of music and mathematics. In these domains we have seen many prodigies, and recent publications examine their development and the unique conditions that facilitate their appearance (Feldman & Goldsmith, 1986). This somewhat puzzling state of affairs calls for a closer examination of the conditions that foster the identification and nurture of precocious talent. The fact that few publications have appeared may not be a true measure of the incidence of early giftedness in the visual arts. To draw attention to their talent, children need a supportive environment eager to foster their skills, and the reported incidence of child prodigies is, in part, a reflection of dominant social and economic currents. To develop precocious talent requires a tremendous investment on the part of parents and the society at large, it is intimately related to shared cultural values and to the prospects of social and financial rewards. A musical prodigy can gain early recognition and stardom with the promise of financial gain, whereas a youngster talented in the graphic domain is less likely to find an equally appreciative audience.

When, quite fortuitously, I discovered some of the remarkable drawings of 3-year-old Eitan who drew vehicles in sophisticated projective systems, my curiosity was aroused and I began a search to locate this child and his family. The questions that intrigued me most concerned the developmental sequence or order in which highly talented children develop their graphic skills. How did Eitan reach this representational sophistication, especially given the young age of this child? Did it appear fullfledged at ages 3 to 4 years, and if not, what were the precursors? This seemed especially important to me because Nadia's virtuosity was said to have arisen spontaneously, without the child having passed through the normal stages of graphic development. Several years after my first encounter with some of Eitan's drawings, I was able to contact Eitan's family.

The parents of Eitan were surprised to hear of my interest in their son's drawings, and at my request invited me to their home where I met them and their four children. Given my special interest in his early work, they had pulled from the attic numerous boxes that housed Eitan's drawings. Of course they appreciated Eitan's graphic talent, but neither the parents nor Eitan had seriously considered an artistic career for this child, and they were amused by my enthusiasm for what the boxes revealed.

The collection of Eitan's drawings, which begins with his second birthday, comprises a continuous record of drawing activity of an unusually gifted child artist, and spans the period from the first representational figures until age 19. Most of the childhood drawings were dated and labeled by his mother, whereas the later ones were identified and dated by Eitan in collaboration with his mother.

Eitan's collection is of particular interest in that he pursued, with an incredible determination for a child that young, his intention to portray objects as faithfully as he could. One can follow in a stepwise fashion how this preschooler taught himself the major projective drawing systems until he mastered the depiction to his satisfaction, and indeed became masterly at it. The collection provides us with an insight into visual thinking and graphic problem solving that is especially valuable because Eitan pursued his goals on his own, without technical aid from adults, and without copying of models. We can follow each one of his solutions, how they were tried out, transformed, or discarded. By the time Eitan was 4 years old, he had mastered horizontal and vertical oblique projection systems, divergent and isometric projection, and began to experiment with convergent perspective.

But beyond the fascinating solutions to the problems of graphic representation, his work is a testimony to the seriousness with which he set himself problems that lead to a deeper understanding of his world, with machines, vehicles, and the mechanics of their operation of central interest. From the volume of his drawings, which run into the thousands, one might surmise that drawing was his childhood passion, and that his quest to represent the important objects and events of his life was motivated by cognitive as well as emotional and aesthetic needs. Eitan's childhood work is unique in terms of the sophisticated drawing systems he invented, the virtuosity of his lines, the originality and expressive power of his composition, which are all signs of artistic sensitivity and talent.

THE FAMILY

Eitan is the oldest of four children and for the first 3 years of his life he was an only child. Both parents—his father an architect, his mother a nursery school teacher—are interested in the visual arts, and have some talent in this domain. Until he was 4 years old Eitan lived in the city of Jerusalem. Thereafter, the family moved to an industrial cooperative village in the northern part of the country.

His parents do not remember whether Eitan ever made scribble pictures. According to his mother, Eitan, an early speaker, started drawing recognizable shapes at the age of 2. His first drawings are of humans that represent Eitan's family, animals, tractors, bicycles, trains, compressors, boats, and hunters. His fine motor coordination was advanced for his age, and he effectively used pencils for drawing, and blocks and small legos for various constructions. His gross motor coordination, however, lagged somewhat behind and he began to walk only at the age of 2. In terms of social interactions with agemates on the playground, Eitan was a somewhat shy child.

Although the parents clearly valued and enjoyed Eitan's drawings, which were dated by the mother and preserved, theirs was a "hands-off approach," an educational philosophy of noninterference, a belief that Eitan should be allowed to pursue his interests at his own pace. In general, however, the family environment encouraged drawing, and father and son spent time together, each one engaged in his brand of drawing: Eitan on his father's lap making his pictures, while the father drew architectural designs.

According to the mother's recollection, Eitan's earliest drawings were made in response to objects encountered on their daily walks through the neighborhood. She views these drawings as Eitan's attempt to take new information in and to make sense of it. Although Eitan also engaged in pretend play, mostly with toy cars, drawing proved to be the major avenue for gaining an understanding of the fascinating world of objects and, perhaps, a means of exerting power over them. Although he spoke early, he was not a very verbal child or one who played with language and created narratives. He was, however, a very observant child whose primary form of expression was in the visual mode.

Between the ages of 2 and 3 years, Eitan spent an average of 15 to 20 minutes at a time drawing. Each of these pencil drawings were made quickly, with light sketchy lines, and in the span of seconds or minutes. Working from memory, Eitan would single out a part, mostly a frontal aspect, and work from there to other parts. He did not draw simple outline figures or construct them in an additive fashion. Instead he developed quite early a fairly complex conception of the whole object that guided the drawing of the parts. He showed an early and abiding interest in cars and knew, even as a 2-year-old, all the models on the road. Eitan was an inquisitive child who asked many questions about objects that interested him, about machinery, cars, and dinosaurs. He also spent long periods of time looking at picture books. He loved his books and liked to "correct" some of the drawings, for example, adding smoke to the chimney of a house. He seemed more interested in the visual aspects of a book, in the drawings and photographs, than in the verbal narrative.

BEGINNINGS

The first drawings in this collection, just as he turns 2 years, are of his family (see Fig. 6.1). The people are tadpoles, composed of a large head, facial features, ears, hair, arms, legs and feet, drawn in a frontal orientation, facing the viewer. They are drawn without regard for the objective shape, size, proportion, or dimensionality of the model, which is quite typical of early childhood drawings. What singles them out is the age of the child, which is 1½–2 years younger than is commonly seen. Despite his young age, Eitan draws his figures with a self-assurance in the way lines and contours are handled, and it is unlikely that they represent his first efforts.

The same quality of line can be seen in the drawing of a fish, at age 2.2. The fish, in side view, is drawn with a sweeping and well-controlled embracing line that ends in a tail, perpendicular to the body. The fish is endowed with facial features and blows air bubbles. Clearly, this 2-year-old already has a graphically differen-

FIG. 6.1. Daddy (age 2.2).

tiated conception of humans and animals. At 2.3, Eitan's humans, no longer tadpoles, boast a differentiated body with limbs extending from the trunk. At the same age he draws a train on its tracks, its wheels crossed with spokes that converge on a center, and overlapping circles for tires. These early drawings reveal Eitan as a careful observer, attentive to the way objects are constructed and to the parts involved in motion. His drawing of a tractor, also at age 2.2, consists of two large wheels, a shaft, exhaust pipe, seat, driver, and steering wheel. The wheels, represented by overlapping circles, suggest the volumetric property of tires (see Fig. 6.2).

These drawings of humans, fish, and tractor are representational achievements that effectively convey their message. Most remarkable is the age of the artist. One month later, at 2.3, the tractor has become more elaborate with spokes crossing the hub of the wheel, and verticals depicting the width of the tire. Two orthographic views of the wheels, a side and a top or rear view, have been juxtaposed, which lends a degree of solidity to the wheels. Other items drawn during this month include a train with its locomotive and many cars, a train on its rail, a ship and its anchor surrounded by fish, a group of hunters, a compressor, and an assortment of cars. The wheels of the cars have been further differentiated and include a set of conspicuous nuts and bolts.

We can follow Eitan's interest in the subjects he draws at 2.4, which include a compressor in frontal view, drawn with self-assured, quickly sketched lines, the

FIG. 6.2. Tractor (age 2.2).

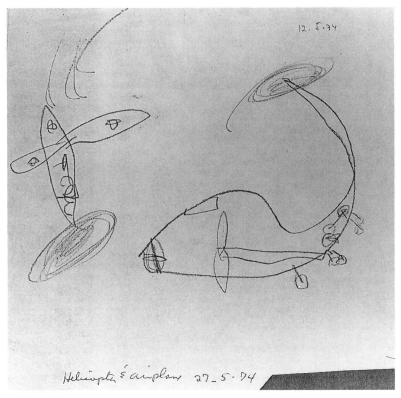

FIG. 6.3. Helicopter and airplane (age 2.4).

wavy lines (smoke) suggesting action and movement. During the same month, he draws helicopters and airplanes stationary or in flight (see Fig. 6.3). The helicopter's rotary movement, so aptly depicted, reveals Eitan's fascination with these powerful machines and their potential action. His attention to such details as rotors, propellers, cockpit, landing gear, and wheels shows how closely he observes these objects, while his ability to capture the characteristic shape of these vehicles and their movement displays an unusual and precocious graphic talent.

The majority of the drawings of vehicles made during the first months following his second birthday employ an orthographic projection system. This means that the object is drawn as if it faces the observer orthogonally, and a single flat, although dominant face comes to represent the totality of the object. From the age of 2.5, Eitan's drawings are based, in part, on a juxtaposition of orthographic projections, in which a frontal view (from the point of view of the observer) is supplemented by one or two side views that are attached to the facade. For example, in the case of the drawing of a car, bumpers, grill, head- and taillights are drawn in the same plane as the body of the car (see Fig. 6.4). This enables the child to represent two or three sides of the object, but the sides are depicted in the horizontal plane. Additional top faces, drawn along the vertical axis of the figure, can also be

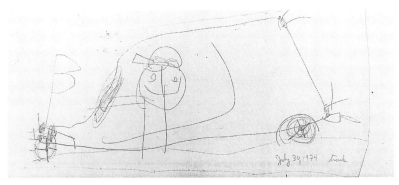

FIG. 6.4. Truck with head- and taillights (age 2.5).

appended to the frontally presented orthographic view. This drawing system soon becomes Eitan's preferred mode of representation. He draws, for example, the head- and taillights of the car at the upper and lower corners of the body; he rotates the bumper vertically upwards or extends it horizontally in an effort to depict more than a single face of the car or truck. In these drawings, cars and their different faces are presented to the observer from more than one viewpoint. Alongside the newly discovered vertical and horizontal oblique projection system (in Willats' (1977) terminology), Eitan continues to use the simple orthographic drawing system.

These early drawings show that Eitan has an agenda, namely, to portray the object as veridically and as completely as he can. Even at this early age, Eitan's drawings give evidence of a probing visual intelligence that observes, records, and analyzes, and is able to invent the graphic means to convey this understanding.

At 2.6 and 2.7, the inventory expands to include a convertible, a jeep, a moving van, cement mixers, trucks, buses, and a striking series of cows. The quickly sketched overlapping lines of the wheels of the jeep convey a sense of motion. The hood of the car is projected vertically, its solidity suggested by a pattern of horizontally and vertically drawn parallels.

The cement mixing trucks drawn at 2.7, are of special interest because they demonstrate so well his success in portraying more than a single face of the object (see Figs. 6.5 and 6.6). The basic side view of the truck is supplemented by a top view of the hood projected upward, a rudimentary frontal view of the grill, bumper, and headlights. Also noteworthy in this drawing is the oval body of the cement mixer. It is marked by a set of curved parallel lines that suggest the roundness or volume of this part. The curling smoke that emanates from the exhaust pipes indicates that the cement mixer is at work and that the vehicle is in motion. In addition to the representational virtuosity displayed by this 2-year-old, the sheer sensory motor mastery of the pencil is astonishing as seen in a moving van with beaming headlights drawn at 2.11.

As soon as he turns 3, Eitan largely abandons orthographic projection. He now consistently represents the third dimension by attaching top and side faces to the

FIG. 6.5. Cement mixer (age 2.7).

FIG. 6.6. Moving van (age 2.11).

178

frontal aspects of his vehicles. Eitan draws an astonishing array of vehicles: sports cars, convertibles, jeeps, police cars, ambulances, trucks, buses, vans, campers, trailers, bulldozers, airplanes, helicopters, an air ballon, and trains. His detailed representation of exhaust pipes, mufflers, gas tanks, differential boxes, and pneumatic brake boxes reveal how carefully he observes these powerful and fascinating machines. His interest in their make-up extends beyond what is visible, and some drawings offer a view of what is underneath the hood or inside a compressor. Looking inside the compressor, we discover its many belts and rotating parts. His helicopters often depict an open door that offers a view of the cockpit, and the open door to the camper reveals a table with chairs and a lamp. Although vehicles are a much favored topic, Eitan includes other items in his drawings, for example, a windmill with sails, a skyscraper, a garage, a guitar, people as drivers or passengers, Eitan and his mother, a birthday cake.

Because Eitan returns time and again to his favorite vehicles, one can literally see the evolution of various drawing strategies. The series of buses and trucks drawn over the next year demonstrate different types of solution which he invents, perfects or discards in his sustained effort to portray the multiple aspects of the vehicle. For Eitan it is clearly not enough to draw the characteristic sideview of, for example, a bus. This 3-year-old is not content until he can represent the long side of the bus with the passengers, the windshield with the driver, the hood, top, and front sides of the bus, the headlights and bumpers, all of which indicate the true shape, volume, and function of the vehicle (see Fig. 6.7). Similar experiments occur with trucks, cars, moving vans, cement mixers, compressors, tractors, and combines (see Fig. 6.8, 6.9, and 6.10).

FIG. 6.7. Bus in isometric projection (age 3.8).

FIG. 6.8. Car in divergent perspective (age 3.8).

FIG. 6.9. Truck in approximately isometric projection (age 3.9).

From his third birthday on, and with a growing repertoire of objects and themes, Eitan now employs three major drawing systems based on horizontal and vertical oblique projection, isometric projection, and divergent perspective. In isometric projection the frontal view of the object, in this case the car, is represented by its true shape (a basically rectangular shape), whereas the top of the car and one of its sides are drawn as parallelograms. The oblique parallel lines of isometric projection represent the edges of the car that extend backward into three-dimensional space. In divergent perspective, divergent diagonal lines are used to represent depth. Such drawings present four aspects or faces of the vehicle: the front, the top, and both sides. Eitan does not always base his drawing on a single system. In some drawings

FIG. 6.10. Compressor in isometric projection (age 3.2).

he uses a mixture of projection systems, for example, a locomotive drawn in horizontal and vertical oblique projection with one car drawn in isometric projection. Although all three systems appear at age 3.0, a more complex horizontal and vertical oblique system tends to displace the earlier and simpler one. A similar trend can be observed for divergent perspective, in which a more comprehensive treatment takes the place of a previously limited employment of this technique. Over the next few months, a combination of isometric and divergent perspective comes to be the system of choice for this 3-year-old. The developmentally less advanced systems, however, are not discarded and he continues to use orthographic and horizontal–vertical oblique projection in drawings of multiple objects for the representation of the nonsalient components of a composition.

In his continuous experimentation with graphic models, Eitan has moved from attaching sides, either vertically or horizontally to the frontal aspect, to a pragmatic experimentation with oblique lines that approximate in an intuitive, although imprecise manner, various projection systems.

Along with the effective use of various drawing systems, Eitan has also mastered the orientation of his vehicles that can face to the left or the right of the page. An amazing drawing of a moving van made at age 3.7 depicts the object in three-quarter view (see Fig. 6.11). The vehicle is drawn in predominantly isometric projection, with several changes in the angle of the parallel lines: Its overall diagonal axis imparts a sense of motion, of an object coming toward the viewer. Another drawing made at 3.7, depicts two people riding a motorcycle, the driver in the driver's seat and his passenger in a separate, although attached, compartment. The motorcycle, depicted from a frontal, somewhat foreshortened view, evokes an impression of

FIG. 6.11. Truck in three quarter view (age 3.7).

movement. Eitan knows how to create tight groupings of figures and their surround, and at times he employs size diminution as is the case in a drawing that depicts a desert scene (see Fig. 6.12). The large car with its driver, prominently displayed in the foreground, is set against a background of hills, dwellings, and vegetation, much reduced in size. Clouds, an airplane, and the jet's contrail complete the composition.

Eitan's line drawings have become increasingly more self-assured in their rendering of shape and volume. He tends to use sketchy, at times scribbly lines that extend into the interior of the shape and endow its object with solidity and vitality. His zig-zag and embracing lines create dynamic representations, whereas his portrayal of the whirls of rotors, jet contrails, exhaust fumes, and speed marks capture the intensity and power of motion.

If we summarize his development so far, we can see that he began his early drawing ventures in the manner of all young children, namely, with topological shapes that yield tadpoles and other simple global representations that are typical

FIG. 6.12. Desert scene (age 3.7).

of all beginners. At first his drawings are remarkable for the young age of Eitan, but very quickly he demonstrates an extraordinary interest, dedication, and skill level in the drawings made before he reaches 2.6. This very observant child who carefully studies those objects that capture his attention is also highly motivated to recreate them in his drawings. His fascination with powerful machines, especially vehicles in motion, is matched by a passion to represent them as completely and accurately as he can. Fortunately, he can capture their outlines and actions in his pencil sketches, and thus begins an intense quest to improve his drawings until they can match his conception of the object and represent it faithfully and comprehensively. In this process, Eitan, who has barely outgrown the toddler status, teaches himself the basic projective systems that can capture the volume and dimensions of his vehicles and of other interesting objects. This achievement is the more remarkable given the finding that, without instruction, even adolescents do not commonly reach this level of three-dimensional depiction.

There is an inherent visual logic to the order in which he acquires these drawing systems, beginning with the simplest and clearest graphic statement in orthographic projection, proceeding to its enrichment via horizontal and vertical oblique projection, and inventing the isometric drawing system which he then perfects to his satisfaction (Arnheim, 1974). This orderly progression, although spectacular in its precocity and autonomous development, is evidence that even the artistic child prodigy does not skip stages but masters them more fully and at a much more rapid pace than his agemates.

Eitan's artistry extends beyond his precocious visual thinking and the technical accomplishments demonstrated, for example, in his invention of effective graphic models, use of size diminution, overlapping parts, shading, and foreshortening. His drawings exhibit an assuredness and vitality of line that captures the essence of his vehicles that come alive under his rule of the pencil.

A YOUNG MASTER AT WORK

Over the next few years, Eitan perfects his strategies for representing his favorite objects and includes in his repertoire humans engaged in various activities, his first profile drawings of a person, animals, and city scenes. A tightly structured drawing of Jerusalem, made at 4.2, depicts the old city with its minarets, towers, and ramparts as seen from a hill or plaza (see Fig. 6.13). The buildings, closely spaced, overlap each other and diminish in size as the eye moves from the right to the left side of the paper. A car drawn in the right bottom corner shows foreshortening and some converging lines. Returning to one of his favorite themes, in a powerful drawing of a cement mixer in three-quarter view made at 4.4, he depicts the rear, side, and top aspects of the vehicle (see Fig. 6.14). This drawing, which is primarily based on isometric projection, is remarkable for its beautifully controlled lines and the self assurance with which Eitan varies their orientation to enhance the effects of volume. His sophisticated use of an elliptical shape for the partially occluded wheels further enhances the three-dimensionality of the scene (see Fig. 6.14). Eitan's vehicles are now mostly drawn in isometric projection, frequently in

FIG. 6.13. Jerusalem (age 4.2).

FIG. 6.14. Cement mixer (age 4.4).

three-quarter view, foreshortened, with a marked diminution in the size of the receding parts. Using this drawing system now in a consistent fashion, he creates powerful images of vehicles and machinery. In place of the earlier and intuitive exploration of various projective approaches, one gets the impression of a deliberate selection of the isometric system that gives him a masterly control over his chosen subject matter.

I have concentrated on Eitan's drawings of vehicles because they occupy a central place in his collection, and demonstrate so well his use of drawing strategies and their transformation. It is important, however, to mention that his repertoire is much richer and includes, among others, children playing, on skis, on tricycles, pushing a doll carriage.

Vehicles and their contents continue to engage Eitan as seen in drawings of a car with a raised hood, a camper, and a magnificent construction scene, all drawn between 5.0 and 5.2 (see Fig. 6.15 and 6.16). The collection from this age reveals an interest in how to assemble things and also includes drawings of the spaceship Apollo. New themes appear and include the depiction of roadways in city scenes, evidence of a broadened conception of urban life. This topic is further developed by the 6-year-old who draws an extensive series of intersecting highways, their traffic patterns and parking lots viewed from various angles, including aerial views (see Fig. 6.17 and 6.18). These are action-packed portrayals of airfields, planes taking off and landing, bombing attacks, near accidents of cars and trucks set

FIG. 6.15. Construction scene (age 5.2).

FIG. 6.16. Car with open hood (age 5.0).

against an urban background (see Fig. 6.17 and 6.18). Some of the more intricately constructed drawings that extend over a large area can take up to 1 hour for their completion. The individual elements that constitute the theme are drawn, as always, very quickly; it is the complexity of the composition and the sheer number of its elements that requires additional time for its planning and execution. A drawing from this period depicts a tornado passing through a city. It is a dynamically balanced composition in which the various elements are organized to convey the

FIG. 6.17. Near accident (age 6.6).

FIG. 6.18. Cement mixer (age 6.7).

tension of the theme. Although his interest is mostly vested in vehicles and the mechanics of their construction and action, he continues to explore other themes, and Eitan reveals an altered conception of the human figure in his portrait of a man with a beard and full lips, perhaps his father, drawn in profile. A cityscape of New York, drawn during a visit to the city at age 7.10, employs a mixture of drawing systems (see Fig. 6.19). Among others, in an attempt to use perspective, Eitan draws the streets with converging lines. The three-dimensionality of the scene is further enhanced by a stacking of buildings that overlap each other, and by the fairly consistent use of diminishing sizes.

A new interest appears in a series of animal drawings made between the ages of 7 and 8. Eitan draws an assortment of animals in the wild, leopards, lions, cheetahs, giraffes, monkeys, deer, elks, elephants, and zebras. They are dramatic action-filled scenes of life in the jungle. In these drawings Eitan tries to depict the various animals in their characteristic stance, in motion and at rest. The pencil drawings of dotted and striped animals display a decorative quality not previously seen. The inspiration for these drawings seems to have come, at least in part, from a calender and an animal puzzle.

In addition to his interest in vehicles, which he has maintained throughout, Eitan makes during this period an extensive series of Superman and Batman drawings, emphasizing the Superman's muscles and the city he flies over, a theme that now captures his imagination. In these drawings he uses black magic markers for the figure and scene, and various colors for Superman's suit.

At ages 10 and 11, following other visits to the United States, Eitan draws a series of city skylines in perspective, with bridges spanning the river (see Fig. 6.20). The drawing captures the elegance and magic of the construction, a poetic vision

FIG. 6.19. New York City (age 7.10).

FIG. 6.20. Cityscape (age 10).

of urban life. His interest in appearances extends to the drawing of maps and of cameras, the faithful recorders of reality, cameras that are open as well as closed, expressing his continued interest in the interior workings of machines that we saw earlier on.

THE ADOLESCENT YEARS

In the early adolescent years, Eitan's interest turns to performers, first the Beatles and then to athletes and rock stars. The portrayal of the Beatles represents Eitan's conscious effort to model the features, to apply shading in new and effective ways that capture the personal characteristics of the musicians.

The theme of athletes and of the muscular-looking human body will continue to engage Eitan's interest over the next few years as he depicts sports events and tries to master the human body in its manifold postures and in its relation to the other players. The same inquisitiveness Eitan showed earlier toward machines and their operation, he now brings to bear on this new field of inquiry. He grapples with the dynamics of motion, the flexing of muscles, and the way shading can enhance the realistic appearance of the body. When the drawings are not meant as mere exercises, which is the case in a series of heads drawn in various orientations, they distinguish themselves by their sense of order and balance in the grouping of figures in action. This series includes sports events in a stadium, with an audience sketched into the background. Athletic events inspire many drawings made over an extended period of years, between the ages of 11 and 16 years, and signify Eitan's admiration for the athletes and his intense interest in the games, some of which he may have attended. Whether real or imagined, he includes in the right corner of one of his compositions, his own hand caught in the act of drawing. The specific athletes portrayed suggest that he has studied the photographs of colorful magazines and newspaper, and is well acquainted with the identity of the players.

Once again we can follow the path Eitan marks out for his conquest of the dynamic shapes of humans in action (see Fig. 6.21 and 6.22). The early portrayals are mostly organized along the horizontal and vertical axes of the page; they concentrate on the different sides of the human body and their proportions, they vary the angles from which a group of players, for example, four men around a basket, can be seen. The figures, carefully outlined, are in motion, straining for the ball. A beautiful drawing of a soccer player depicts the athlete, in color, in a central position facing the viewer and against a background of horizontally arranged rows of fans, depicted by specks of color. As was the case earlier with vehicles, buildings, and machinery, Eitan's ambition is to capture appearances with precision and fidelity to the model. Gradually, the portrait of the athlete and the composition of

FIG. 6.21. Athletes (age 12–13).

FIG. 6.22. Athletes (age 12–13).

the team becomes more complex and captures the dynamics of individual as well as group action (see Fig. 6.23 and 6.24). His drawings, studies of parts as well as compositions, demonstrate a more intimate knowledge of the muscles that come into play, and his lines contrast the darker body contours with those that move into the interior spaces of limbs and torso, with shading highlighting areas of importance to the action.

Throughout the changing of topics he selects for drawing, for example, animals, cities, batman, beetles, rock stars, and athletes, Eitan maintains his interest in cars. The car drawings made during this period are mainly of cross-sections that depict the mechanical parts of the engine, the crankshaft, pistons, steering column, caliper brakes, fan, electric wiring, and the inner springs of seats. Others focus on stylistic

FIG. 6.23. Athletes (age 16).

differences between various car models. These drawings emphasize mechanical precision and, not surprisingly, their lines are sparse and somewhat lusterless, as is the case with catalogues. They contrast sharply with his drawings of athletes, of basketball and soccer players whom he presents in a seemingly unending array of postures.

Although Eitan shows a great concern with anatomical fidelity, and has taught himself much about the workings of the human body, his interest extends beyond the body in motion to the human face and its diverse expressions. As he experiments with different facial orientations, one sees the beginnings of a more psychological portrayal of the athlete.

Other themes that engage Eitan and thus enter his drawings are rock groups, figures from the Dungeons and Dragons game, the Beatles in various disguises, for

FIG. 6.24. Athletes (age 16).

example in Dungeons and Dragons garb. Political caricatures appear during the last years of high school, and we see the first sketches of teenage girls and young women. Not surprisingly, cars continue to engage him, and he creates his own designs, presented from different vantage points.

By the age of 17, drawing no longer serves as a major source of information about the way the world looks and operates. Eitan now draws for relaxation, for self-entertainment, often while listening to music. Art and drawing are relegated to the realm of a hobby that makes no demands on him. His talent allows him to play with whatever elements of reality he might be momentarily engaged in.

Over the years, his relationship to drawing has changed from a compelling desire to master the depiction of fascinating objects and scenes, and thus to control them, to an activity engaged in for his own amusement. But even in the early years, when he drew a great deal and with intense concentration, drawing was a playful and enjoyable activity. Eitan has been consistent in rejecting formal instruction. Earlier, as a 12-year-old, he insisted that he could teach himself whatever he needed to know by looking at photographs. Although at some point during his high school years he was registered for two courses in art, he quickly dropped one of them, an indication that he had no desire for formal training, and did not wish to subject his drawings to outside criteria.

This need to exercise autonomy over his drawing talent is similar to his approach to music. According to his music teacher, Eitan is highly gifted in this domain and could pursue a professional career if he devoted himself to music, but he refused lessons and plays the guitar by ear. During his years of service in the army, Eitan stopped drawing altogether, and took up playing the guitar. He has taught himself to play this instrument by listening to recordings of favorite rock musicians, and he feels challenged to reproduce the music exactly as he hears it. Perhaps, in analogy to drawing, there is the same love and fascination, and the ability to reproduce very closely the sounds of the music he has heard.

Eitan was a good student in high school, especially in mathematics, computer science, and English, although, in his own words "I was an average student ... I didn't really devote myself to school, and I had, like most of the boys, other things in mind." At 18, before his induction into the army, he considered as possible career choices architecture or automotive design. Following his recent discharge from the army, at the age of 21, these are still the two options he is considering, with industrial design a likely choice, thus joining his long-standing interest in the workings and designs of machines with his graphic talent.

A CHILD PRODIGY GROWS UP

Eitan's development documents quite clearly that this unusually gifted child did not skip stages. In his childhood he taught himself how to draw the objects that fascinated him until he could represent them as fully and as clearly as he desired. For Eitan to draw is to know and understand and early on he set himself the task to render his favorite objects with as much fidelity to their looks and function as he could master. By virtue of his tenacity, talent, and commitment, he found solutions that satisfied him. It is quite breathtaking to see how Eitan transformed the simple drawing systems until they suited his purposes. One can see how his solutions came about and note the orderly fashion in which these drawing systems evolved. Their adoption followed in broad outlines the developmental progression delineated by Arnheim (1974), and provides empirical support for his theoretical analysis. In Eitan's case we can say that he acquired complex projective drawing systems without recourse to copying or instruction.

According to his mother, Eitan never copied from a model. The art that was prominently displayed in his home did not seem to inspire Eitan's drawings. The walls displayed large, colorful abstract paintings, the work of his father. Eitan preferred lead pencils, and most of his childhood drawings were monochromatic pencil drawings that aspire toward realism. Of course, pencil affords the artist optimal control over line and contour, and is a most useful tool in architectural drawings.

The marvelous early drawings reflect this child's love of vehicles and an intense determination to understand his world, with a special fascination for its mechanical aspects. This effort to understand and to master new knowlege in conjunction with his drawing talent yielded the exquisite drawings Eitan made between the age of 4 to 6. These drawings are not merely cognitive exercises, their expression carries an affective charge that conveys the fascination, admiration, and perhaps fear of the young child in the presence of these awesome machines. To make an image means exercising control over the object and staking out a claim for its possession, a powerful tool for a child, and one that Eitan developed to perfection.

What are the common themes that motivated such intense dedication to drawing, and what might be the reason for the presently diminished urge to represent his relationship to the world and its meaning in graphic form? Quite striking is Eitan's choice of subjects that exemplify power, energy, and destructive potentials: vehicles and machinery, traffic patterns and accidents, tornados, wild animals, Superman, the Beatles and rock stars, and athletes with their extraordinary skill and strength. These subjects carry a tremendous appeal for all children and also many adults, but in the case of the child the contrast between his or her vulnerability, weakness, and powerlessness and the world of adults and their powerful machines is so much greater. Eitan was fortunate to have exceptional visual and graphic abilities that enabled him to take a stance vis-à-vis this world, to tame it as he represented it with ever greater clarity and aesthetic delight. Given that he was a somewhat shy child, who did not use language as the preferred mode for relating to others or to himself, drawing assumed special significance. As Eitan's world expanded, so did his interests, and the many ways in which he could now cast his understanding. Thus, gradually, drawing lost the urgency that had motivated the younger child.

As a teenager, Eitan engaged in sports, chess, music, and worked in his free time as a draftsman in his father's architectural firm. Of course he knew that he had a talent for drawing, and that he was admired for his skill, but he felt no need or desire to pursue a career in the fine arts. The earlier compelling need to draw had petered out.

In many ways, Eitan and Varda, the artist discussed in chapter 3, are studies in contrast. Eitan's interest was focused on the outer world, its appearance and mechanics, and he set out to study it and master it via his drawings. Eitan is not an introspective person, and questions about his interests in the arts, how he feels about his talent in the past and present time, do not engender self-reflection and articulation of subjective feelings. These questions receive short and simple answers and suggest that he is not comfortable talking about himself. His answers indicate that he was well aware that his parents liked his work, but he does not believe that it played a major role in his pursuits. Drawing was not the only preferred activity, he liked it along with others, for example, constructing models with legos, and playing basketball. From an early age he knew that he would choose a profession related to graphics. He still finds drawing rewarding and assumes that it will play a significant role in whatever career he will choose, perhaps architecture or graphic design. During his service in the army he had no time for drawing, and when he came home for short visits he preferred to see his friends and have some fun. As these responses indicate, Eitan does not feel a compelling need to draw, the emotional drive is absent. Drawing expresses momentary interests that are quite age appropriate, for example, in sports, rock stars and girls, but do not connect with deeper levels of his personality.

As Eitan's development so clearly demonstrates, exceptional artistic talent in childhood and a highly supportive environment do not predict adult artistic creativity. In Eitan's case, there is no inner necessity that dictates the choice of an artist's career, and he is free to consider a range of options. For Eitan, who is so richly endowed with visual intelligence and graphic talent, there are many avenues for using his gifts productively.

REFERENCES

Arnheim, R. (1974). *Art and visual perception*. Berkeley: University of California Press.

Feldman, D. H., & Goldsmith, L. T. (1986). *Nature's gambit: Child prodigies and the development of human potential*. New York: Basic Books.

Goodenough, F. L. (1926). *Measurement of intelligence by drawings*. New York: Harcourt, Brace & World.

Kerschensteiner, G. (1905). *Die Entwicklung der zeichnerischen Begabung* [The development of graphic talent]. Munich: Gerber.

Selfe, L. (1977). *Nadia: A case of extraordinary drawing ability in an autistic child*. London: Academic Press.

Willats, J. (1977). How children learn to draw realistic pictures. *Quarterly Journal of Experimental Psychology, 29*, 367–382.

7

Nadia Reconsidered

Lorna Selfe
Hereford and Worcester County Psychological Service, England

In this chapter, I describe my more than 20-year involvement with an autistic child with extraordinary drawing ability. I also discuss the evolution of the explanatory theories that could be proposed to account for the phenomenon she represented. It is impossible to approach any "wonder" without speculating how or why. This seems to me to be the natural human response and the root of all scientific endeavor. So, throughout this chapter, I share the development of my theories and confusions alongside a description of the facts of my inquiries into this and other cases. It is also very difficult to sustain any claim for total objectivity in reporting facts—the selection, weight, and presentation of such facts belie any such claim. It may well be helpful, therefore, for the reader to know a little about my perspective. I was originally trained as a teacher specializing in child development at an infant/junior level and after teaching infants for a number of years I obtained a degree in psychology at a British university renowned for its empirical and scientific approach. My later training was as a clinician under the direction of professors of psychology who are thorough-going scientists but have an eclectic and humanistic interest. I present theory and facts together from this perspective.

In 1974, a very worried mother contacted Professors John and Elizabeth Newson in the Child Development Research Unit at the University of Nottingham, England. She asked if they would be prepared to see her then 6-year-old daughter, Nadia, because most areas of the child's development were severely retarded. The Newson's agreed to see the child at one of their Thursday afternoon clinics. I was one of their postgraduate students, at that time, and I volunteered to work with Nadia in the special observation unit.

Despite Nadia's normal appearance, it quickly became evident to all the psychologists present that afternoon that she had a number of severe learning difficulties, especially in the field of language and motor development. However, toward the end of the session, her mother produced a bundle of drawings and, in stark contrast to Nadia's severe difficulties, it was claimed that she had a truly remarkable ability to draw.

In the discussion session after Nadia and her mother had left, the drawings were examined in stunned silence, for these were not the drawings of a normal or even a very gifted child. They were like the free sketches of a seemingly mature artist. They defied all that was known by the assembled child psychologists of the normal development of the representational drawing of children. Instead of the usual schematic and symbolic representations of an object, typical of a 6-year-old child, Nadia's drawings were of one stationary fixed view of objects, usually animals, in linear perspective, where foreshortening was used. Proportions were invariably accurate, diminishing size with distance was used reliably and essential characteristics of an object, not visible from a fixed viewpoint, were occluded. All these features of representational drawing are associated with later stages of graphic representational development, not usually achieved until all sorts of subskills are mastered and the stage of visual realism attained. Most developmental psychologists believe that such stages relate to general intellectual maturation and are only attained in a progressive way based on known developmental processes. (Buhler, 1930; Bruner, Olver, & Greenfield, 1966; Eng, 1931; Freeman, 1980; Goodenough, 1926; Harris, 1963; Luquet, 1927; and Sully, 1896, represent just a selection of eminent child psychologists who have made a special study of children's drawings and subscribed to a maturational and developmental view.) The first reaction was therefore to doubt the authenticity of the drawings, but all doubts were dispelled when I visited Nadia's school 2 days later and witnessed her drawing. Nadia and her unique ability became the subject of a 5-month research study and later of a book (Selfe, 1977).

Nadia was born in Nottingham to Ukrainian emigré parents. She is the second child in a family of three children. Her brother and sister are normal bright people but Nadia failed to develop language properly. The few words she had acquired by 12 months of age disappeared; she was unusually passive as a baby, had poor muscle tone, and learned to walk late. As she grew older, it became evident that Nadia's language development was severely delayed but her difficulties extended beyond verbal expression. Instead of the usual process of language acceleration or the generative stage that occurs around the age of 2 in normal children, the single words Nadia had mastered disappeared and she became virtually mute. Her verbal comprehension, too, was limited and she seemed to lack many of the prerequisites needed for normal language development, such as gesture and pointing, symbolic play, social responsivity, and imitation. By the age of 6 she had a very limited vocabulary of single words. She was extremely clumsy and poorly coordinated, could not dress herself, but on some visual matching tasks (such as jigsaw puzzles) Nadia's ability appeared to be average for her age.

At the age of 3½, Nadia suddenly displayed her extraordinary drawing ability, which was marked at the outset by very good motor coordination and manual dexterity and a quality of reproduction well beyond her years. However, this skill became apparent only when she was given fine-line pens, such as biros or sharp pencils with which to draw. Her drawing, even at this age, was in perspective, proportions between and within elements, usually of animals, were correct. She could use occlusion, eliminate lines hidden from view and the whole production was realistic, as if it had been drawn from one single fixed viewpoint, rather like a photograph. However, she was also able to imbue the subject with a sense of movement and vitality (see Fig. 7.1–7.7). The drawings were not copied from pictures, but were drawn entirely from memory, although on rare occasions she also appeared to draw from life. Generally, the inspiration for the drawings came from children's picture books, often where the quality of the picture was rather crude. She would study such pictures with close attention and then days or weeks later she would execute a similar drawing from memory. However, her drawings showed changes and embellishments from the original including changes of orientation, so that any explanation in terms of simple imaging or eidetic imaging must be regarded with extreme caution.

Over a 5-month period when Nadia was 6 years old, I saw her drawing many times. I was able to videotape the production of many drawings and analyze her technique at leisure. Nadia drew quickly with her head very close to the paper and became very animated, gurgling, vocalizing, and laughing as she drew, again in stark contrast to her normal slow and almost lethargic behavior. Nadia was left handed and her very strong preference was for a biro and a fine point. She would use a pencil if a biro was not available, but as she was interested in the verisimilitude of the line above all, she would quickly abandon attempts to draw with crayon, chalk, or even felt pen. She held the biro in a competent and adult manner between her thumb and index finger using her second finger for support. This was in marked contrast to other fine motor movements that were often executed with a whole fist grip in an immature manner. Her fine motor control when drawing was highly developed judged by her speed, accuracy, and general deftness. She did not need to track the progress of the line with the eye as many immature drawers do. Her lines were firm and confidently executed. She could stop a line where it met another line precisely, despite the speed of execution. She could change the direction of a line and draw lines at any angle toward and away from her body. She set down lines as if she were swiftly tracing round an outline, moving here and there, until the figure emerged to the astonishment of the onlooker. Unlike all young artists, her production did not appear to be governed by the previously drawn lines but by a very strong image of the finished product. Occasionally, it was evident that the line she had executed was not to her liking (usually incorrectly placed in relation to the rest of the figure), she would then make scolding noises and she would either repeat the line, searching for the correct position, move to another section of the drawing, or abandon the work in evident displeasure. At times, the search for the line became very dominant and she would go over and over an area until the production looked as if she had employed shading (see Fig. 7.2). With the same impulse to achieve

FIG. 7.1. Nadia, age 3½.

FIG. 7.2. Nadia, age 5½.

FIG. 7.3. Nadia, age 4.

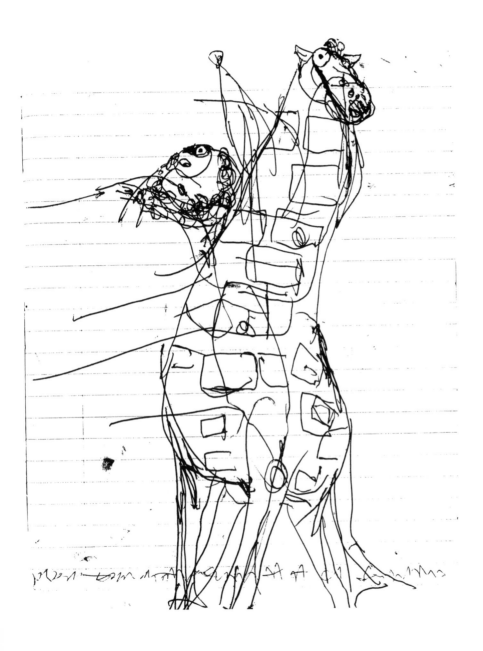

FIG. 7.4. Nadia, age 5–6.

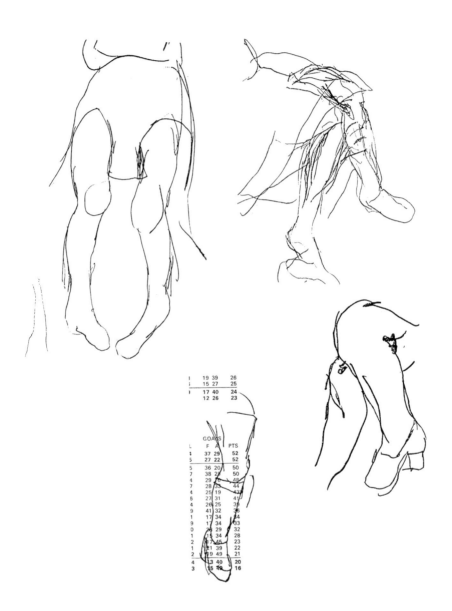

FIG. 7.5. Nadia, age 6.

FIG. 7.6. Nadia, age 6.

FIG. 7.7. Nadia, age 6½.

the correct line, Nadia would occasionally pick up an old drawing and correct it. She could spoil some good drawings in the process and occasionally I felt impelled to intervene. She usually displayed annoyance and frustration at such times, and it is possible that this frustrated search for perfection in her terms would lead her eventually to regard drawing as more frustrating than pleasurable. Nadia very occasionally employed shading in her drawings usually to depict tone or variations in color on an animal's skin (see Fig. 7.3 and 7.4).

Nadia drew intensively in short bursts, usually up to 1 minute in duration, but occasionally, when a drawing was going especially well, for longer. She would then sit back to survey her work moving her head to vary the viewing angle. This usually gave her great pleasure and she would shake her hands and knees in glee gurgling and babbling. If she was happy with the drawing she would quickly return to work but she would seldom repeat this process of intense work and inspection on the same drawing, although there were a few drawings (see Fig. 7.2) where Nadia became engrossed and worked for more than 30 minutes. Nadia's mother frequently gave her just one or two pieces of good quality paper to try to encourage her to persist at one effort. This had limited success. She appeared to be happiest with an unrestricted supply that may well have encouraged her to achieve verisimilitude. When she had plenty of paper at hand, usually after a second or, occasionally, third session the drawing was complete to her satisfaction. She would often swiftly turn the page and begin again, frequently on the same subject. If she was unhappy with a drawing or if she was evidently losing interest and concentration she would often lapse into a staring reverie that frequently signaled the end of the session. Nadia gobbled up paper using up to 30 sheets in a 20-minute session. Her parents found it difficult to keep her supplied with paper and she did the majority of her drawing at home. Some of her early drawings were executed on scraps of paper, cartons, advertisements, and even in picture books on top of other illustrations (Fig. 7.5).

Nadia's favorite subject throughout this period remained horses and horses with riders (see Fig. 7.1–7.3). She also drew fierce cockerels and I witnessed the evolution of one series of cockerels. From an interest in a crude drawing of a cockerel in a child's coloring book, a few days later she produced a recognizable copy characterized by the same stance, orientation, and size. Over the next few weeks she experimented with the image, changing the size and orientation, and adding details such as a tongue. She experimented with orientations of beaks. I regard this as almost defying rational explanation because her experience of real chickens or cockerels was extremely limited, yet she demonstrated an intimate understanding of the shape and dimensions of the bird and all its features (see Fig. 7.6). Other subjects appeared and were slowly discarded in a similar manner. She saw a picture of a pelican and carefully scribbled over the lines of the image. Days later she drew the image from memory and she produced the drawing four or five times more over the next week. She also had a period of drawing legs and shoes. (I suspected that this was sparked off by the great interest in the emerging new fashion for shoes with high wedged soles and heels.) Human figure drawings had appeared from time to time, and in the period when I was working intensively with her they appeared intermittently, usually as riders. She started to experiment with smaller and smaller heads on her figures until she produced headless figures and riders (see Fig. 7.7). Although she usually drew from memory, I also witnessed her drawing from life, or rather with the subject of her drawing before her. She showed a great deal of versatility in both her choice of subject as well as her models. The idea that she may have had a very limited repertoire of well-rehearsed subjects is entirely erroneous.

Nadia was diagnosed at the Child Development Research Unit as suffering from autism and severe learning difficulties. Shortly after I had concluded the original study, Nadia was transferred to a special school for autistic children. This school, Sutherland House in Nottingham, is considered to be one of the best schools for autistic children in Britain, pioneering new educational programs and therapies. Nadia was placed on a special individualized program. It was decided that her prime need was to develop communication skills, and language development formed a major part of her program; within months she made very good progress in this respect. Over the next 2 or 3 years I saw Nadia regularly, usually at home. The teachers and psychologists in her school gave her a great deal of encouragement to draw, providing her with art books of all descriptions, especially reproductions of paintings of horses. As she was brought into closer communication with others she began to imitate the drawings of her peers and to reflect their interests. Doll-like fashion drawings emerged at one period (see Fig. 7.8). She did not lose her old ability and flair and she could produce wonderful drawings of horses and cows on one day, and cartoonlike drawings of people and teachers on the next, but her

FIG. 7.8. Nadia, age 8–9.

interest in photographically realistic representations was visibly waning (see Fig. 7.9). Another disastrous occurrence for the whole family was the death of Nadia's mother in 1976. She had drawn with her mother and mainly at home. When I saw Nadia shortly after her mother's death she became very distressed and started shouting "Mummy, Mummy." I had always been "Nadia's drawing lady" to the family and I realized then the great store that Mrs. Chomyn had placed in Nadia's drawing ability. Nadia demonstrated this in such a painfully eloquent way. Nadia clearly associated me with her mother as it was her mother who had especially

FIG. 7.9. Nadia, age 8–9.

valued my friendship through my appreciation of her daughter's one remarkable talent. In retrospect, two events marked the beginning of a decline in Nadia's interest and ability to draw; the death of her mother and the development of communication skills.

Nadia continued to draw with intermittent interest and her drawings at the age of 12 remained highly skilled and unusual (see Fig. 7.10–7.12). However, as most 12-year-olds can make use of most of the graphic devices of perspective drawing, her drawings were no longer remarkable except that she remained a very retarded person with severe learning difficulties. Unfortunately, her skill had shown no real development, and at this stage I feared that her ability to "sketch round an image" was less confident and her productions were more tentative and frequently showed visually degraded images (see Fig. 7.12). As a teenager she attended a local school for autistic adolescents, progressing on to a residential school. Again, every effort was made to foster her ability and she was now having regular drawing and art lessons. When I worked with her at this period it was evident that drawing no longer enthralled her. The animation and excitement of earlier years was totally absent. She patiently cooperated but very soon she simply ignored my entreaties.

The original study of Nadia at the age of 6 was produced as a book that appeared in 1977. The book attracted many reviews and commentaries, perhaps the most notable ones being from Arnheim (1980), Gregory (1977), Pariser (1979), and Nigel Dennis (1978). Walter Cronkite brought a television team from the United States to interview Nadia. Most commentators shared our original reaction of astonishment and perplexity. Dennis' long review in the *New York Review of Books* was decidedly controversial. He criticized all of the psychologists in the Child Development Research Unit who had any connection with Nadia for a failure to treat her "genius" with more sensitivity. I believe that he quite understandably failed to appreciate the severity of her handicaps. The drawings inevitably mislead. I, therefore, plead "not guilty" to his accusation, but guilty and unrepentant to the charge of attempting to make some sense of her genius. Nadia's drawings have traveled Britain as an exhibition and they have crossed the Atlantic to appear in an exhibition in Chicago. The drawings are now in a permanent special archive at the Institute of Psychiatry, the Maudsley and Royal Bethlehem Hospital, in London.

I went on to conduct a further piece of research that involved a study of a very small group of autistic savant children who showed a similar, although not as spectacular ability in representational drawing as Nadia. Her progress was reviewed in that study, which appeared in 1983. This involved a review of the autistic syndrome and attempts were made to link what was known of autism to explain the extraordinary phenomenon. The study also reviewed the cognitive processes involved in children's drawings.

It is now 10 years since this work was concluded. A great deal of discussion about the phenomenon of autistic artistic savants has been conducted as a result of the discovery of Nadia and this is variously described in Park (1978), Pariser (1979), Gardner (1980), Sacks (1985), Howe (1987), Thomas and Silk (1990), Golomb (1992a), and Cox (1993). The case is also frequently quoted in textbooks on developmental psychology and has become a standard classic.

FIG. 7.10. Nadia, age 12.

FIG. 7.11. Nadia, age 12.

211

FIG. 7.12. Nadia, age 12.

There has also been a plethora of research into autism in Great Britain and the United States, but of particular interest to a better understanding of autistic savants is the work of O'Connor and Hermelin (1987a, 1987b); Frith (1989); and Baron-Cohen, Leslie, and Frith (1985, 1987). Finally, there has been a great deal of research and some developments in our understanding of theories of representational drawing in ordinary children (see, in particular, Freeman & Cox, 1985, and Thomas & Silk, 1990). It is therefore opportune to look again at the phenomenon that Nadia represents in the light of these new developments. In the mid-1980s, we did not know as much about the etiology of autism nor did we have sufficiently elaborated theories explaining representational drawing in children as we do today. What then is the situation in the mid-1990s?

In the original study of Nadia (Selfe, 1977), I reviewed the theories that had been proposed to account for those adults and children with severe learning difficulties who had special abilities up to that date. These individuals used to be termed *idiot savants*, but Howe (1989) rightly referred to such people as *retarded savants*. I concluded that the best of them gave no satisfactory insight into Nadia's particular skill. Jaensch (1930) described a study of a calender calculator who claimed to be able to read off the correct date by visualizing a calendar in "his mind's eye." But on close appraisal of the evidence on eidetic imagery it was concluded that it was not a sufficient explanation for Nadia's extraordinary skill. Her drawings not only showed an imaging ability but she displayed interpretation; the original image was placed in a new orientation, details were added or omitted, and sizes varied. Also eidetics are not noted for their drawing ability, and although imaging must be involved in the drawing process, the mechanics of getting the image in the head on to a two-dimensional surface must be far more complex.

Attention was then turned to the attempt to find an explanation for Nadia's extraordinary ability by scrutinizing her other abnormalities and their effect on cognitive functions. Nadia had many "soft" neurological signs of brain damage and it was tentatively suggested that possible damage to her left cerebral hemisphere (usually claimed to be involved in controlling the language function) had resulted in a compensatory development of right hemisphere functions (the hemisphere claimed to be more specialized for spatial processes). I ultimately abandoned this hypothesis, although others have resurrected it since (see Cox, 1993; Edwards, 1979), because this model is highly controversial and philosophically flawed. Howe (1989) pointed out that there is no explanatory force in terms of underlying neurological mechanisms in a physiological explanation and the arguments advanced are often circular. The major difficulty, however, is that the evidence for the cerebral lateralization of functions is contradictory and, in any case, the evidence that was available about Nadia's cerebral functioning conflicted with the model because she showed abnormal electrical discharges on the right side of the brain. Finally, subsequent studies of other autistic savant artists further confounded this theory because a number had well-developed language skills, some were right handed and some were left handed, there was no evidence of brain dysfunction, and no simple physiological model could account for all the findings.

Finally, as a psychologist I naturally felt more at home seeking explanations within my own discipline. It was possible to build an explanation based on cognitive processes alone. I had attempted to investigate Nadia's ability to match objects with perceptual and conceptual similarities. She had no difficulty in matching pictures of objects to their silhouettes, but she was unable to group objects in the same conceptual class for example, kitchen chair to armchair to deck chair. Normal children's drawings are essentially conceptual where the essential defining features are represented. Nadia's drawings were not like this, and the distinction between normal children's conceptual or symbolic representations and the fixed single viewpoint anomalous drawing demonstrated by Nadia was explored in my further studies.

In the conclusions to *Normal and Anomalous Representational Drawing in Children* (Selfe, 1983), I reviewed the evidence as presented by the drawings of a small number of autistic savants together with what was known of autism and theories of representational drawing, and I proposed a hypothetical explanation for the phenomenon.

In the first half of that book, theories of the normal development of graphic representation were reviewed. It has been demonstrated by many researchers that children up to the age of 8 have major difficulties representing features of photographic realism. Devices such as occlusion, perspective, foreshortening, and so on representing photographic realism in children's drawings, are gradually acquired. Normal children up to the age of about 7–8 are best described as drawing symbolic or canonical representations of objects (Freeman, 1980). Children with high intelligence can sometimes show an accelerated development with regard to the acquisition of these devices, and a correlation between the degree of elaboration and the inclusion of these devices and children's intellectual maturity has been described, in particular by Goodenough (1926) and Harris (1963).

The book then described the small group of children who showed outstanding representational ability in their drawings from a very young age, and who also shared severe intellectual impairments. The specific differences in the drawing ability of these children and normal children were isolated. The differences were found to be the use of photographically realistic proportions, the depiction of apparently diminishing size with distance, and the depiction of occlusion or overlap.

This type of depiction was discussed in terms of photographic realism because the drawings had many of the qualities of the photograph. However, the main characteristic was that the drawing depicted as if from a fixed single viewpoint. Light (1985) discussed this difference in terms of an "array-specific" depiction as against a "view-specific" depiction, the former characterizing young children's drawings because their representations are canonical and symbolic.

Of the eight children studied in detail, five were already diagnosed as autistic and the remaining three showed many of the essential features of autism. As this ability to depict a single fixed viewpoint using linear perspective at an early age (before the age of 8) does not usually occur in the ordinary population or indeed even in the highly gifted population, it was reasonable to conclude that the phenomenon is a pathological one connected to the deficits seen in autism. A review of the research on the cognitive deficits in autism was therefore undertaken (Rutter & Schopler, 1978). Ten years ago there was some consensus, but not unanimity, that autism resulted from a central cognitive deficit probably with a physiological origin, which involved retarded and/or abnormal language development, but which was thought not to be just confined to the language function alone, because motor, perceptual, and social functions were also affected. Hermelin and O'Connor (1970) argued that autistic children had difficulty in transposing coded information between internal representational modalities. In a series of experiments, they showed that autistic children were inflexible in transposing between modalities on a range of tasks where auditory or spatial stimuli were presented, and where responses had to be given in the alternative mode.

In Selfe (1983), I argued that normal young children's drawings reflect dominant cognitive and developmental processes. This is a well-established, noncontroversial view. Bruner et al. (1966) suggested that after the age of 2, an iconic stage of development is superseded by a symbolic stage. The well-established view that normal young children represent the characteristic rather than the idiosyncratic features of an object and that their drawing is essentially symbolic or conceptual was also cited. The argument then continued by making a parallel with language development, where language is characterized by Piaget, Vygotsky, and Bruner as preeminently a categorizing and symbolizing activity whereby the whelter of perceptual and sensory experience is ordered and reduced. In attempting to draw out this parallel, I argued that the special group of autistic savants were better able or more concerned to draw single viewpoint, static spatial configurations due to the fact that their symbolic and discursive abilities were very restricted, and that transposition between cognitive modalities was very limited in these individuals. Using Paivio's (1971) work, where he elaborated a dual coding hypothesis in human cognition, it was conjectured that these autistic savants had well-developed imaginal thought processes involving visual imagery, but that their verbal and discursive thought processes were defective. Normal drawing development results from the integration of both forms of thinking, thus it was reasoned that autism and its attributive cognitive defects account for the special spatial characteristics of the drawings of these children. The claim was made that these autistic savants were able to draw photographically realistic spatial configurations not because of an accelerated development or the attainment of more advanced representational ability in their drawing, but because of a profound deficit in the normal symbolic, canonical, or conceptualizing process.

At the end of the book it was acknowledged that there are many flaws with this hypothetical explanation and that it may prove to be a "house of cards." The first obvious difficulty is that not all autistic children show any special ability with representational drawing, in fact most show a retarded development, drawing at their mental age level. My eight subjects were a special subgroup and it may be something quite apart from autism that unites them in their common skill. Furthermore, dual coding models of human cognition have been heavily criticized (Pylyshyn, 1973). The relationship between drawing and cognitive processes is as yet poorly understood; although the product of drawing is a spatial configuration, the process involves a discursive, sequentially organized series of motor movements. I concluded the study by admitting that the phenomenon remained a great puzzle.

In this chapter, I propose to look afresh at this hypothesis in the light of the new researches and developments that have occurred. But first, it might be instructive to take another look at the original evidence. What of Nadia herself? She now represents the opportunity for a longitudinal study of an autistic savant. Nadia's current status in developmental and cognitive terms may support or detract from the claims and the inferences arising from the original hypothetical explanation.

In order to discover more about Nadia's present status, her father kindly cooperated in completing a factual questionnaire. From his answers a clear picture emerges. Nadia is now in her 20s. She lives in a special residential home for adults with severe learning difficulties and she will require a degree of supervision and support throughout her life. In terms of basic self-sufficiency, there are several skills that she has mastered satisfactorily. She can feed herself competently and without assistance and needs no special help at table. She can drink in a normal fashion and has good table manners. She can bathe or shower without supervision and can wash and dry herself. She will clean her teeth without being told and care for herself at toilets, including washing her hands. She can dress and undress unaided and appropriately. Also, she can look after minor health problems appropriately. The only thing she cannot manage in this category of basic skills is to care for her hair unaided. However, in other respects, her abilities in and around the home remain limited. Although she can prepare a simple meal by herself, she cannot carry out simple household activities without help, nor can she wash, dry, or iron clothes appropriately and she cannot carry out basic repairs to clothes. One of her major leisure activities is the playing of records, which she can undertake unaided. She also particularly enjoys horseback riding, which she does under close supervision.

It is clear that Nadia's ability to lead an independent life in the immediate community is very restricted. She cannot plan and carry out simple activities (e.g., visiting local shops) without close supervision. She cannot locate items in a supermarket or other shop and pay as required. Nor can she use public transport independently. She cannot use a telephone, thus she cannot contact anyone for help or advice, whether family or the emergency services. She can, however, ask for the toilet in unfamiliar situations. Nadia has no clear concept of the use or value of money, so that she cannot use it accurately or meaningfully. She cannot check change. She cannot tell the time, although she does seem to understand the significance of time in terms of daily routines. Unfortunately, Nadia cannot read any single words so the simplest of books is denied to her. She acquired a very small sight vocabulary at one period but as reading skills failed to progress, this too waned. She cannot count and so cannot add numbers below 10.

Her interest in spontaneous drawing has waned into virtual extinction. She shows no interest in drawing without supervision, but she can be coaxed into some rather stereotyped and unremarkable productions (see Fig. 7.13–7.15). It is almost as if she realizes and is pained by the gradual withering of her once prodigious talent; but this may be to impute too much to her. Certainly, drawing holds none of the excitement and pleasure for her that it did when she was 6 years old.

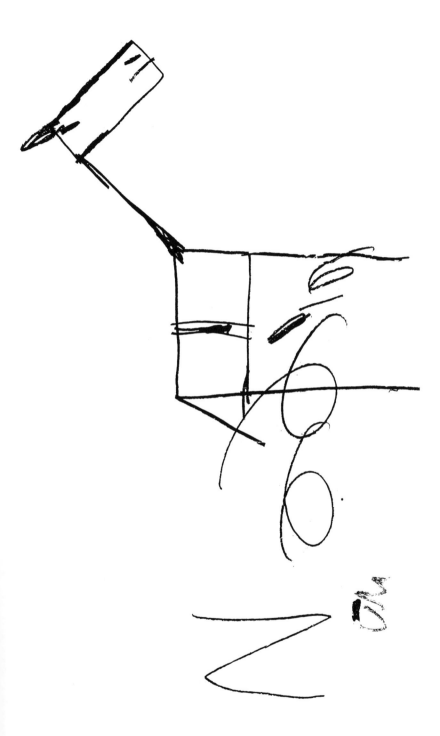

FIG. 7.13. Nadia, age 25.

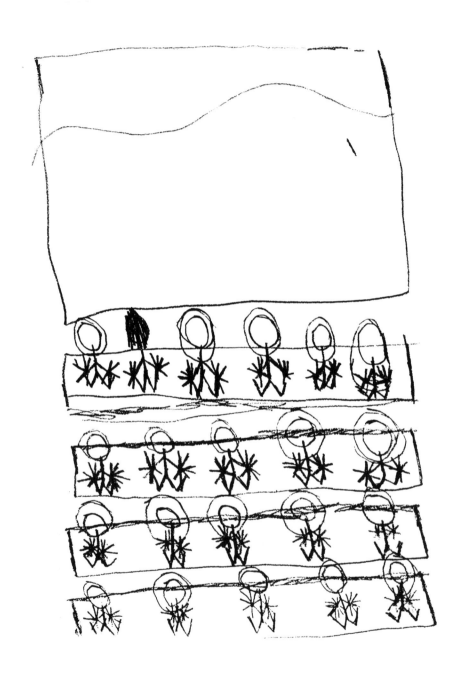

FIG. 7.14. Nadia, age 25.

FIG. 7.15. Nadia, age 24.

And finally, what of Nadia's language development? Nadia can now only hold the simplest of conversations. In such conversations she can make her basic needs known; she can give her name on request and can follow reasonably simple instructions, such as "Go and get a knife and fork" where a familiar context plays a part. She can also name at least four colors accurately. However, she does not know her age, her birthday, nor her address. She certainly cannot join in any normal kind of conversation or convey a simple message accurately to someone else. She cannot explain her simplest action or why something has happened (e.g., why a houseplant without water has withered and died). She cannot follow stories on television or on the radio or indeed those which have been told to her with any sign of comprehension or interest. Although she still shows interest in pictures and drawings in books, she is apparently unaware that her own work has been published and that it is of interest to other people.

The picture that emerges of Nadia now is of a severely handicapped individual who has some basic but limited self-sufficiency skills, but requires high levels of care and supervision in all the more complex day-to-day activities. As previously mentioned, one or two of the reviewers who commented on the original book when it was first published failed to comprehend the severity of her learning difficulties. This was an understandable reaction given the impact of her extraordinary drawings. Dennis (1978) described Nadia as a genius and Howe (1989) picked up the word in his excellent book about retarded savants entitled *Fragments of Genius.* Howe proposed, along with Gardner (1984), that cognitive abilities or skills may be much more independent than previously thought. The problem is that Nadia's one remarkable ability appears to have had very little impact on any other skill area and has, in any case, virtually disappeared. One might have hoped that her visual skills would have transferred to the acquisition of a basic sight vocabulary, for example. But in spite of years of training this has not been accomplished. Arnheim (1970) made special claims for visual imagery suggesting that most thinking operates in this mode and language merely helps this process. Dennis created a view of Nadia as an isolated genius who would not deign to cooperate with her teachers and therapists. Autistic children are always a puzzle, and a frequently voiced feeling from parents and therapists is wanting to find the key to unlock the person's cooperation. I fear, then, that it is safe to conclude that it is not that Nadia will not cooperate, it is that she cannot, and the responses to this up-to-date questionnaire strengthen this conclusion.

The question of the role of language of Nadia's prolonged inability to speak, the subsequent development of some very basic level of verbal comprehension and speech, and the coincidental decline in her drawing ability is an intriguing one. Several other commentators have attempted to explore this (Howe, 1989; Pariser, 1979; Thomas & Silk, 1990). It does appear that, as language has developed, Nadia's interest and/or her ability to draw has waned and again the responses to the questionnaire confirm this. But this is a complex issue and one that is considered again later in the chapter.

Nadia has regular art therapy in the residential home. If left to her own devices she spends time in art lessons scribbling concentric circles in circular patterns. Representational drawings are only done on request and she frequently simply refuses to cooperate. When she can be persuaded, most of her productions are crude and childlike canonical representations (Fig. 7.13–7.15). These correspond very approximately with her mental age (5–6 years). They are unremarkable and typical of the work of many mentally handicapped adults. But they are remarkable if one considers how she drew when she was 6 years old. What has happened to the old ability, to the skills of representing animals so accurately and in linear perspective? Can such talent be irretrievably lost? Most notions of skill acquisition are challenged if we think of Nadia as actively and consciously learning to draw, acquiring devices, and solving planning problems in the manner described by Freeman (1980). But perhaps her original drawing was not like this, but was more like an infantile, unconscious reflex that was doomed to disappear with maturation—swallowed up by a more conscious approach to drawing. Another parallel is the acquisition of a second language in a very young child that is then lost through disuse.

Occasionally, a drawing will appear that has echoes of Nadia's old skills (Fig. 7.15). Lines, too, have a fluidity and assurance that suggests mastery (Fig. 7.15). But that wonderful burgeoning talent has not been fulfilled and not from lack of opportunity or nurturing. Nadia has had a series of excellent, dedicated teachers who have taken pains to encourage her. One cannot but feel dismay comparing her drawings then and now, contemplating withered promise. But the story must be told and now with such an ending we have a new enigma. Why such a disastrous withering? It suggests to me, yet again, that the original drawing was not the result of a burgeoning talent, the work of an isolated "genius," but was the amazing result of a pathological process. But this is one among several guesses. It is just conceivable that Nadia is producing canonical drawings in that "tyranny to conform," to be like her peers. And, again, her mother's death marks a decline in interest in drawing coincidental with the development of verbal communication.

It is now timely to attempt to review some of the relevant research that has been conducted since the 1980s. The six subjects I was able to discover with extraordinary drawing ability had a number of common features. What seemed to me to be most significant, however, was that they all were either diagnosed as autistic or had autistic features. Since these cases were reported, several others have been published and in all cases the subjects have been autistic. (Morishima, 1974; Park, 1978; Sacks, 1985; Wiltshire, 1987). The case of Stephen Wiltshire is perhaps the most interesting insofar that, now in his late teens, he is a formidable artist (and I use the word with all due caution) whose skill, far from waning, is improving. He is an autistic boy whose drawings first appeared in print when he was 12. He draws very fine, detailed architectural scenes (see Fig. 7.16). His ability was first noticed when he was 9 and it has continued to develop since then. He learned to speak late and he remains retarded in many aspects of cognitive development including verbal processes. Of all autistic savants that I have encountered, however, Nadia remains the most extraordinary example because of her age. None have shown exceptional ability so early. Some of her outstanding drawings were done at the age of 3. In view of the fact that her skill has so dramatically waned, it is possible that Nadia is not at the extreme end of a continuum but is a case apart.

Reading Howe's (1989) book, *Fragments of Genius,* I was struck by his many descriptions of what he termed *retarded savants.* So many of these individuals displayed autistic as well as retarded characteristics. He cited the case of outstanding musical ability in a man with severe learning difficulties reported by Anastasi and Levee (1960), and he gave a long description of the man that reads like a textbook description of autism, although Howe did not use the word. Howe questioned whether all savants are autistic, but he is not convinced that a distinction between retarded and autistic is useful. He limited himself to an old and very restricted view of autism quoting Kanner's (1943) original definitions. My experiences in finding subjects for my sample of very talented young drawers led me to consider

FIG. 7.16. The Kremlin Palace. Drawn by Stephen Wiltshire, age 17.

autism as central to extraordinary skill in graphic production. One 5-year-old subject had no diagnosis of autism, his reported history appeared to be normal, and he was attending an ordinary school. He was drawing buildings in linear perspective from memory and I believed that I might have found a very gifted ordinary child until I met him. After the usual introduction he danced on tip toes over to the window and spent the next hour twiddling objects in the light in his peripheral vision. This was not the behavior of an ordinary boy, and it quickly became apparent that he showed many other features of autism.

Of course the problem in positing a link between autism and special skills is that it is a tiny minority of autistic children who have any unusual ability (Charman & Baron-Cohen, 1993; O'Connor & Hermelin, 1987a, 1987b). However, I remain convinced that this remains a fruitful conjecture. In the first place, I have not yet found a case of idiot savant or retarded savant who does not display autistic features and, judging from a search through the available evidence, many of the documented cases of idiot savants or retarded savants have indications that the subject has autistic characteristics (these are outlined later). Not all gifted child artists are autistic, as Golomb's chapter on Eitan indicates. Eitan was a precociously gifted child artist who was also a highly intelligent normal child. Nevertheless, in the case of autistic children, it is well established that they frequently have wide discrepancies in their profile of abilities. Characteristically, the profile of subtest scores on tests such as the Wechsler Intelligence Scale for Children shows a wide variation in intrasubject scores (Frith, 1989, 1991). Frequently, verbal subtest scores are significantly lower than performance subtest scores. Skills involving visual organization such as object assembly and block design are frequently relatively well developed compared with skills involving verbal categorization such as similarities where the child is required to say how two words are alike or similar (e.g., a rose and a tulip). In some cases of autism, then, it appears that the supposed underlying neurological dysfunctions implicated in the condition are selective and discrete, allowing other areas of the brain to function relatively normally. Autism can exist in association with global retardation, but there are also very able autistic people (now being recognized as having Asperger's syndrome; Frith, 1991) who can be highly intelligent but have profound difficulties especially in the social domain. It is likely that autism is in marked contrast to other syndromes involving brain dysfunction where the dysfunction is all pervasive as in, for example, Down syndrome. The fact that in autism deficits can coexist with highly developed skills and abilities is obviously supportive of the conjectural link.

Finally, there is the striking parallel between autism with all its connotations of idiosyncratic isolation and the idiosyncratic, single, fixed viewpoint portrayed in the drawings of Nadia and other autistic savants such as Stephen Wiltshire. Photographic realism necessarily involves one lone viewer surveying a scene from one fixed spot. Such an image of autism is a poetically compelling one if not a specifically defined scientific one. And for this there need not be any apology, Camus pointed out that when scientists are asked to explain high level theories their explanations are invariably metaphorical.

If there is a link between autism and this special drawing skill, it is useful to examine what is currently known about autism that might be relevant to our understanding of Nadia and what has changed since the 1980s.

The major change that is discernible in the current literature on autism is the shift to consensus on what are the essential features of autism and, therefore, on the underlying nature of the disorder. Articles from the late 1970s and 1980s claiming that language disorder was the principal deficit in autism (Churchill, 1978) were appearing at the same time as papers examining perceptual deficits as the major handicap (DeMyer, 1979). Most leading experts now claim that the essential deficit is in the child's social development. Thus, the American Psychiatric Association (1987), emphasized the importance for diagnosis of impairments in social interaction, in social communication, imaginative play, and the presence of repetitive stereotyped routines. Newson (1977) was one of the first in Britain to recognize that the core deficits in autism were in social development that involved impairment in the development of imagination and pretend play. Her four criteria for diagnosis of autism are impairment of all modes of communication; impairment of social relationships, in particular, a failure of social empathy; evidence of rigidity and inflexibility of thought processes; and onset before 30 months. Other experts in this country provide very similar criteria (Wing, 1992). In a related theory, Frith (1989, 1991) attempted to sketch a cognitive account of autism based on her own research as well as on the work of others. She first pointed out that autistic people appear to lack the ability to pull information together in an overall meaning. There appears to be a fragmentation of abilities, as well as behavior, and a lack of coherence. These observations were developed into a theory of the inability of autistic people to extract relevance (Sperber & Wilson, 1986). This accounts for many of the peculiarities in verbal communication evident in autistic subjects, namely, their pedantic and tangential replies to questions; their failure to "read between the lines," and problems with grasping the point.

One of Frith's associates, Baron-Cohen, further developed the cognitive explanation for autism. He chose to focus on the autistic child's lack of pretend play and he asked the question "what role does imaginative play have in the development of social interaction and communication?" In an elegant series of experiments Baron-Cohen et al. (1985) demonstrated that the autistic child's notions about another person's beliefs were severely defective. The autistic child appears to be limited or egocentric in being unable to attribute reasons and beliefs to others. Baron-Cohen et al. (1985) undertook a study with autistic subjects and their nonautistic, matched controls surveying an incident involving two girls, Sally and Ann. Sally has a basket and Ann has a box. Sally places her marble in her basket and she goes out of the room. When she is out, Ann takes Sally's marble and hides it in her box. Sally returns and at this stage the subjects are asked where Sally will look for her marble. Nonautistic subjects have no problem in understanding that Sally would look where she believes the marble to be, but the autistic subjects are unable to disassociate from what they know and have seen, from what Sally would know. They expect Sally to know that the marble has been transferred.

Evidence such as this is accumulating to show that autistic individuals have great difficulty in conceiving of mental states such as "believing" and "knowing" in other people. Interestingly, autistic subjects perform similarly to their nonautistic matched controls in experiments such as Piaget's three mountains experiment, in which the child has to select a view to match another person's viewpoint. The child appears to understand another's viewpoint about the physical world but the child has little conception of another's internal mental representations. Frith claimed that one of the consequences of this deficit is that the understanding of their own, as well as the emotions of others, would be very limited. This theory of autism's central deficit is linked to what is known in the developmental literature as the child's theory of mind.

How does this theory and the isolation of essential characteristics of autism relate to Nadia and to the other gifted drawers? At the most superficial level it is easy to see that drawing as an isolated, asocial activity would appeal to autistic children whose choice of subjects to draw is almost invariably unusual in so far as the human figure is rarely depicted. But it is difficult to envisage how deficits in social comprehension and particularly problems in conceiving of others beliefs might relate to the ability to produce single fixed viewpoint drawings. One suspects that there must be some other, deeper deficit operating at another level that would link the two. The original conjecture of a failure in forming internal symbolic representations remains largely unexplored although a recent study calls it into question. Evidence from Charman and Baron-Cohen (1993) showed that, in the main, autistic children's drawings show no special features but generally reflect their mental age level on measures of visual intelligence, although this is not a surprising finding and was anticipated in my earlier writings (Selfe, 1977, 1983), their study deserves a closer analysis as it raises many complex issues.

Charman and Baron-Cohen engaged three groups of children: normal children with a mean chronological age of 5 years and of normal intelligence; autistic children with a mean chronological age of 13 years but with a nonverbal mental age of 7.9 years and a verbal mental age of 5.3 years. The final group comprised nonautistic mentally retarded children matched for chronological age (14 years) and overall mental age (approximately 5 years). (The problems of finding matched controls for autistic children is amply demonstrated by this.) All the subjects were tested using a standardized procedure and each subject was required to draw a mug with its handle occluded, a ball behind a wall, and a cube with different colors on its six sides. All these tasks have been used by other experimenters to investigate whether subjects draw what they see (visual realism) or what they know (intellectual realism). For example, at the earlier stage of intellectual realism, a child will draw a mug with its handle even when the mug is presented with its handle not visible to the viewer, and the child is instructed to draw exactly what he or she sees.

The drawings of the subjects in this experiment were scored as to whether their production was visually realistic or intellectually realistic. The results showed no significant difference in the production of intellectually or visually real drawings produced by subjects with autism as compared to other subjects of an equivalent mental age. However, on a composite score of predominantly visual realism, there were significantly fewer subjects with mental handicaps who were visual realists than there were in the other two groups. The authors attributed this finding to the fact that the autistic subjects had consistently higher nonverbal intelligence scores than the mentally handicapped group. They also reported that the developmental shift from intellectual to visual realism occurred in the autistic group in much the same way as in the other groups when nonverbal mental age was taken into account. Autistic children with a nonverbal mental age below 6 produced drawings predominantly intellectually real, and mental age over 6 years, predominantly visually real. (The authors themselves pointed to differences in performance in the autistic group that confirms the view that it is difficult to make generalizations about these highly individualistic children.)

These results confirm that my group of artists are atypical. Most autistic children are not at all gifted at representational drawing, although a trend to be more able with nonverbal skills is clearly discernible in the results of this experiment. The authors also mentioned that there was one outstanding autistic teenager who drew in a very detailed and visually real manner. Perhaps this is the right moment to raise the question of the possibility of the existence of a special subgroup of autistic children who have this special ability and who have different characteristics from other autistic children. One might conjecture that a particularly wide discrepancy between verbal and nonverbal skills may exist in these individuals.

There is one further important observation that should be made about the foregoing experiment and that is that the evidence shows conclusively that most autistic children are capable of producing intellectually real drawings. The significance of this is easily overlooked but it may prove to be difficult to reconcile this finding with my original conjectures. Autistic subjects can produce symbolic or canonical representations of what they know about objects. So my original conjecture that autistic children draw view specific representations because they cannot produce symbolic representations does not apply to all autistic children. It appears that autistic children can draw symbolically or, to put it another way, can draw objects as concepts; as representations of classes of objects. In order to be able to sustain my original conjectures one would have to confine this to my autistic savants alone and not extend the claim to autistic children in general. This appears to weaken any link between this special ability and autism.

Concluding this section on the role of autism in an explanation of the special ability of the group of autistic artists, it can be seen that a lot of progress has been made in our understanding of autism. Evidence for the neurological basis of the disorder has also been amassing so that there is little doubt now that autism results from brain dysfunction due to an inherited disorder, disease, or injury acquired before, during, or shortly after birth. It seems very likely that autism results from dysfunction in those areas of the brain that are involved in social development; although where those centers are located or what the psychological mechanisms are involved in socialization is hazy conjecture. Autism varies in its severity and some autistic individuals are highly intelligent. It can also occur in conjunction with global brain damage and severe learning difficulties. Autistic individuals do not form a homogeneous group and one can already discern subgroups emerging from a continuum of autistic disorders. Studies on autism have, however, failed to shed much light on a better understanding of our autistic artists. It has been established that most autistic children's graphic representational skills are unexceptional: They follow the normal developmental progress of drawing ability albeit at a pace that reflects their mental rather than chronological age. My small group of autistic savants may represent a subgroup within the autistic continuum who share substantially different features from other autistic children. This would have more conviction if my group resembled each other in other substantial ways but they do not. Some of the research into autism using groups of autistic children can be very misleading because autistic subjects differ substantially from one another. Autistic savants are extremely puzzling but this bewilderment is a reflection of the confusions and contradictions that parents, clinicians, and researchers encounter within autism itself, and I still believe that the key to understanding Nadia lies in a better understanding of autism.

Some new light on autistic artists has been generated from research that has been undertaken since the 1980s that has examined the development of drawing in ordinary children. Fortunately, there has been a revival of interest in children's drawings since the 1970s. Rather little research was conducted in the late 1960s and early 1970s and Harris' (1963) book, *Children's Drawings as Measures of Intellectual Maturity,* remained the influential text throughout this period. Harris was able to build on the work of Luquet and Piaget and particularly on Goodenough (1926). These writers had plotted a clear developmental progression in children's drawings and Goodenough developed this systematic progression detail and drawing devices into a test for measuring the intellectual maturity of the child. Harris updated and extended her work.

Freeman (1980) was almost the lone researcher in Britain during the 1970s and his book, *Strategies of Representation in Young Children,* sparked a great deal of interest and new research. In the United States, Goodnow (1977) and Golomb (1974) were just ahead of Freeman producing books. Both these researchers took a new direction in analyzing children's drawings. Hitherto, drawings had been described as if they are a print out of internal mental images and, in a behaviorist climate, interest in the subject had withered. Freeman, especially, considered drawings as constructions whose final forms depended on the plans and strategies used by children to produce them. This view has helped to restore children's drawings to a central position in developmental cognitive psychology. The planning strategies used by children in making drawings can be experimentally analyzed; children have to solve a variety of sequencing, organizing, and orientation problems in setting down the lines of a representational drawing. A developmental progression in the acquisition of subskills can be discerned. In this way we can understand why, to use Freeman's terms, "children's drawings look so queer."

It should be noted, however, that there is a view that derives from Arnheim (1980) and that is best expounded recently by Golomb (1992a). This view offers a much qualified view of developmental stages and prefers to view the child's graphic depictions not so much in terms of age and stage limitations but as reflecting the child's "visual logic."

Later, Freeman (Freeman & Cox, 1985) was also to challenge the assumption that the well-documented developmental progression was quite as rigid or inevitable as had been claimed. A number of researchers had shown that, under certain circumstances, it was possible to promote view specific drawing in children under the age of 7. Light (1985) demonstrated that the type of drawing produced was influenced by the instructions children were given. In most experimental situations where the child is requested to draw an object the instructions are ambiguous. Freeman suggested that the predominance of canonical representations in young children is due more to "inflexibility in their choice of options, rather than an inherent inability to produce view specific drawings" (pp. 209–210). Although it is clear that the old maxim that "young children draw what they know rather than what they see" needed a great deal of clarification and qualifying, in an eagerness to disprove some of the rigidities of Piaget's stage conception, we may be in danger of throwing out the baby with the bath water. The baby in this case, being the well-documented progression of skill acquisition seen across and within individuals and across cultures in children's representational drawing.

Many researchers have followed Freeman's lead and much research has appeared since the 1980s describing strategies of representation and illuminating children's problem-solving abilities in the process of drawing. Much of this work is described in Thomas and Silk (1990). Most of the experimental studies confirm my original perplexity; for what is a hard won laborious process of trial and error and gradual mastery for normal young children, is apparently effortlessly achieved in these few autistic artists. Freeman (1980) gave a beautiful description of the skills that are needed to draw in perspective. He summarized them at the beginning of his discussion. He wrote:

> One is a grasp of the idea that the observer has to play an active role in construction so that the final representation is a recombination of aspects of real objects which explains their structure and relationships. Another is some degree of abstract understanding that the best way of explaining a scene is to rescale it and even to violate isolated aspects of its appearance. Thirdly, he has to have a grasp of measurement and geometry for these are the key aspects of scaling and coordinating scales. Finally, he has to understand something about the structure of space, the relationships in the "external frame of reference," within which he occupies but one position which is not a privileged one but one whose consequences have to be worked out in the context of the external relationships. (p. 209)

On reading this one turns again to the drawings of Nadia or Stephen Wiltshire with a renewed sense of wonder. The natural perspective evident in Stephen's architectural drawings had to wait until the 15th century to be laboriously invented by Alberti and other Renaissance painters. I am led to conclude that such drawings are not evidence of the accelerated progress of normal development but are something quite apart. It must be remembered that these autistic artists are otherwise very handicapped people who score well below average on any usual composite measure of intelligence. Howe (1989) suggested that human skills may be far more independent than assumed by the original creators of the IQ tests. These gifted, retarded individuals may have passed through the initial stages in the development of graphic skills at lightening speed, but I was unable to find any evidence of early immature drawings with Nadia. This point is examined in more detail later.

Thomas and Silk (1989) included a very useful discussion of autistic artists in their book. They quoted from O'Connor and Hermelin (1987b), who compared a small group of people with severe learning difficulties, all of whom had exceptional drawing talent, with IQ-matched controls. The group with exceptional drawing talent showed a significantly superior ability to identify incomplete pictures. Elsewhere, O'Connor and Hermelin (1987a) discussed the possibility that visual processes have developed at a quicker rate in such individuals as a compensation for retarded language development. Very simply, such people may have become autistic observers, whereas their normal peers are listeners as well as observers. Thomas and Silk made two more important observations in their discussion of these autistic artists. In reviewing the notion derived from Paivio (1971) and developed in my work (Selfe, 1983) that verbal coding interferes with the development of view-centered representations, they noted that unlike Nadia, whose drawing declined as her speech developed, Stephen's drawing has continued to improve as his language developed from the age of 5. As a result of these and other findings, I would want to modify my original notions. I suspect that the interaction of verbal and imaginal processes in development is subtle and influenced by developmental sensitivities. The lack of normal language development may have encouraged view specific drawings initially, which then became well practiced and elaborated in both children. The waning of skill in Nadia may have been due to quite other effects, such as the death of her mother who took a great interest in the development of this one skill in her daughter, or by a limited reinforcement of drawing. Stephen, by contrast, had the enormous reinforcement of media attention, drawing exhibitions, and artistic expeditions around the world. Moreover, Stephen is not nearly as handicapped as Nadia; he understands and appreciates the attention that his drawing ability has brought him. Nadia would have been confused and possibly frightened by such attention.

Second, Thomas and Silk made the point that the drawings of these anomalous subjects show a very accurate sense of perspective but no more than that. They wrote:

> Unlike the drawings of talented normal youngsters the artwork of autistic children seldom conveys anything more than visual appearance. There is seldom, for example, any expression of emotion or of personal relationships. ... Such a lack of emotional expression is, of course, consistent with the topics which many autistic artists choose to draw—buildings rather than people. (p. 139)

The question of whether one can consider the productions of these autistic savants to be "works of art" was considered in my previous books. I share Thomas and Silk's doubts and concur with Pariser (1979), who commented that the same aesthetic effects do not always come from the aesthetic aims. But the case of

Stephen is special. He is much more of an artist in Gombrich's terms—someone who depicts his vision of the world through a draft that he is constantly practicing and revising. Furthermore, he clearly took great pleasure in communicating in this manner. Nadia took great pleasure in drawing but was apparently oblivious to anyone else's interest in them.

Coincidentally to the discovery of Nadia, Freeman's work on what he termed *canonicality,* or the intellectually real representation of an object, had started a train of experimental work. This work is very ably reviewed and discussed by Davies (1985), and the issue is of significance to a consideration of autistic artists because of the apparent absence of this stage in their productions. One particularly pertinent line of inquiry has been into the effect that instructions about the object to be drawn have on the canonical bias. In one study that is likely to become a classic, Phillips, Hobbs, and Pratt (1978) gave six 7-year-old children a line drawing of a cube and one of a nonrepresentational figure but of similar complexity in terms of the number of lines. The cube was drawn much less accurately than the nonrepresentational figure. The children tended to draw all the faces of the cubes as squares but had no difficulty in drawing acute angles in their copies of the nonrepresentational figure. These results were interpreted to suggest that if children can describe to themselves what an object is, this will guide the way in which they will draw. The child knows that all the angles in a cube are right angles and this will tend to govern the production.

Bremner and Moore (1984) returned to one of Freeman's original experiments in asking young children to draw a coffee mug presented with its handle out of sight but they did not allow any prior inspection of the mug, so that the subjects did not see the handle. Half of the children were asked to name the object before they had drawn it and the other half after they had drawn it. Nearly all the children in the first group drew mugs with handles, but most of the children in the second group omitted handles, although they later identified the object as a mug. Naming the object appears to induce canonical drawings and the absence of naming produces more view-specific drawings.

There has been one series of studies of drawing in ordinary children that is of particular relevance to our understanding of autistic artists and all the issues raised here. These were conducted by Lee (1989). She described five experiments using groups of normal children to examine the nature and extent of errors in drawing. In the first experiment she asked her subjects to copy drawings in various projections of a table as well as drawing a table from imagination. The projections used were those suggested by Willats (1977); namely, orthographic, vertical oblique, oblique, naive perspective, and perspective. Her subjects were aged 4 to 14. She was able to score the preferred depiction device used by each subject (no implicit depth, oblique depth, and perspective depth). She was also able to vary presentations of the stimuli in order to determine if children could change their drawing device according to the stimulus used. She was able to confirm that the use of more advanced drawing systems increased with age. Her younger subjects had difficulty in copying a table top and table legs in oblique projection. Having a stimulus to copy as opposed to drawing from imagination alone elicited more correct responses, but the children usually drew in the same projection system.

The next experiments asked subjects to copy parts of the line drawings of tables presented as meaningless lines. Lee's most important finding as far as this chapter is concerned, is that all her subjects, including those aged 4, were able to produce the lines of an accurate oblique as well as a perspective projection when presented as lines only. Lee also discussed her results in terms of figural biases and showed that young children's apparent problems with the depiction of oblique projections was not due to such biases.

In the final experiment, the stimuli given to the subjects were precisely the same meaningless line drawings given in the previous experiments but the children were told that the lines were part of the drawing of a table. The children were aged between 4 and 7. Lee was then able to measure the effect of the verbal instructions that had translated lines in certain orientations into an object. She found that there was now a significant difference between the way in which her subjects depicted the lines. The knowledge that they were drawing lines as part of a table dramatically altered the subjects' response on two otherwise identical tasks. To quote from Lee:

> It would appear that when the subjects appreciate that the stimuli might not just be a collection of lines, but could represent part of a table, they unwittingly attempt to represent the three dimensionality that is now associated with these lines. Their performance on the task is now similar to the way subjects of their particular age are known to represent three dimensionality, in that young children no longer copy the stimuli accurately and produce the same errors as if they were drawing a three-dimensional object. (p. 31)

Furthermore, Lee made the link between this finding and both the hypothesis described at length earlier and the work of Baron-Cohen and his associates. She interpreted Baron-Cohen et al.'s (1985, 1987) experiments as indicating that autistic children "fail at conceptual perspective taking as opposed to perceptual perspective taking tasks." And she concluded that it is plausible that this cognitive deficit in autistic children is related to their lack of attendance to the symbolic or conceptual aspects of visual experience that accounts for the ability of some autistic subjects to draw in perspective at an unusually early age. Similarly normal children's failure to copy lines that have been presented as an object is due to the dominance of certain conceptual and symbolic schemas at an early stage in the development of graphic representation.

However, from my understanding of Baron-Cohen et al.'s experiments, I am not sure that one is justified in making quite such a claim as Lee does for the link between the theory of mind and conceptual processes. Baron-Cohen et al. described differences in autistic children's understanding of mechanical processes in a series of pictures depicting, for example, a snowball rolling down a hill, as opposed to their understanding of people's intentions in a similar pictorial sequence. I am, therefore, unsure whether there is a parallel between mechanical and imaginal processes on the one hand and conceptual and intentional processes on the other.

As I have already discussed, any substantial connection between Baron-Cohen's theory of mind and my previous notions of the role of symbolic or conceptual processes is extremely tenuous and difficult to sustain. Perhaps the best that can be said is that understanding another's beliefs and intentions and the ability to form concepts is in the same general domain, both require abstraction.

Another important contribution to the debate about autistic artists has been made by Howe (1989). His work is in its own special category. He has been mentioned in this chapter on several occasions because he has examined the phenomenon of the idiot savant and autistic savants in detail, including Nadia. He offered his own reflections on previous explanations for the phenomenon in general and he presented new and interesting suggestions. He reviewed many fascinating cases of retarded individuals with outstanding musical ability, calendar calculators, and feats of memory as well as autistic artists. He found the general explanations offered for these isolated skills unsatisfactory. He pointed out that explanations implicating physiological or neurological dysfunctioning frequently tend to be circular and not illuminating. Attributing disabilities and special talents to brain damage doesn't help us to understand the underlying mechanisms of the disorders. Howe also reviewed psychoanalytical theories and he was clearly unhappy about the untestable nature of many of their propositions.

Howe asked a series of fundamental questions that are highly pertinent. How can somebody who has evolved a skill to such a high level of achievement be so deficient in other areas of functioning? How are the feats actually done? He continues by asking searching rejoinders. Why do we assume that the divergence in skills needs to be explained? To quote: "Why shouldn't a person's different skills be autonomous and fragmentary, and why are we so surprised to find that they are?" He suggested that the answer to these latter questions rests on our traditional notions of intelligence. Notions of intelligence have been dominated by IQ measurement and the belief that there is a general intelligence factor (or g factor) underlying the acquisition of all human skills. Howe reviewed evidence that challenges these notions and in this he echoed the trend in educational psychology that recognizes that every individual has a profile of different abilities and skills that cannot be simply reflected in one composite score. Howe argued that despite these seemingly common-sense notions of intelligence, it is quite possible for isolated mental skills to exist at all levels of ability, which are largely independent of the individual's measured intelligence. He showed that large discrepancies in abilities occur in people who are considered to be very bright and reasoned that the same discrepancies should also occur in retarded individuals. Howe correctly pointed out that psychologists, for good practical reasons relating to educational placement and prediction, have been concerned to discover similarities in abilities rather than differences. As I am a practitioner of many years standing this argument finds a very receptive ear. From my direct experience I know that, even within the very narrow spectrum of skills measured by the best IQ tests, children's abilities can vary widely. Howe concluded by offering support for an alternative notion of intelligence. He favored Gardner's (1984) view, put forward in his book, *Frames of Mind,* according to which each person has a number of separate and largely autonomous intelligences. Howe proposed that retarded savants may well have developed their one particular skill independent of their other abilities and he accounted for their skills by suggesting that they have been constantly and whole-heartedly engrossed in that one activity. He said:

> this, more than any other single factor, provides the key to the savants' achievements we marvel at—the capacity to be constantly and wholeheartedly engrossed in whatever they put their minds to, to concentrate and drive out distractions and competing interests, in short … to inhabit for long periods of time a mental world in which nothing but the object of their interest, or perhaps obsession, is allowed to exist. (p. 159)

Golomb (1992a), too, speculated on Nadia's drawing ability and is unconvinced that Nadia's development is truly anomalous and that her ability should be viewed as pathological. She challenged the "presumed absence of precursors to the astonishing realism of her drawings at age three." She pointed out that Nadia's mother may well have selected only Nadia's best drawings for preservation and her immature drawings may well have been lost. She also argued that Nadia's work showed considerable development between the ages of 3 and 6 particularly with her horse theme. Golomb also rightly pointed out that Nadia's decline in interest in drawing coincided with the development of sociability and language. She expressed the view that the precocity of some gifted but normal child artists such as her own study of Eitan (Golomb, 1992b), should alert us to the fact that it is possible to pass through the stage of graphic development very quickly and that we should be guarded in "pathologizing" an extraordinary talent, even in a child with autism. She concluded, along with Gardner, that Nadia may represent the development of one specific intelligence to a very high level.

Howe (1989) devoted a chapter of his book to a consideration of the puzzle presented by Nadia. A great deal of his analysis of retarded savant is applicable to her. She had an independent and autonomous skill and in keeping with autism, she showed an early obsessional interest with one achievement. It is conceivable that she could have been practicing drawing in her head, to the exclusion of everything else. But, as Howe acknowledged, Nadia is a very special case because there is something else to be accounted for; her drawings at the age of 3 are well beyond the most gifted normal intelligence. There is no evidence that she passed through the normal stages at an accelerated rate. Her parents and teachers denied any such development and they were questioned closely. There are some canonical productions among her early drawings, but these cropped up at odd intervals alongside view-specific productions, and her very earliest productions were realistic not canonical. Also, there are examples of the degradation of images rather than their development. Nadia cannot be so easily explained away and it is equally puzzling how a seemingly highly developed, well-rehearsed skill has dwindled to well below the original level of competence. Howe agreed that an explanation for Nadia's drawing ability may well be tied to her underlying pathological condition rather than to the development of a special isolated talent.

The conclusions I reached in this chapter both reaffirm some of my earlier views and lead me to some amendments and reconsiderations. First, I am still of the opinion that in considering Nadia's drawings, what at first glance may appear to be drawings of "frozen intelligence" or of a "genius," may in fact be a symptom of pathological development. In the assessment and diagnosis of autism, as part of my everyday work, I now always ask about drawing and any indication of view specific drawing before the age of 5 is added to my checklist of positive indicators. Nadia may well prove to be "a case apart" at the extreme end of the autistic continuum where view-specific drawing at a very early age is possible only because of the paucity of conceptualization. At the other end of the continuum is Stephen Wiltshire whose development of drawing skills has been much more "normal" and who shows an outstanding and developing ability to observe and record the visual world.

Second, my original model has needed some qualification particularly with regard to recent research in autism. It would appear that autistic children can draw intellectually real drawings so that my group of autistic savants are a special case. Also research into autism has suggested that autistic children have very specific difficulties with conceptual processes. They fail to understand other peoples intentions and beliefs, but they have no difficulty in understanding another child's perspective on the physical world. I find this all very puzzling and no doubt future research will illuminate these questions.

Third, the research on representational drawing in ordinary children is yielding some very promising leads. The fact that children draw differently, and far more accurately, in terms of projection systems, when they have not named an object or do not know that the lines to be copied can depict an object, is substantial evidence that poorly developed language and conceptualization may have accurately aided my autistic savants in their view-specific depictions. But again, much clarification and qualification will be needed before any confident model can be proposed. It seems very likely that there is a correlational relationship, if not a causal one between the cognitive deficits of autism and view-specific drawing in very young subjects.

Finally, a new puzzle has also been emerging as the full story of Nadia has unfolded. It is now clear that Nadia has lost much of her original skill in drawing, not that her original ability has stood still, it has atrophied. Her drawings now are the canonical representations so notably absent in her early years. Has this resulted from emotional trauma, cognitive maturation, or from her pathological condition?

The supports of my original explanatory structure seem far less solid and I think that it may be altogether wiser to offer merely a tentative plan, pointing to possible connections, lines of inquiry, and structural defects. I have tried to present a plan for the structure of an explanation for this fascinating but enigmatic phenomenon but Nadia remains a puzzle. She will undoubtedly continue to challenge other more critical and more creative psychologists. In Bacon's *Novum Organum,* he distinguished between three types of scientific inquirer in a lovely analogy with the insect world. There are, he said, the ants who gather facts assiduously but in a random fashion. Then there are the spiders who collect very little but sit spinning "webs out of their own substance" and finally, there are Bacon's favorites, the bees, who spend their time busily collecting and then organizing and building enduring systems. The perils of Bacon's metaphor are obvious. There is a danger of collecting new and possibly relevant experiments and data ad infinitum. Equally, there is a temptation to sit and build wonderful theories of intricacy and complexity and no real substance. The need to understand may well be vain and even foolish, but it is the natural impulse of science.

ACKNOWLEDGMENTS

I acknowledge the help of Nadia's father, Mr. Chomyn; Alison Wooten; Denise Knill; and Paul Selfe in the preparation of this chapter. I acknowledge the kind permission of the Stephen Wiltshire Trust in the reproduction of one of his beautiful drawings.

REFERENCES

American Psychiatric Association. (1987). *Diagnostic and statistical manual of mental disorders* (3rd rev. ed.). Washington DC: Author.

Anastasi, A., & Levee, J. (1960). Intellectual defect and musical talent: A case report. *American Journal of Mental Deficiency, 64,* 659–705.

Arnheim, R. (1970). *Visual thinking.* London: Faber & Faber.

Arnheim, R. (1980). The puzzle of Nadia's drawings. *The Arts in Psychotherapy, 7,* 79–85.

Baron-Cohen, S., Leslie, A., & Frith, U. (1985). Does the autistic child have a "theory of mind"? *Cognition, 21,* 37–46.

Baron-Cohen, S., Leslie, A., & Frith, U. (1987). Mechanical, behavioural and intentional understanding of picture stories in autistic children. *British Journal of Developmental Psychology, 4,* 113–125.

Bremner, J., & Moore, S. (1984). Prior visual inspection and object naming: Two factors that enhance hidden feature inclusion in young children's drawings. *British Journal of Developmental Psychology, 2,* 371–376.

Bruner, J., Olver, R., & Greenfield, P. (1966). *Studies in cognitive growth.* New York: Wiley.

Buhler, K. (1930). *The mental development of the child.* London: Routledge & Kegan Paul.

Charman, A., & Baron-Cohen, S. (1993). Drawing development in autism: The intellectual to visual realism shift. *British Journal of Developmental Psychology, 11,* 171–186.

Churchill, D. (1978). Language: The problem beyond conditioning. In M. Rutter & E. Schopler (Eds.), *Autism: A reappraisal of concepts and treatment.* New York: Plenum.

Cox, M. (1993). *Children's drawings.* Harmondsworth: Penguin.

Davies, A. (1985). The canonical bias. In N. Freeman & M. Cox (Eds.), *Visual order* (pp. 202–214). Cambridge: Cambridge University Press.

DeMyer, M. (1979). *Parents and children in autism.* Washington, DC: Winston.

Dennis, N. (1978, May). Book review of Selfe, L. "Nadia." *New York Review of Books.*

Edwards, B. (1979). *Drawing on the right side of the brain.* Los Angeles: J. Tarcher.

Eng, H. (1931). *The psychology of children's drawings.* London: Routledge & Kegan Paul.

Freeman, N. (1980). *Strategies of representation in young children: Analysis of spatial skills and drawing processes.* London: Academic Press.

Freeman, N., & Cox, M. (Eds.). (1985). *Visual order, the nature and development of pictorial representation.* Cambridge: Cambridge University Press.

Frith, U. (1989). *Autism: Explaining the enigma.* Oxford: Blackwell.

Frith, U. (Ed.). (1991). *Autism and Asperger syndrome.* Cambridge: Cambridge University Press.

Gardner, H. (1980). *Artful scribbles: The significance of children's drawings.* London: Jill Norman.

Gardner, H. (1984). *Frames of mind.* London: Heinemann.

Golomb, C. (1974). *Young children's sculpture and drawings.* Cambridge, MA: Harvard University Press.

Golomb, C. (1992a). *The child's creation of a pictorial world*. Berkeley: University of California Press.

Golomb, C. (1992b). Eitan: The development of a precociously gifted child. *The Creativity Research Journal, 5*(3), 265–279.

Goodenough, F. (1926). *Measurement of intelligence by drawings*. New York: Harcourt, Brace & World.

Goodnow, J. (1977). *Children's drawings*. Cambridge, MA: Harvard University Press.

Gregory, R. (1977). Book review "An isolated talent." *New Scientist, 76*, 577.

Harris, D. (1963). *Children's drawings as measures of intellectual maturity*. New York: Harcourt, Brace & World.

Hermelin, B., & O'Connor, N. (1970). *Psychological experiments with autistic children*. London: Pergamon.

Howe, M. (1989). *Fragments of genius*. London: Routledge.

Jaensch, E. (1930). *Eidetic imagery and typological methods of investigation*. London: Routledge & Kegan Paul.

Kanner, L. (1943). Autistic disturbances of affective contact. *Nervous Child, 2*, 217–250.

Lee, M. (1989). When is an object not an object? The effect of meaning upon the copying of line drawings. *British Journal of Psychology, 80*, 15–37.

Light, P. (1985). The development of view-specific representation. In N. Freeman & M. Cox (Eds.), *Visual order* (pp. 214–231). Cambridge: Cambridge University Press.

Luquet, G. (1927). *Le Dessin d'un Enfantin* [Children's drawings]. Paris: Alcan.

Moore, V. (1987). The influence of experience on children's drawings of a familiar and unfamiliar object. *British Journal of Developmental Psychology, 5*, 221–229.

Morishima, A. (1974). Another Van Gogh of Japan: The superior artwork of a retarded boy. *Exceptional Children, 41*, 92–96.

Newson, E. (1977). Diagnosis and early problems of autistic children. *Communication, 11*.

O'Connor, N., & Hermelin, B. (1987a). Visual and graphic abilities of the idiot savant artist. *Psychological Medicine, 17*, 81–92.

O'Connor, N., & Hermelin, B. (1987b). Visual memory and motor programmes: Their use by idiot savant artists and controls. *British Journal of Psychology, 78*, 307–323.

Paivio, A. (1971). *Imagery and verbal processes*. New York: Holt, Reinhart & Winston.

Park, C. (1978). Book review of "Nadia: A case of extraordinary drawing ability in an autistic child." *Journal of Autism and Childhood Schizophrenia, 8*(4), 457–472.

Pariser, D. (1979). *A discussion of Nadia* (Tech. Rep. No. 9). Cambridge, MA: Harvard University Project Zero.

Phillips, W., Hobbs, S., & Pratt, F. (1978). Intellectual realism in children's drawings of cubes. *Cognition, 6*, 15–33.

Pylyshyn, Z. (1973). What the mind's eye tells the mind's brain: A critique of mental imagery. *Psychological Bulletin, 80*, 1–24.

Rutter, M., & Schopler, E. (1978). *Autism—A reappraisal of concepts and treatment*. New York: Plenum.

Sacks, O. (1985). *The man who mistook his wife for a hat*. England: Duckworth.

Selfe, L. (1977). *Nadia: A case of extraordinary drawing ability in an autistic child*. London: Academic Press.

Selfe, L. (1983). *Normal and anomalous representational drawing ability in childen*. London: Academic Press.

Sperber, D., & Wilson, D. (1986). *Relevance: Communication and cognition*. Oxford: Blackwell.

Sully, J. (1896). *Studies of childhood*. New York: Appleton.

Thomas, G., & Silk, A. (1990). *An introduction to the psychology of children's drawings*. London: Harvester Wheatsheaf.

Willats, J. (1977). How children learn to draw realistic pictures. *Quarterly Journal of Experimental Psychology, 29*, 367–382.

Wiltshire, S. (1987). *Drawings*. London: Dent.

Wing, L. (1992). *Autistic continuum disorders: An aid to diagnosis*. London: The National Autistic Society.

8

Exclusive Profiles: Tentatively Sketching Giftedness

Ronald N. MacGregor
University of British Columbia

Almost every art educator I know who has children has assiduously built up a collection of their work, from first scribbles through the time they cease to draw or construct images. These collections are often made specifically for instructional purposes, to be shown to student teachers along with anecdotes designed to reveal how the circumstances surrounding the construction of the work affect one's understanding of it. The priority for the instructor is to show a range of work that students will recognize as typical of what may be expected of children.

The collection of work by gifted students, as Golomb observes earlier in this book, is much less common. Part of the reason may be that although an educator's collection of child art is usually the subject of classroom discussion, and never need achieve formal documentation in written or photographic form, the atypicality of gifted child art invites a research focus and informed reference to a literature not normally explored in education methods classes.

The reluctance of art educators to become involved in the question of what distinguishes gifted art from "typical" art may well be in part a reflection of a historical preoccupation with large numbers in art rooms in schools, with a consequent tendency in educational research to focus on large group studies. Narrative writing, the preferred form for detailing individual differences, has been only recently accepted in education as a valid form of presenting information. The single-case study, an essential form for the study of exceptionality, was for years placed at the outer fringes of educational research. Now brought in from that chilly periphery, its legitimation may encourage more in-depth investigations of gifted and talented students.

Should educators be persuaded to contribute formally to the pool of knowledge on the gifted and talented in art, they will rapidly find how useful good recordkeeping is in providing a context for the pictorial material. All the chapters in this book are evidence of the importance of collaboration between author/collector and subject/narrator, with the body of the work acting as the medium for reflection, interpretation, and evaluation.

The topic of gifted child artists presents a special problem for the researcher in that one has no way of knowing at the outset whether a child selected for study will turn out to exhibit above normal ability. Ex post facto interpretation of a body of work originally preserved by family members for largely sentimental and personal reasons is therefore the norm. The researcher must draw conclusions on the basis of situations imperfectly recalled, or for which no background exists. The result, as in Duncum's (1984) investigation of how 35 children living between the 18th and 20th century learned to draw, is inevitably fragmented.

Another problem is that, for reasons directly related to the values brought by the researcher to the investigation, who is or is not gifted may not be readily apparent. The "discovery" of women artists after centuries of "invisibility" is an analogous case; whereas even the grounds by which gifted children might be identified among North American aboriginal groups are not at present formally articulated.

My task is to offer some reflections on the chapters that make up this book, and to add commentary on what it may mean to be gifted in art. My narrative, I fear, rambles. Whether this is the natural consequence of dealing with a variety of manifestations and instances of unusual behavior, or simply a lack of incisiveness on my part, the reader must judge.

TOWARD SOME DEFINITIONS

Words like *talent* and *creativity* have, over the years, been defined in terms of process and product, as personality traits and socially desirable characteristics. Perhaps mirroring recent general tendencies to place the individual in a particular context, Csikszentmihalyi (1988) and others described creativity as a function of the social and historical world into which an individual is born, and of the cultural values that the social world supports. Although there is a certain circularity in the idea that society rewards for being creative those whom it considers creative, the focus on sociocultural determinants of creativity helps to explain why some persons are rewarded by society while others are marginalized.

The case of two Canadian inventors makes the point. J. Armand Bombardier, inventor of tracked vehicles including the snowmobile, earned the gratitude of the military, who needed reliable transport in winter conditions; business (particularly oil and mineral companies, for whom all-terrain vehicles offered a distinct market edge in year-round exploration); farmers, peoples living above the Arctic Circle, and adherents to a new form of winter sports activity. By contrast, Reginald Fessenden, who had determined at least 30 years ahead of Rutherford and Bohr that atoms possessed positive and negative charges that held them together, and who applied this to problems where friction or fusion was prevented, by substituting the suspect part with another with a different chemical profile, was and is almost unknown. The difference in the reception accorded these two is readily explained by the positive and visible effects on people's lives of Bombardier's invention, and the comparative inaccessability of Fessenden's research.

Not surprisingly, then, similar expectations and preferences have influenced adult notions of children's art. In chapter 1, Diana Korzenik argues that children are identified as having characteristics deemed "childlike," and are then provided with those materials and experiences that encourage these characteristics. In her words, "Adults keep tapping and admiring in young people whatever they can get them to make that will resemble the current art world's taste." I recall as a junior high school teacher in the 1960s being thoroughly dejected during an exhibition of districtwide work by a display of sparkling paintings in the abstract expressionist idiom, contributed by an elementary school: paintings that had all the casual grace and sumptuous surface qualities largely absent from my own students' work. Only later did I realize I had been been the victim of an infinite number of monkeys/infinite number of typewriters stratagem: initial instructions to "the workers" to cover as many surfaces as possible, with final selection and cropping made by an art teacher as admiring of abstract expressionism as I was.

Terminology contributes to defining these social states and contexts. Subtle hierarchies of relations among aspects of work and aspects of class may be seen in the relative frequency with which *gifted* is applied to a musician, but not to a carpenter, where *talented* is more likely to be the descriptor. There are gifted orators, accomplished equestrians, creative cooks, and clever lawyers: adjectives not bestowed by chance. However the terms *gifted, talented,* and *creative* are defined, they should be seen as provisional, and to some extent arbitrary.

Nevertheless, if the concepts derived from the chapters in this book are to be discussed, some attempt at definition is necessary. The literature has tended to follow the language of the Marland Report (1972), wherein six types of giftedness were identified: general intellectual ability, specific academic ability, creative or productive thinking, leadership ability, talent in the visual and performing arts, and psychomotor ability. Gardner's (1983) list of multiple intelligences is a similar manifestation of differentiation among talents, and a rejection of unitary conceptions of intelligence. Gardner's list includes the potential for giftedness in language, music, logic/mathematics, visuospatial relating, bodily/kinaesthetic applications, and intrapersonal and interpersonal connecting.

Everyone, it seems, has a particular definition, which gives me the latitude to attempt my own. In print, the gifted and talented are often lumped together, like Gilbert and Sullivan. But like these two apparently synonymous but really quite different characters, the gifted and the talented deserve separate consideration.

The gifted are characterized by an ability to solve problems, often by reframing them. They manifest this consistently, sometimes in spite of themselves. It is as if they are incapable of accepting wisdom at face value, but instead are impelled to recast it in unconventional ways. They are infinitely beguiled by notions, ideas, and roads that may lead nowhere but that are too intriguing to be left alone.

The talented person derives satisfaction from doing something well. Improvement in technique and competence, rather than the chase after the ineffable, is the preferred objective. Talent is consistent across situations, where those situations form a family of linked behaviors (i.e., the talented person develops a repertoire of strategies adaptable to several stages of problem solving). As Pirsig (1974/1981) noted:

> The craftsman isn't ever following a single line of instruction. He's making decisions as he goes along ... the nature of the material at hand determines his thoughts and motions, which simultaneously change the nature of the material at hand. The material and his thoughts are changing together in a progression of changes until his mind's at rest at the same time as the material's right. (p. 148)

As for creativity, it may be an expected practice of gifted and talented persons, but it is not confined to that group. Anyone, as any teacher will confirm, can on occasion be creative. Indeed, one of the rewards of teaching is to have unlikely persons surprise everyone, including themselves, by suggesting unforeseen but appropriate directions for action. Creative acts are situation-specific and relatively random as to origin.

ESTABLISHING A FLOOR

Gifted, talented, and creative individuals may be identified in any subject field, or indeed in any area of activity. Pye (1964) remarked that a person who is capable of invention as an artist

> is commonly capable also of useful invention. Leonardo's exceptional genius in both useful and artistic invention seems to have fostered the idea that he was exceptional also in combining these two talents. But this is not so. The combination is usual rather than exceptional, so usual in fact that one is led to suspect that both are really different expressions of one potentiality. (p. 72)

Were those art educators referred to at the beginning of this chapter to come together so that each one might show slides and talk about the work of their offspring (an event that may be better to contemplate in theory than to sit through in practice) one might expect, in light of these definitions, and putting aside parental pride, that they would agree that some of the children whose work was shown have an advantage over the remainder, be it in terms of the amount of work they produce or in the way they organize and interpret their ideas and experiences in art forms. But the evaluative scale would be ordinal, not ratio: There is no absolute floor, no case of zero talent.

The floor is rather that which is called *common sense.* Geertz (1983) described common sense as stemming from "the desire to render the world distinct" (p. 77) and characterized it by *naturalness, practicalness, literalness,* and *accessibleness.* Naturalness is a product of the degree of comfort felt about a situation or a belief, expressed in such phrases as "That's just the way it is." Practicalness is knowing what one has to in order to move around sensibly in society. Literalness (or, to use Geertz' term, *thinness*) is what results from describing something unequivocally, so that it has one denotation and no other. And accessibleness implies that the commonplace world is available to anyone expending minimum effort.

On this common-sense floor, cases for giftedness, talent, and creativity may be built. Against these common-sense attributes, the particular qualities of the gifted may be contrasted and their unique contributions understood. It is not that the gifted and talented lack common sense; rather, they transcend the state of accepting things as they are, or doing only as much as is necessary to get by.

This is the assumption on which the preceding chapters in this book may be examined. The question motivating such examination is voiced by Korzenik, who asks concerning the artist Washington Allston whether knowing and predicting his giftedness would have made any difference to his life. In Allston's case, circumstances combined to enable him to succeed. But suppose circumstances had been different. Might history have shown that Allston's successful career in art was directly attributable to his being identified as special by his school art teacher, and provided with opportunities to exercise his talents?

The contributors to this book provide examples from which guidelines for the identification of talent may be inferred, and discuss those ways in which the subjects of their studies stand out against the common sensical everyday world. There are at least eight categories under which the contributions may be grouped. Each is now discussed in some detail.

A SENSE OF IDENTITY

A theme running through several of the chapters is that of establishing and maintaining control over one's ideas and their execution. The thought that children might have a distinct identity and a sense of their own destiny, although promulgated since the 19th century, has only taken partial root in public school education. The reasons are well known: large classes, indifferent or overworked teachers, bureaucratic caution, instruction geared to a largely silent majority. One may see, then, how readily the kind of change to which Eric (see Zimmerman, chapter 5, this volume) responds can be deflected in the interest of keeping the class moving slowly toward a predetermined conclusion. Eric saw competition, surpassing his peers, as very important. He wanted to be the best, and the only way he could feel he was the best was through knowing that the other students were giving 100%. His impatience at what he perceived as slackness on the part of his peers is the reaction of someone trying to accommodate a Porsche to the snaillike tempo of downtown traffic.

Varda's (see Golomb & Haas, chapter 7, this volume) sense of being in control arose not from competition with peers, but rather from the necessity to excel autonomously. Left to her own devices, she disciplined herself to "control every motion, to be precise and exercise mastery over the conditions." The willingness of the gifted or talented individual to invest time and effort in "getting it right" is mentioned frequently throughout the text, although the means to achieve it are most evident in Nadia's (see Selfe, chapter 7, this volume) repetitive drawing habits.

Gifted children are voracious gatherers of information and produce large quantities of work, thus it is not surprising that their progress is marked by cycles of acquisition and discarding of directions, techniques, and media. Assessing the worth of holding on to an idea inevitably involves asking questions about its validity, which is what all students are supposed to do, according to educational theory, but which is often absent in practice. Teachers may be forgiven for shying away from discussion of the relative worth of material for study; the question, "Why do we have to do this?" is just as often asked as a diversion as it is out of genuine inquisitiveness.

A problem for the child working toward self-identity noted by several of the contributors is that adults determine standards of giftedness and then look for corroborative evidence in children's behavior. Korzenik mentions the cult of primitivism, and the adult perception of the child as artist-in-embryo, both of which resulted in hands-off attitudes on the part of teachers, and in immense frustration for those talented students who were not in the least interested in naive expression, but who instead wanted to know how to draw the road so it would lie down.

David Pariser (chapter 2, this volume) refers to the "crystallizing experience," that moment of epiphany when a person sees clearly, for the first time, the road ahead and how it is to be traveled. Levi-Strauss (1978) described one of those experiences as he looked for a line of contact between two geological features in the Languedoc, in southern France.

> Every landscape appears first of all as a vast chaos, which leaves one free to choose the meaning one wants to give it. But over and above agricultural considerations, geographical irregularities and the various accidents of history and prehistory, the most majestic meaning of all is that which precedes, commands and, to large extent, explains the others. (p. 56)

Levi-Strauss transferred that experience to what was to be his life's work: mapping the geology of belief systems expressed through myth; looking for the conceptual strata that form a unity, despite local irregularities introduced by time, place, and circumstances. Levi-Strauss' sense of identity, how he was thereafter to see his mission, was formed from a relating of events that resulted in new meaning: a metaphor to live by.

In addition to acquiring a metaphor to live by, the gifted person may enjoy access to a range of metaphors that vivify situations. The 19th-century historian Francis Parkman draws the reader into the milieu of the British and French colonial wars in North America by describing the landscape as a migrating goose might have seen it: the Hudson River, the untouched forests, the mountain wilderness of the Adirondacks, the flicker of the Bourbon flag on Fort Ticonderoga (Tuchman, 1981). The vivid three-dimensional description of the landscape is a particular tribute to Parkman's metaphoric power, because it was totally a mental projection. Writing well before the Wright brothers flew, Parkman could not have seen what is routinely available to the traveling public today.

For Varda, the crystallizing experience seems to have been human suffering, first experienced at secondhand via the television screen, but latterly explored firsthand through personal tragedies and resolutions. For her, it marks a coming to terms with existence.

Out of these common behaviors—a sense of challenge, an appetite for investigation, an openness to new experience, and the acquisition and development of personal metaphors—gifted-and-talented children forge their individual identities. Their art provides them with a means to orient themselves in the shifting sands of life as lived and life as told.

DIALECTICS OF THE FIELD

How individuals define their places in society requires a sense of self, and of other. Murphy (1971) took the position that the relationship of the individual to society is dialectical, although elastic. At times, the fit between the individual and society seems snug and more like a complementarity than two polarities; at others, the gap is large, and the individual "rattles around," in Murphy's phrase, more or less alienated.

The notion of an elastic dialectic is quite reasonable if one agrees that the seeds of each polarity inhere in the other: Life has the meaning it does because death is not only its opposite but part of it; classicism has its romantic undertow, and vice versa. As well as providing pointers to help in the identification of gifted-and-talented individuals, the authors of the preceding chapters have introduced material that may be considered as establishing boundaries within which the creative magic occurs (or, if that seems too fanciful, within which the artists who are the subject of the chapters have chosen to work).

Pariser uses Arnheim's discrimination of the perception of effect (or emotional impact) and the perception of form (or structural contribution) to describe Lautrec's precocity. Although in children in general the first precedes the second; and although formal analysis may enlighten some children, inform others, and make no impact at all on still others, in Lautrec's case effect and form were interactive, manifested in his literal illustrative style and grotesque subject matter.

The case of Nadia presents a paradox in this regard, as it does in so many others. Selfe's hunch is that, although children normally present the characteristic features of an object rather than its idiosyncratic features, autistic children tend to rely on imaginal presentation: the object, rather than the idea of the object. It may be so. Yet, when I first saw Nadia's drawings, I recall how closely they resembled, in their loose, swashbuckling vigor, those of Feliks Topolski, a Polish artist of the first half of the 20th century. Was it possible to claim that Topolski's work had emotional and structural authority, whereas Nadia's, closely related as it was in appearance, lacked that authority? And if it was, wherein, then, resided the authority?

Varda's work, by contrast, shows consistent evidence of applying dialectical contrasts, both structurally, in inside–outside, light–dark relationships, and emotively, in fluid–immobile elements, or in themes of separation and connectedness. It extends even to the inward-looking character of her later work, contrasting with the outward-looking, diverse subject matter of her early childhood.

FINDING ONE'S PLACE

Although art offers an avenue for the expression of creative thinking, it is one of several possibilities on which the gifted individual may draw. For gifted children, the reservoir of resources is large. Either they find that out by energetically questing about, or they assume (it transpires, correctly) that whatever they need will simply present itself for use when the occasion demands. Words and images are plentiful in the resource reservoir, and language-related activity offers ready parallels with art. Selfe points to the correlation between the ability to name an object and the ability to draw it, a correlation that has received increased attention in elementary schools in recent years through the development of whole language programs.

Founded on the assumption that language is learned holistically, in the context of everyday situations and with an emphasis on oral communication, whole language programs frequently make use of drama or art activities to encourage discourse. Rather than process leading to product, activity is cyclical, with essays, drawings, videotaped performances the by-products of interaction among students and media.

Historically, one of the most gifted proponents of image and narrative complementarity was Edward Lear. As a boy brought up in 19th century England, prevented from attending regular school by recurring epilectic seizures, Lear gave much of his attention to poetry, natural history, and painting. In his adult life he used all three to advantage: as a zoological and botanical illustrator, as a landscape painter, and as the inventor of limericks and nonsense poetry that captivated young audiences. Lear's use of puns, invented words, and whimsical advice (he devised an illustrated nonsense botany, while another work dealt with cookery) falls squarely within the definition of the gifted person as one who transcends the world of common sense. As Lehmann (1977) wrote in a biography of Lear, "All nonsense, whether by Lear or [Lewis] Carroll or any one of their modern successors, is a parody or standing-on-its-head of the strict and rational world in which we have to live, and so momentarily releases us from its chains" (p. 51).

In Henri de Toulouse-Lautrec's work, the relationships of image and text were a recurring source of invention; as they were for the illustrators of medieval manuscripts and as they are for Joel (see Milbrath, chapter 4, this volume), Varda, and Eric in this book. Joel's classification of Geeples, Progees, and Goregons is in the tradition of Lear's "runcible spoons" and Lewis Carroll's "frabjous days." They depend on our common-sense knowledge that nouns have adjectives and that graphic objects have relational contexts. Then they stand those precepts on their heads; the ground rules change. Knowing that one can change the ground rules is what sets apart gifted students. They experience a progression from "How do I fit into the game plan?" to "What is the game plan?" to "What is my game plan?" whereas their peers may never move beyond the first step of finding out how to fit in.

Adams' (1979) *A Hitchhiker's Guide to the Galaxy* (1979) is full of such incidents. Indeed, the entire book depends on them. In one episode, the protagonists, Arthur and Ford, are ejected from a space craft and caught up in the Improbability Drive.

> Arthur had jammed himself against the door to the cubicle, trying to hold it closed, but it was ill-fitting. Tiny furry hands were squeezing themselves through the cracks, their fingers were ink-stained; tiny voices chattered insanely.
>
> Arthur looked up.
>
> "Ford!" he said, "there's an infinite number of monkeys outside who want to talk to us about this script for 'Hamlet' they've worked out." (p. 84)

If one doesn't know the old joke about the infinite number of monkeys and the infinite number of typewriters that it would take to write "Hamlet," this passage is just one more in the series of extraordinary and mystifying events that make up this book. The author not only writes the script, but writes the rules for the script simultaneously. The gifted student often has this capacity to digest information collected omnivorously, and to re-shape it in a way that reflects a personal game plan for others to discern, or not.

Out of interest, and as means to determine what makes certain things behave in particular ways, Eric is led to undertake study in visual perception, in the same tradition that led Turner to study and lecture on light, or Eakins to anatomical dissection. It led Eric to recast the human digestive system as a game, and one might speculate that enthusiasm for game playing may have led him to his current fascination with computers. Although those early games fit within the category of bending the commonplace into more interesting shapes, these lead (in Varda's case, as well) into reconceptualizing existing notions and ideas; into progressively more adequate or fulfilling matrices.

THE CHARACTER OF THE WORK

In reading the accounts in the previous chapters, one is struck by the intuition displayed by these youngsters of what is required to bring the work into being. In Nadia's case, it is as if she searches for the correct line, making and correcting her marks until a satisfactory placement is found. The impression given in the narrative is that memory plays a part in this: Incidents are recalled where she would scribble over the lines of an image, then reproduce those lines as her own image later. This kind of rehearsal is common in children; what sets apart the gifted child like Joel is an ability to discover the final product in a first sketch. Once the plan is established, much that follows is a combination of what Golomb and Haas call "playful ornamentation" and "serious, meditative expression."

Along with clarity in visualization, gifted and talented children show their special abilities in the depth of their technical repertoires. Persons who can impart the impression of movement in what are static images; who can show how objects and figures may appear from different angles, using a variety of perspective systems; who can use occlusion, foreshortening and other means to create liveliness and complexity: These abilities excite our admiration and respect.

A third characteristic of work by gifted-and-talented students is the attention paid to detail. In *Children's Drawing,* Goodnow (1977) spoke of the young child's tendency to find the most economical solution to problems of drawing; they were, she wrote, thrifty in their use of graphic signs, and conservative in the changes they were prepared to make to suit individual circumstances. By contrast, the children featured in the preceding chapters commonly claim to be interested in details, and in getting those details right. Eitan (see Golomb, chapter 6, this volume) showed an early interest in details; his vehicles bristle with switches and wires and tie-rods, and his purpose is exposition rather than economy. Joel follows a similar path with his dinosaurs, his details extending to those landscape features that make up the dinosaur habitat. In the drawing of the lambesaurus, water droplets run off its tail into the water. One might expect to find that kind of engaging detail as a single memorable feature in a child's otherwise predictable drawing, but in Joel's case it is one of a dozen similar instances of keen observation. The difference between most children and children like Joel may be that, although most children record some detail that has particularly caught their attention, Joel's vision embraces the totality of those parts that make up the scene. It may be a truism to say that one cannot focus on figure and ground at once, but what constitutes figure, and what makes up ground, seems relatively less arbitrary in the case of the gifted child, and their attention is more equitably distributed.

That same richness extends to the subject matter: In Varda's case, her subjects include an insect, a dead bird, a woman giving birth, and Biafran children, all done with the kind of assurance that speaks to depth as well as breadth in repertoire. The initial obvious difference between Varda's expressiveness and Eitan's information-processing recalls the distinction alluded to by Gardner (1980) in his discussion of *patterners* and *dramatists.* Patterners are fascinated by the physical attributes of objects. They experiment with and elaborate on the forms they create. Dramatists are more likely to find their enjoyment in storytelling, drawing their themes from interpersonal relationships. Patterning and dramatizing represent polarities of the dialectical kind referred to earlier. It is clear from the examples of Eitan's and Varda's work illustrated in this book that Varda's position is close to the middle of the continuum, whereas Eitan's is much closer to the patterning end.

UNIQUENESS AND GENERALIZABILITY

The traditional argument made against case studies is that when their findings are all added together, they tell us little more than we knew before. Each case is different: true, but hardly conducive to progress. Yet, if researchers continue to do case studies, it is surely so that pattern will eventually emerge out of the data.

Does the value of the chapters in this book reside in the commonalities that are discovered? Pariser claims that "ultimately ... nomothetic formulations would be very satisfying." But for what? Or for whom?

The story of Nadia offers a firsthand look into autism, but Selfe is at pains to warn the reader that autism is not a generalizable condition. Rather, it is specific in its gifts and liabilities. The relationship between the child and the professional caregiver, for example, can significantly affect what a child will do.

Howe's question (cited in Selfe, chapter 7, this volume), "Why shouldn't a person's different skills be autonomous and fragmentary, and why are we so surprised to find that they are?" raises a different but related matter. Life, someone once said, is just one damn thing after another. That being so, and because the next damn thing is unlikely to resemble its predecessor or its successor, human beings develop bundles of skills that evolution ensures will be more or less adequate to get by. The lessons of one situation, applied to others and found to be appropriate or not, are not stored in isolation. They are applied to others, creating effective strategies for day-to-day living. Continuing crosstalk across the brain's corpus callosum results in a conceptual profile where one knows a lot about some things and a little about lots of things. What makes Nadia so interesting is that her profile is like one of those jigsaw puzzles where there are some brilliant fragments that seem to have no relationship to the rest. There is not much to generalize here.

One group that would no doubt welcome generalizable data on the gifted and talented is the teaching force. The literature can refer to evidence supporting claims that gifted persons are competitive, have a strong sense of what they want to do, benefit from mentoring, and are interested in moral rules and positions (Clark, 1992). All those traits have been mentioned at some point in the chapters that make up this book, and they may therefore be said to have general relevance for the teacher. The most comprehensive recipe for success was articulated by Zimmerman (chapter 5, this volume):

> Successful teachers of highly able students who are knowledgeable about their subject matter and able to communicate instruction effectively select important learning experiences and lead their students to attain mastery level achievements.

Although one might chip away at what those "important learning experiences" might be, it does seem as if this statement hits just the right balance between the particular and the general, the idiosyncratic and the nomothetic.

FORMAL AND INFORMAL INSTRUCTION

Armed with Zimmerman's definition, the educator might contemplate the advantages of formal and informal modes of instruction for the gifted student. Certainly, in Eric's case, his propensity for making connections among subject areas was to some extent satisfied by exposure to a formal curriculum, offered by persons aware of how their own area of expertise was related to others. But in his junior year in high school, deprived of that stimulation, he quickly became bored.

The cause of a number of problems encountered by gifted children in school was identified on one occasion succinctly by a student in a graduate seminar. We had been discussing Parsons' (1987) five stages of critical responding. Talk had centered on the probability that only a small number of elementary school students would attain Level 5, where the viewer is capable of assuming the artist's stance, while realizing that artistic values change in changing historical circumstances. The graduate student offered the opinion that numbers of elementary school teachers were nowhere close to that level of proficiency, so one might well expect frustration and even hostility on the part of those few students who are at Level 5 toward someone who, although purportedly a teacher, nevertheless "just didn't get it."

Those gifted students whose level of tolerance is not high in the first place are likely to have trouble dealing with a less gifted teacher. Stress will be compounded if the teacher retreats behind the authority of office offered by a formal setting.

Woods (1987) reinforced this point in a study she conducted among 30 persons who held prominent positions in the art community of a middle-sized city. She asked them about their early experiences with art teachers. One said, "The fortunate thing for me in terms of my later thinking about art is that I never associated what they called art in school with what I later began to think of as art. What they called art was stupid. It was all rote" (p. 69). Another referred to "a lot of nonsense with patterns. I was very bored by it all" (p. 81).

By contrast, those who respected their teachers came to appreciate the subject they taught. "The lifestyle of the teacher made an impression. Art wasn't part of my environment. This teacher was the first person to encourage me to go into art instead of engineering" (p. 83).

Some of the young persons described in the preceding chapters may claim similar incentives. It seems not to matter whether formal instruction in art was available: Varda and Eitan, in common with Lautrec, had little or none. In Eitan's case, his parents were content to let him find his own way; whereas Eric's parents were actively involved in his decision making. Lautrec's career reflects his desire to extract from persons and institutions what he felt might improve his skills, while having no desire to acquire formal recognition or credentials. For years, art schools catered to this attitude, accepting students on the evidence of their portfolios and making no demands on how students should organize their programs of study. Lately, however, the art school has edged closer to the university in its requirement that students take prescribed content as well as electives, and the scholar gypsy finds it increasingly difficult to follow personal inclination.

THE FUGITIVE GIFT

Time alters circumstances, and for the gifted young persons whose narratives are recorded in this book, those alterations have frequently seen a diminution of their art activity. Varda's horizons have solidified into domesticity; Eric has transferred his interests to computers; Eitan the soldier has little time for drawing. Sometimes the field of interest by which one has been defined as gifted changes; at others, it vanishes. Nadia's case is particularly poignant. In a reversal of normal behavior, she who drew at 3 like a 25-year-old now at 25 draws like a 3-year-old. *Giftedness,* a slippery concept to define, proves equally difficult to hold on to.

History is riddled with cases where promising young persons soared like Icarus, only to fall like him, leaving a momentary ripple, then nothing. Much less common are instances where persons, after half a lifetime of unremarkable acts, suddenly assume the trappings of genius. Accumulated wisdom may confer advantages to age, but being wise is not the same as being gifted. It begins, it seems, early in life, although circumstances may prevent its recognition until later.

Being gifted and being motivated enjoy a certain synonymy, but the relationship is not as robust as it is for the talented individual. Talented persons—the ballroom dancer, the newspaper editor, the boat builder—although experiencing a certain rustiness after a period where practice has been allowed to lapse, can revive their expertise by working at it. The gifted person's loss of momentum is much more difficult to reactivate. Although talent may be reengaged by the exercise of determination, not all the determination in the world can resurrect the spontaneous curiosity that is fundamental to giftedness.

THE BROADER CONTEXT

Gathering information on the nature of giftedness may in theory be achieved by adopting either a close-up or a broad focus. A close-up approach is typically that taken by those who would seek answers from examining the brain itself, or that much less tangible entity, the mind.

The directions taken by research into the organization and operations of the brain have brought rewards in some cases, and frustration in others. Accessibility determines progress. Hence, neuroanatomists and neurophysiologists aided by bundles of microelectrodes and (if not infinite numbers of monkeys) large numbers of laboratory animals have made impressive progress in mapping the architecture of the cortex. Neurochemists have been able to verify the effects of various transmitter substances on the ability to think and to act. But the neuropsychologist remains on the outside, while thinking happens on the inside. After decades of trying to discern what happens to visual input after it leaves the visual cortex, all that researchers can say with assurance is that neurons are activated in several areas of the brain, and that activity varies with the kind of input experienced.

Without a working knowledge of what thinking entails, it makes no sense to speculate on how the gifted brain varies in physiological terms from the average brain. Broca and Einstein are still materially present in that their brains lie preserved in formaldehyde, presumably waiting for the day when someone will be able to show which cortical convolutions are subtly but crucially different from those of the average citizen. Even then, to infer anything from that would be like trying to infer the nature of medieval Christianity from the shapes of the columns in a Gothic cathedral.

Much more is known about deficits: the causes of blindness or loss of motor control. The brain in death, sliced, stained, and presented on slides so that the effects of trauma are plain to see, is more informative than it is in life, where EEGs may record goings on, but not what is going on.

The brain's hemisphericity has latterly been used as a plank on which to build political and social agendas. Loose talk about male and female brains, creative (right hemisphere), and prosaic (left hemisphere) activity have the same speculative character that René Descartes resorted to in placing the soul in the pineal gland. The field does not need speculation.

Instead, it seems more profitable to adopt a broad focus, examining how giftedness and creativity are regarded from group to group. North America's largely immigrant population has invited various descriptions, but it is fair to say that melting pot metaphors have given way to something closer to the mosaic, as a contemporary characterization. One effect has been to call attention to alternative ways in which special qualities are recognized among groups. Talent is a universal, although which talents are prized varies from one group to the next. In every community, certain persons are identified as being able to do things well. But giftedness may be applied in some communities only to those who are able to transcend everyday existence through quasi-religious experience; in others, creativity may simply not be a discussable state.

Recent attempts to accommodate immigrant and aboriginal lifestyles in North America have had the effect of drawing attention to those alternatives. Woliver and Woliver (1991) characterized Asian behavioral priorities as learning respect for elders, avoiding calling attention to oneself, desiring to act as part of the group rather than individually, and being prone to agree out of politeness rather than argue out of inquisitiveness. Hawaiian children are described as learning "to obtain assistance from parents by remaining unobtrusive and watching for cues of the adult's receptivity to an approach" (p. 252).

Van Tassel-Baska (1992) added to this list of intercultural differences variations in attitude, different notions of social integration, different conceptions of time and affect, and what is held as a world view itself. Education under those conditions takes on a different character from the discussion-centered, transactional, open-ended models favored by many North American educators, and advocated by them as particularly suited to creative interchange.

A further dimension, this time linking social and physical factors, includes those students who, like Nadia, have learning disabilities, and those with speech, hearing, and visual impairments. Those form the category of the gifted handicapped. Bibby (1993) noted that teachers identify gifted students within this category by more or less the same characteristics that describe gifted students in general: the ability to understand quickly, to use expressive language, to show superior powers of recall, and to reason intelligently. According to Bibby's 12 informants, all of whom were teachers of hearing impaired students, teacher understanding of how characteristics of giftedness might be manifested depends on teacher beliefs and biases arising out of past experiences with a variety of students. A teacher's interactions with a particular student might persuade the teacher that the child falls into the category of *gifted,* but Bibby pointed out that *gifted* is simply a convenient term to cover an untidy collection of traits and attitudes. She remarked that the teachers "appeared to have no need to label these students and were more concerned with meeting their individual needs, both in terms of the demands of the effects of having a hearing loss and being gifted" (p. 262).

Firsthand testimony to the tension between the mental state of giftedness and the effects of physical deficit is provided by MacKarell (1990), a British art educator who developed multiple sclerosis that resulted in physical degeneration and eventually, death. MacKarell was an illustrator and a painter, possessed of a formidable technical repertoire. As his illness progressed, not being able to use the technical fluency that had been second nature was very frustrating for MacKarell, who had to adapt not only to what was conceivable but to what could physically be done.

> Expression not only includes aesthetic matters but it also embraces such matters as finding a way past basic problems, such as how you make the mark and with what you make it. This becomes vital if there are problems with perception and motor control which in normal circumstances simply do not present difficulties. (p. 54)

In sum, whether the study of the group is set in the context of cultural norms, or whether physical constraints set the parameters, certain individuals will come to the notice of their peers or other interested parties, as exhibiting superior performance, however that is defined. How these persons are treated thereafter depends on where social priorities lie. For the teachers in Bibby's study, helping the gifted and nongifted alike was a priority. In less nurturing times and places, the gifted individual has faced ostracism and at times physical harm, the gifts of God and the Devil being sometimes difficult to distinguish within the narrow perspectives of local orthodoxy.

Even in so short a period as 25 years, the effects of social and cultural changes are evident in how the gifted are viewed. A study by Schaefer (1970) of 10 creative young women gives a picture of gifted characteristics identified then, and offers grounds for comparison with how they might be identified in the 1990s. Schaefer's sample of nine Whites and one Asian would in many metropolitan areas today be regarded as atypical and nonrepresentative—although in fairness, ethnic representativeness was probably not a priority for him. The subjects, identified early as creative, and showing consistent evidence of creativity particularly in art and writing, would in that respect be no different from their counterparts in the 1990s. Their characteristic openness to change, aggressiveness, sense of autonomy, and imaginative approach to problems might be recast for a contemporary sample by taking account of the more varied contexts in which creativity is anticipated. Aggressive in some situations, translates as adept at working proactively in others; autonomous, in some cases to the point of alienated, is what in other situations may be termed tenacious in seeking alternatives to the conventional solution. Certainly, participants in this kind of study in the 1990s would be more conscious that their destiny is no longer determined by how tactfully they can effect compromises with expectations set by males for males: Something that was a concern for the 1970 sample.

CONCLUSION

Naturalness, practicalness, literalness, and accessibleness were what Geertz (1983) offered as building blocks for matter-of-fact interaction. They are removed in spirit from the incongruous, whimsical, metaphorical, and recondite behaviors exhibited by the young persons whose stories make up this book, and by the actions of those other characters whom I introduced to make a point or provide an example. It remains to speculate briefly on whether formal education allows sufficient flexibility for the gifted student. Good teachers, as has been shown, try to accommodate the unusual student; while the school provides a greater array of resources than are normally available to individuals in alternative settings. When the community is part of the school's resource bank, the situation is even more favorable. The writers of the preceding chapters are agreed that the subjects of their study benefitted from situations where they could exercise independence while taking advantage of available resources. For the school, that seems a small outlay for potentially impressive returns.

REFERENCES

Adams, D. (1979). *A hitchhiker's guide to the galaxy.* New York: Harmony.

Bibby, M. A. W. (1993). *Conceptions of giftedness among students who are deaf or hard of hearing.* Unpublished doctoral dissertation, University of British Columbia, Vancouver, Canada.

Clark, B. (1992). *Growing up gifted.* New York: Merrill.

Csikszentmihalyi, M. (1988). Society, culture and person: A systems view of creativity. In R. J. Sternberg (Ed.), *The nature of creativity: Contemporary psychological perspectives* (pp. 325–340). Cambridge: Cambridge University Press.

Duncum, P. (1984). How 35 children born between 1724 and 1900 learned to draw. *Studies in Art Education, 26*(2), 93–102.

Gardner, H. (1980). *Artful scribbles: The significance of children's drawings.* New York: Basic Books.

Gardner, H. (1983). Artistic intelligences. *Art Education, 36*(2), 47–49.

Geertz, C. (1983). *Local knowledge.* New York: Basic Books.

Goodnow, J. (1977). *Children's drawing.* Cambridge, MA: Harvard University Press.

Lehmann, J. (1977). *Edward Lear and his world.* New York: Charles Scribner's Sons.

Levi-Strauss, C. (1978). *Tristes tropiques.* New York: Atheneum.

MacKarell, P. (1990). *Depictions of an odyssey.* Corsham: NSEAD.

Marland, S. J. (1972). *Education of the gifted and talented* (Report to the Congress of the United States by the U. S. Commissioner of Education). Washington, DC: U. S. Government Printing Office.

Murphy, R. (1971). *The dialectics of social life.* New York: Columbia University Press.

Parsons, M. J. (1987). *How we understand art: A cognitive developmental account of aesthetic experience.* Cambridge: Cambridge University Press.

Pirsig, R. M. (1981). *Zen and the art of motorcycle maintenance.* New York: Bantam. (Original work published 1974)

Pye, D. (1964). *The nature of design.* London: Studio Vista.

Schaefer, C. E. (1970). A psychological study of 10 exceptionally creative adolescent girls. *Exceptional Children, 36*(6), 431–440.

Tuchman, B. W. (1981). *Practicing history.* New York: Knopf.

Van Tassel-Baska, J. (1992). *Planning effective curriculum for gifted learners.* Denver, CO: Lowe.

Woliver, R., & Woliver, G. M. (1991). Gifted adolescents in the emerging minorities: Asians and Pacific Islanders. In M. Bireley & J. Genshaft (Eds.), *Understanding the gifted adolescent* (pp. 248–257). New York: Teachers College Press, Columbia University.

Woods, J. H. (1987). *Enlightened cherishing of art: Formative influences and their relevance to British Columbia art curricula.* Unpublished master's thesis, University of British Columbia, Vancouver, Canada.

Author Index

Subject Index